SEXUAL CONDUCT

OBSERVATIONS
A series edited by Howard S. Becker
Northwestern University

SEXUAL CONDUCT
the social sources of human sexuality

John H. Gagnon
State University of New York
Stony Brook

William Simon
Institute for Juvenile Research
Chicago

Aldine Publishing Company / Chicago

ABOUT THE AUTHORS

John H. Gagnon is Professor in the Departments of Sociology and Psychiatry at the State University of New York, Stony Brook. William Simon is Program Supervisor, Sociology and Anthropology, at the Institute for Juvenile Research in Chicago. Both Dr. Gagnon and Dr. Simon received their Ph.D's in sociology from the University of Chicago, and have been associated as research sociologists with the Institute for Sex Research at Indiana University. They have published extensively in the area of human sexuality, including *The Sexual Scene* and *The End of Adolescence: The College Experience* (in press).

First published 1973 by
Aldine Publishing Company
529 South Wabash Avenue
Chicago, Illinois 60605

ISBN 0-202-30261-X Cloth
       0-202-30262-8 Paper

Library of Congress Catalog Number 73-84930

Printed in the United States of America

First paperback edition, 1974
Second Printing, 1974
Third printing, 1977

To our children

Andreé	David
Chris	Jonathan
	Adam

Contents

Acknowledgments

As social scientists, as well as social actors, both of the authors experienced their "intellectual coming of age" in a world that has been described, with considerable justification, as "post-Freudian" and "post-Kinseyan." While frequently critical of both of these monumental figures, we also recognize that the work that follows, as a social and intellectual possibility, derives from the heritage they left. There are few circumstances where the image of "pygmies standing on the shoulders of giants" can be invoked with greater justification. To Alfred C. Kinsey we owe an additional debt; many of the ideas developed in this volume found their initial formulation while the authors collaborated in research at the Institute he created at Indiana University.

Numerous debts are also owed to a contemporary cohort of researchers. Preeminent among these are William Masters and Virginia Johnson, who—among other contributions—made female sexuality less an eternal mystery. We must also cite the work of John Money, Robert Stoller, and Richard Green, whose contributions to the study of gender identity formation became something of a script within which our own thinking about sexual scirpts began to develop. Similarly, Evelyn Hooker, Albert J. Reiss, Ira Reiss, Lee Rainwater, Laud Humphreys, Martin Hoffman, and Martin S. Weinberg not only provided significant contributions to the intellectual landscape within which we worked, but also provided effective models of a concern for the sexual that was effectively disciplined by a compelling sense of professional responsibility.

More than any mere citation can convey, the work of Kenneth Burke profoundly shaped our sense of the symbolic in both human behavior and the human view of nonhuman behavior. It is perhaps appropriate that the work of an individual who has illuminated so many diverse areas of intellectual endeavor should provide much of the organizing perspective of a work on sex, itself a topic that has engaged all of these areas.

Much of the content of the present work did not emerge from abstract theorizing, but developed in the course of an intense research experience. Virtually all of this research was generously supported by both the National Institute of Mental Health and the National Institute of Child Health and Human Development. This period of support, it must be noted, occured during a time when the responses from alternative sources of funding could only, with the utmost of charity, be termed timid. And these government agencies are not abstract entities, but the work of individuals whose courage and assistance ought to be acknowledged. John Eberhardt of NIMH gave us a great deal of early encouragement, advice, and support. Of the numerous other NICHD or NIMH staff members who made substantial contributions we would like particularly to mention David Kallen, formerly of NICHD, James Lieberman, formerly of NIMH, and Jack Weiner, still with NIMH.

An additional source of support was the Hugh M. Hefner Foundation which provided early financial support that made much of the research that followed possible. The grant was made on the most permissive terms with the assumption, at the time, that it would not be publicly acknowledged.

Several chapters of this book are much revised versions of material that first appeared as indicated below.

Chapter One, "The Social Origins of Sexual Development," is a revised combination of "On Psychosexual Development" from *Handbook of Socialization Theory and Research* edited by David A. Goslin (New York: Rand McNally, 1969) and "Sex Talk: Public and Private," from *ETC. A Review of General Semantics*, Vol. 25 (1968).

Chapter Four, "The Pedagogy of Sex," is a combination of an article by the same title that appeared in *The Saturday Review* (November 18, 1967) and "Sex Education and Human Development," a chapter from

Human Sexual Function and Dysfunction edited by Paul J. Fink (Philadelphia: F. A. Davis, 1969).

Chapter Five, "Male Homosexuality," was published in an earlier version as "Homosexuality: The Formulation of A Sociological Perspective," *The Journal of Health and Social Behavior*, Vol. 8 (1967).

Chapter Six, "A Conformity Greater than Deviance: The Lesbian," is a revised combination of "The Lesbians: A Preliminary Overview," from *Sexual Deviance: A Reader* (New York: Harper and Row, 1967) and an article, "Femininity in the Lesbian Community," from *Social Problems*, Vol. 15 (1967).

Chapter Seven, "The Prostitution of Females," is an expanded version of "Prostitution" from the *Encyclopedia of Social Science* (London: Collier-Macmillan Ltd.)

Chapter Eight, "Homosexual Conduct in Prison," is a revised version of "The Social Meaning of Prison Homosexuality," from *Federal Probation*, Vol. 32 (1968).

We have enjoyed and benefited from the association with numerous colleagues and students—many more than can be mentioned here. Among them were David Sonenschein, who provided most of the interview material utilized in chapter 5; Daniel Offer who constantly attempted to steer us away from an overly-stereotyped view of Freud, though he may not feel that he has succeeded as much as he would have liked; John McHale for helping us view the future less nervously; Alan Berger, who played an invaluable role in moving much of the uncompleted research for this book to completion; and David Goslin, who, at critical moments, helped us feel less lost in the margins. Much of the final work on the manuscript was done with the authors at separate sites—Simon at the Institute for Juvenile Research, and Gagnon at the State University of New York at Stony Brook. While this complicated the process somewhat, it also enlarged the available pool of colleagues offering stimulation, support, and criticism. At IJR this included the late Noel Jenkin, Zena Smith Blau, Calvert Cotrell, Patricia Y. Miller, Gary Schwartz, Joseph Puntil, Merton S. Kraus, and Frank Rafferty; at Stony Brook, Gerald Davison, David McWhirter, Hanan Selvin, Stanley Yolles, and Eugene Weinstein.

Lastly, Howard S. Becker and Sheldon Messinger provided a critical reading of an earlier version, and our publisher, Alex Morin, is responsible for reorganizing and arranging the final version. Curt Johnson and Nanci Connors, our editors at Aldine, have our appreciation.

John H. Gagnon
Churchill College, Cambridge

William Simon
IJR, Chicago

1

The Social Origins of Sexual Development

Introduction

Underlying all human activity, regardless of the field or its stage of development, there exist metaphors or informing imageries—commonly unnamed until they lose their potency—that shape thought, experiment, and the directions of research. In the earliest days of the development of what is now modern physics, the metaphorical content of Newtonian mechanics could be found not only in the sciences, but in religion, philosophy and the widest range of activities of educated men.[1] The Newtonian (or Descartian) metaphor of the universe as a large clock running its immutable course after having been designed and wound up by the creator was widely and easily accepted far beyond the narrow domain of physics. The content of the mental life of educated men, whether in the sciences or not, for that brief moment overlapped and the metaphors of the larger society and the paradigms of the sciences interpenetrated.

Once that central and organizing paradigm had been selected, as Kuhn points out, there began the separation of physics and then the other natural sciences from an immediate accessibility to even educated men.[2] The content of the sciences has become increasingly

1. Murray Turbayne, *The Myth of Metaphor* (New Haven: Yale University Press, 1962).
2. Thomas Kuhn, *The Structure of Scientific Revolutions* (Chicago: University of Chicago Press, 1962).

limited to scientists and the generation of useful metaphors from scientific formulations has declined as the sciences separate from the society at large. Most recently it is argued that with the increased difficulty of translating the mathematical formulations of modern physics into usable social coinage, the field of physics has ceased to have any serious effect on the way most men think about the world.[3]

Such unrecognized conceptions and metaphors are still characteristic of modern studies of man, however, and these continue to draw upon conventional historical thought and upon folk wisdom to develop their modes of thought. In this important sense the study of man and society is close to pre-paradigmatic; that is, there is no organizing scheme which directs our activities. Thus, central to the study of social life is a commonly unspoken belief in the existence of natural man, a man who has innate transhistorical and transcultural attributes and needs. A dependence on the constancy of the human seems to be a necessary element in our desire to understand the past and in our belief in our capacity to control the future. A commitment to a fixed psychological (in some cases, physiological) nature of man allows us to see all of the actors of history as operating with our motives, concerns, and goals, so that Moses and Luther, Michelangelo and Manet, Dante and Joyce, are equivalent figures removed from each other only by the exterior accidents of time and culture. At the higher cultural levels this tyranny of the present over the past is represented most vividly in Marxist and Freudian reinterpretations of history which involve profound assumptions not only about the past, but the present as well; in its more vulgar form it is in those cinematic personifications that allow Charlton Heston to be Moses, Michelangelo, and Ben Hur and serve as the crucial condensate of our cultural heritage. Taken together, the high and low cultural responses are variants of two historical fallacies pointed out by David Fischer, the idealist fallacy (resting upon a narrow and exclusive concept of homo sapiens), and the fallacy of universal man. As Fischer argues:

3. Hannah Arendt, *The Human Condition* (Chicago: University of Chicago Press, 1958).

People, in various places and times, have not merely thought different things. They have thought them differently. It is probable that their most fundamental cerebral processes have changed through time. Their deepest emotional drives and desires may themselves have been transformed. Significant elements of continuity cannot be understood without the discontinuities, too. . . . There is accumulating evidence of expressions of thought and feeling that make no sense unless we allow a wide latitude for change in the nature of cerebral activity through space and time. The range of this change is as obscure as its nature. But its existence is, in my opinion a historical fact which is established beyond a reasonable doubt.[4]

This rummaging through the past for useful arguments and ideologies to introduce cultural and social innovation in the present has been a characteristic of modern societies, and the impulse to connect ourselves no matter how tenuously with the past is in part an attempt to cast wider the net of a common humanity. However, it is in quest for (motivational) immortality that the modern impulse to use the past is converted into an attempt to psychologically colonize the future. High culture and low again combine in Committees on the Year 2000, Institutes for the Future, movies such as *2001 A.D.,* and television shows such as *Star Trek.*

At no point in human history has the historical-cultural specificity of the human personality and the concept of what is human been more evident, and at the same time there are extraordinary pressures against such a changed conception of the human. Committing the ethological fallacy, wherein we are warned that our hunting-gathering natures are the central themes around which modern man must organize his marriage and reproductive life or in which we are instructed to consider our common attributes with other primates, is an example of an unwillingness to live with the existential and changing nature of man at an individual and collective level. Continuity is sought with all living things until one has an urge to plead for the theory of special creation.[5]

At no point is the belief in the natural and universal human more

4. David H. Fischer, *Historical Fallacies* (New York: Harper Torch Books, Harper & Row, 1970), pp. 203-24.
5. Lionel Tiger, *Men in Groups* (New York: Random House, 1969).

entrenched than in the study of sexuality. The critical significance
of reproduction in species survival is made central to a model of
man and woman in which biological arrangements are translated
into sociocultural imperatives. In consequence it is not surprising
that it is in the study of the sexual that there exists a prepotent concern with the power of biology and nature as opposed to an understanding of the capacities of social life.

Naturalness and the Body

In an important sense our concern with the natural in sexual conduct is ambiguous. At one level our view of sex insists that it is a
natural function, growing out of biological or evolutionary or species needs or imperatives. It is this view that supplies us a belief in
cultural, historical, and transpecies comparisons. At another level,
however, the natural also exists in opposition to the unnatural; of
the wide variety of sexual expressions there are those that are natural (i.e., contribute to species survival, virtuous in the eyes of God,
or mental-health enhancing) and those that are unnatural (i.e., reduce species survival, are sinful or vicious, or involve mental path-
ologies). There is a linkage between these two levels, but more
often we move from one to the other confusing our ideological inher-
itances about the sexual (as well as our ideologies about evolution,
species survival, virtue, and mental health) in order to conserve one
or another of our cultural-historical values.

In large measure our distinctions between the *natural* and the *unnatural* in sex behavior is directly based on the physical activities in
which people engage when they are doing what are conventionally
described as sexual acts. For most persons (even the most liberated
of the post-Freudians) most of the time, it is the assembly of bodies
in time and space that is the primary defining characteristic of normalcy or perversion, health or sickness, virtue or vice, conformity
or deviance. Our laws embody our felt margin between those acts
that are natural and those that are crimes against nature, delineat-
ing a narrow domain of *de jure* legitimacy by constraining the age,
gender, legal, and kin relationships between sexual actors, as well as
setting limits on the sites of behavior and the connections between
organs. Even if one leaves aside the legal allowances for the mar-

ried, a status which clearly normalizes many aspects of sexual activity, coitus in the "missionary position" (the male above prone, the female below supine) is the physical arrangement of bodies that calls forth our greatest sense of comfort in thinking about the physical aspects of sex. To move beyond this arrangement of bodies either in fantasy or fact is to move into a more shadowy realm where anxiety, guilt, and eroticism await. Indeed, to think about sex in terms of what bodies do is to begin to perform a sexual act—an act with its own norms and constraints, but at the same time an act that provokes the physiological beginnings of what Masters and Johnson have classified as sexual excitement.

It is perhaps startling to consider that when we think about the sexual, nearly our entire imagery is drawn from the physical activities of bodies. Our sense of normalcy derives from organs being placed in legitimate orifices. We have allowed the organs, the orifices, and the gender of the actors to personify or embody or exhaust nearly all of the meanings that exist in the sexual situation. Rarely do we turn from a consideration of the organs themselves to the sources of the meanings that are attached to them, the ways in which the physical activities of sex are learned, and the ways in which these activities are integrated into larger social scripts and social arrangements where meaning and sexual behavior come together to create sexual conduct.[6]

It is this assembly of the reality of the body and the social and cultural sources of attributed meaning that is missing in the two greatest modern students of sexuality in the West. In Freud we find a world dominated by the search for motivation, a world in which the body never seems to be very problematic since it is both the source of naturalness (anatomy becomes destiny) and the passive recipient of meanings attributed to it. At no point in psychoanalytic theory is there an extended consideration of the physical activities of sexual behavior and the ways in which these physical activities themselves require systematic linkage to social roles and social meanings. Sexual arousal lies in nature; the social world responds and shapes but does not initiate. In Freud sex itself seems disembodied and we are left with a world full of ideas and psychic struc-

6. Ernest W. Burgess, "The Sociologic Theory of Psychosexual Behavior," in *Psychosexual Development in Health and Disease,* eds. Paul H. Hoch and Joseph Zubin (New York: Grune and Stratton, 1949) pp. 227–43.

tures only tangentially related to the bodies that are performing the acts.[7]

In the work of Kinsey we see the opposite thrust. Here we have sexual man in the decorticated state; the bodies arrange themselves, orgasm occurs, one counts it seeking a continuum of rates where normalcy is a function of location on a distribution scale. Once again in our search for the natural sources of behavior, the meanings that actors attribute to their own behavior and that the society collectively organizes are left out. In the Kinsey reports sexual activity among primates and primitive societies, in the historical past and the present, are functional equivalents because the arrangement of organs and orifices appear similar. Thus, each instance of the presence or absence of homosexuality in various cultures is counted as an identical manifestation of evolutionary principles rather than being examined within the complex of meanings that a physical sexual relationship between persons of the same gender may have in various circumstances, at various moments in history, and in various subgroupings in a society. The physical sexual activity of two males when one of them is defined as *berdache* among the Western Plains Indians is identical with the sexual activity of two men in ancient Greece or in a modern Western society; but the meanings attached to the behavior and its functions for the society are so disparate in these cases that seeing them as aspects of the same phenomena except in the most superficial way is to vitiate all we know about social analysis.

Of the two figures, Freud has surely been of greater influence in shaping theoretical models of development and in the penetration of his ideas into the cultural ambiance. It is in the work of Kinsey, however, that we find the largest body of empirical data about sexual behavior. Despite the predominance of these two men in the discussion of the sexual, there is, from the point of view of the history of science, a curiously nonconsequential quality about their work. While the status of their ideas as cultural events has been substantial, there has been a painful lack of scientific follow-up of either their concepts or their data. This is not to say that there is not a substantial literature that has developed out of the psychoan-

7. Sigmund Freud, "Three Essays on Sexuality," *Complete Psychological Works,* vol. 7 (London: Hogarth Press, 1953) pp. 135–245.

alytic tradition, but in the largest part it has been narrowly concerned with the Talmudic imposition of Freud's original models on clinical case histories or the reading of collective and sociocultural events.[8]

Kinsey's scientific fate has perhaps been ruder than Freud's, since very little research of any sort has followed upon the publication of his two major works, perhaps no more than two to three papers of merit each year. His two large volumes continue to be for the most part undigested lumps in the craw of the research community. While Kinsey's work had serious consequences in changing and creating cultural attitude, in bringing the language of sex into general public discussion (as Freud had done among intellectuals a generation before), there has been only a minimal increase in activity at the level of science, most of that preoccupied with the burdens of social bookkeeping, at the most significant points providing a context of cultural journalism.[9]

To some degree this failure to develop a research concern for sexual matters in the conventional disciplines can be laid at the door of scientific and cultural prudery, but it is equally a function of two other forces: the historical (and perhaps reactive) self-insulation of "sexological" researches and researchers from the mainstream disciplines, and the continued commitment—shared by both Freud and Kinsey—to a belief in "biological knowingness" or to the wisdom of nature in the explanation of sexual behavior and development.

The very idea of "sexology" tends to insulate those interested in sexual behavior from theoretical and methodological developments that occur on a broad front within the human sciences. Because sex is culturally isolated in general, researchers often claim exemption from normal methodological strictures and become deeply and de-

---

8. While the deeply beleaguered condition of psychoanalysis as a movement accounts for at least some of the sectarian politics of its earlier days, the adherence to doctrinal purity on the part of younger analysts may be equally attributed to the ambiguous conditions under which therapy is practiced. See John H. Gagnon, "Beyond Freud," *Partisan Review* 34 (Summer 1967): 400–14.

9. The publication of the two volumes by Masters and Johnson appear at some level to be as noncumulative as Kinsey's and to be similar kinds of cultural rather than scientific events.

fensively invested in the substantive content of sexuality while remaining indifferent to the rest of social life. The very specialness of sex makes its students special, both to themselves and others, and their possession of secret cultural knowledge is in itself sometimes intellectually disabling, since it often is used as a device to disarm criticism.

It is the most suspect of the expository literature about sex that attempts in a limited way to bring together feelings about sex with descriptions of sexual activity. Though most written pornography may appear to be (in the words of Steven Marcus) "organ grinding," it does indicate a crude psychology and set of motivations for those who are performing the sexual acts.[10] As we argue elsewhere (see chap. 9), there is more social life in literary pornography than those who wish to contrast it to "literature" are wont to notice. In order for the sexual activity described or observed to have erotic stimulus value for the reader, the actors involved must be playing out some sociosexual script that has significance for the reader. The capacity for arousal itself (including physical tumescense) depends on the presence of culturally appropriate eliciting stimuli composed of persons, motives, and activities combined to produce significant sexual actors in sexual situations. For all practical purposes, until the 1960s it was only pornography that made available descriptions of some of the physical aspects of sexual behavior. While limited in complexity and with a limited sensibility, the characters in pornography actually felt skin, smelled each other's odors, tasted bodily fluids, and did sexual things.

Only recently in the scientific literature and only now in "higher" art is a significant component of physicality present in the descriptions of sexual activity. Because we possess theories of sexual behavior based on the immediate connection between explicit sexual descriptions and overt behavior, our analysis of the erotic does not come to terms with the fact that these descriptions are received into already existing complex cognitive and emotional structures. As a result of our commitment to nature and to the sexual organs as the primary sources of meaning, we fail to observe that the doing of sex

10. Steven Marcus, *The Other Victorians* (New York: Basic Books, 1966), pp. 292ff.

(even when alone) requires elaborated and sequential learning that is largely taken from other domains of life and a resultant etiquette that allows for the coordination of bodies and meanings in a wide variety of circumstances.

The complex outcome which is marital coitus, the most common form of sexual conduct in our society, involves a vast array of human learning and the coordination of physiological, psychological, and social elements, practically none of which can be attributed to nature writ large as evolution or nature writ small as a morality play based on glandular secretions. Our concern here is to understand sexual activities of all kinds (however defined, good or evil, deviant or conforming, normal or pathological, criminal or noncriminal) as the outcome of a complex psychosocial process of development, and it is only because they are embedded in social scripts that the physical acts themselves become possible. This combination of various periods of development into the articulate behavioral sequence that leads to orgasm is not fated or ordained at any level; it is neither fixed by nature or by the organs themselves. The very experience of sexual excitement that seems to orginate from hidden internal sources is in fact a learned process and it is only our insistence on the myth of naturalness that hides these social components from us.

The Sexual Tradition

The most important set of images for sex or eroticism in the modern West, either for scientists or in conventional educated speech, derives from the language of psychoanalysis. It would be difficult to overstate the coercive power of Freud's innovative verbal reformulations of a whole range of early conceptualizations about the role of sexuality in its biological, personal, and societal contexts. In an important sense Freud remains the superego of nearly all researchers into the sexual, since we must in some measure either conform to or rebel against his body of ideas. As with most great innovators, Freud began with the available set of contemporary ideas that were part of the heritage of the eighteenth and nineteenth centuries. It is difficult for those in the 1970s, for whom Freud is received wisdom and whose conservative postures are now most evident and empha-

sized, to recognize his role as a radical theorist of sexuality as well
as representing a force for sociopolitical liberalism. The emphasis
on the instinctual basis for the experience of the sexual and the universality of man's sexual experience, though possibly wrong in fact
and theory, served to introduce a great change in sexual values at
the turn of the century. Perhaps more important, by asserting the
universality of the human experience, Freud significantly helped
erode the dubious anthropology that imperial Europe used to describe its colonial subjects.

The Freudian codification provided for modern, educated, Western man a set of verbal categories through which he might describe
his internal states, explain the origins of his sexual proclivities, describe his own and others' motives, and ultimately reanalyze literature, histories, and societies as well as individual lives. The cultural
assimilation of much of psychoanalytic theory, especially on a popular level, resides in its essential continuity with popular wisdom
about the instinctive nature of sexuality. This version of sexuality as
an innate and dangerous instinct is shared not only by the man in
the street, but also by psychological theorists deeply opposed to
Freudian thought, as well as by sociologists whose rejection of analytic theory is nearly total. Hence the language of Kingsley Davis:

> The development and maintenance of a stable competitive order with
> respect to sex is extremely difficult because sexual desire itself is in-
> herently unstable and anarchic. Erotic relations are subject to con-
> stant danger—a change of whim, a loss of interest, a third party, a
> misunderstanding. Competition for the same sexual object inflames
> passions, and stirs conflicts; failure injures ones self-esteem. The in-
> tertwining of sex and society is a fertile ground for paranoia, for
> homicide and suicide.[11]

The seventeenth-century political image of the individual against
the state is translated by the Romantic tradition into a contest between the individual and his culture. The Hobbesian contest between natural instinct and imposed constraint was moved by Freud
(as well as many other post-Romantic innovators) from the arena

11. Kingsley Davis, "Sexual Behavior," in *Contemporary Social Problems*
eds. R. K. Merton and R. Nisbet (New York: Harcourt Brace Jovanovich,
1971), p. 317.

of the state, power conflicts, and the social contract to the arena of the mind, sexuality, and the parent-child contract. The sexual instinct presses against cultural controls, pleasure contests with reality, as the sociocultural forces in the form of parents (Leviathan writ small) block, shape, and organize the sexual drive and convert it from lust to love, from societal destruction to social service.

This tradition is surely present in Freud with his emphasis on a drive model of development, a libidinal thrust that sequentially organizes intra- and extra-psychic life as well as the very meaning of the parts of the body. This direct relation between the external signs of physiological events and necessary motivational and cognitive states is a given for nearly all students of sexual behavior, whose frequent error is to confuse the outcomes of sexual learning with their apparent origins.

The Freudian or Kinseyian traditions share the prevailing image of the sexual drive as a basic biological mandate that presses against and must be controlled by the cultural and social matrix. This drive reduction model of sexual behavior as mediated by cultural and social controls is preeminent in "sexological" literature. Explanations of sexual behavior that flow from this model are relatively simple. The sex drive is thought to exist at some constant level in any cohort of the population, with rising and falling levels in the individual's life cycle. It presses for expression, and in the absence of controls, which exist either in laws and mores or in appropriate internalized repressions learned in early socialization, there will be outbreaks of "abnormal sexual activity." In the more primitive versions of this drive theory, there is a remarkable congruence between the potentiating mechanisms for specifically sexual and generally sinful behavior. The organism is inherently sexual (sinful) and its behavior is controlled by the presence of inhibitory training and channeling, internalized injunctions, and the absence of temptation. If these mechanisms fail, there will certainly be sexual misconduct (sin). More sophisticated models can be found in functional theories in sociology or in revisionist psychoanalytic models, but fundamental to each is a drive reduction notion that sees sex as having necessary collective and individual consequences because of its biological origins.

What is truly innovative about Freud's thought is not his utilization of prior constructs about sexuality and the nature of man, but his placement of these ideas about sexuality at the center of human concerns, beginning in infancy, an essential to normal human development. As Erik Erikson has observed, prior to Freud, "sexology" tended to see sexuality as suddenly appearing with the onset of adolescence.[12] From Erikson's point of view, Freud's discovery of infantile and childhood expressions of sexuality was a crucial part of his contribution. Libido—the generation of psychosexual energies—was viewed after Freud as a fundamental element of the human experience from its very inception, beginning at the latest with birth and possibly prior to birth. Libido was conceived as something essential to the organism, representing a kind of constitutional factor with which forms of social life at all levels of sociocultural organization and development, as well as personality structure at each point in the individual life cycle, had to cope.

In Freud's view the human infant and child behaved in ways that were intrinsically sexual and these early behaviors remained in effective and influential continuity with later forms of psychosexual development.[13] Implicit in this view was the assumption that the relations between available sexual energies and emergent motives and attachments would be complex but direct. In some aspects of psychoanalytic thinking, both adolescent and adult sexuality were viewed as being in some measure a reenactment of sexual commitments developed, learned, or acquired during infancy and childhood.[14]

From the vantage point of the late twentieth century, it is apparent that this point of view presents both an epistemological and a sociolinguistic problem. Freud's descriptive language for sexuality was the language of adults describing their current and childhood

12. E. H. Erikson, *Childhood and Society,* 2nd ed. (New York: Norton, 1963).

13. Sigmund Freud, "Three Essays on Sexuality," *Complete Psychological Works,* vol. 7 (London: Hogarth, 1953), pp. 135–245. Also, E. Jones, "Freud's Conception of Libido," in *Human Sexual Behavior: A Book of Readings,* ed. Bernhardt Lieberman (New York: John Wiley & Sons, Inc., 1971), pp. 42–60; P. Chodoff, "Critique of Freud's Theory of Infantile Sexuality," *American Journal of Psychiatry* 123 (1966): 507–18.

14. Sigmund Freud, *A General Introduction to Psychoanalysis* (New York: Liveright, 1935), pp. 283–84.

"sexual" experience (as transmuted through psychoanalytic interviews), which was then imposed upon the "apparent" behavior and "assumed" responses, feelings, and cognitions of infants and children. Acts and feelings are described as sexual, not because of the child's sense of the experience, but because of the meanings attached to those acts by adult observers or interpreters whose only available language is that of adult sexual experience.

It is important to note here the extraordinary difficulties of all developmental research in getting accurate data and also that research on infancy and childhood through adulthood faces a problem which most of the psychoanalytic literature obscures. Part of the problem is faulty recall, some of which is locatable in the problem of inaccurate memories, but another source of error is located in the existentalist insight that instead of the past determining the character of the present, the present significantly reshapes the past as we reconstruct our biographies in an effort to bring them into greater congruence with our current identities, roles, situations, and available vocabularies. Indeed, the role of the analyst in providing an alternative self-conception for patients by creating a new vocabulary of motives is central to the therapeutic impulse and opposed to the gathering of accurate information about the past.

The other major problem of data quality control results from attempting to gather data either from children who are, because of their stage of development, ill-equipped to report on their internal states or from adults who were asked to report about periods in their life when complex vocabularies for internal states did not exist for them.[15] How can the researcher determine what is being felt or thought when the researcher is confronted with organisms whose restricted language skills may preclude certain feelings and thoughts? The child in this situation possesses internal states that in a verbal sense are meaningless and that will begin to be named and organized only during later development. The adult loses access to that inchoate period of his own experience by learning new ways of attributing meaning to experiences. The organism cannot hold onto both sets of experiences at once. Indeed, this may be the central meaning of development, that the acquisition of new categories for

---

15. E. Schachtel, *Metamorphosis* (New York: Basic Books, 1959).

experience erase the past. Opie and Opie report that adolescents quickly forget childhood games. How much more quickly do we forget earlier and more diffuse experiences?[16]

The assumption of an identity between perception based upon a adult terminology for the description of a child's behavior and the meaning of that behavior for the child must be treated with extreme caution. The dilemma is in distinguishing between the sources of specific actions, gestures, and bodily movements and the ways in which they are labeled as sexual at various stages of development. For the infant touching his penis, the activity cannot be sexual in the same sense as adult masturbation but is merely a diffusely pleasurable activity, like many other activities. Only through maturing and learning these adult labels for his experience and activity can the child come to masturbate in the adult sense of that word. The complexity of adult masturbation as an act is enormous, requiring the close coordination of physical, psychological, and social resources, all of which change dynamically after puberty. It is through the developmental process of converting external labels into internal capacities for naming that activities become more precisely defined and linked to a structure of sociocultural expectations and needs that define what is sexual. The naive external observer of this behavior often imputes to the child the complex set of motivational states that are generally associated (often wrongly) with physically homologous adult activities.

In the Freudian schema, this gap between observer and observed, between the language of adult experience and the lived experience of the child is bridged by locating an instinctual sexual energy source within the infant. The child is seen as possessed of certain emergent sexual characteristics that express themselves regardless

---

16. There is a body of evidence that among young children there is a large amount of game and folklore material that is rapidly forgotten after puberty. A certain amount of this material is sexual, but the folklorists who work with children usually fail to keep records of this, or if they do so, do not publish it. An interesting aspect of this material is its eternal character —that is, it is passed on from generation to generation. For example, children in England are currently singing a recognizable variant of a song about Bonaparte popular in the early nineteenth century. See Iona Opie and Peter Opie, *The Lore and Language of School Children* (London: Oxford Press, 1959), pp. 98–99.

of parental action systems. These actions of the child are viewed as being rooted in the constitutional nature of the organism. Consequent upon this primitive Freudian position is an over generalized presumption that all contacts with or stimulation of the end organs of the infant have a protosexual or completely sexual meaning.

To suggest that infant or childhood experience, even that which is identified as genital, is prototypical of or determines adult patterns is to credit the biological organism with more wisdom than we normally do in other areas where the biological and sociocultural intersect. Undeniably, what we conventionally describe as sexual behavior is rooted in biological capacities and processes, but no more than other forms of behavior. Admitting the existence of a biological substrate for sex in no way allows a greater degree of biological determinism than is true of other areas of corresponding intersection. Indeed, the reverse is more likely to be true: the sexual area may be precisely that realm wherein the superordinate position of the sociocultural over the biological level is most complete.[17]

The unproven assumption in psychoanalytic theory (and much conventional wisdom) of the "power" of the psychosexual drive as a fixed biological attribute may prove to be the major obstacle to the understanding of psychosexual development. In its more specific psychoanalytic formulation, we find little evidence to suggest that such a "drive" need find expression in specific sexual acts or categories of sexual acts.[18] Similarly, we must call into question the even more dubious assumption that there are innate sexual capacities or specific experiences that tend to translate immediately into a kind of universal wisdom, that sexuality possesses a magical ability allowing biological drives to seek direct expression in psychosocial

17. Even on the level of organismic needs and gratification, the linking of these to the sexual or protosexual may be too limited, too simple. Robert White has argued cogently that during infancy and early childhood an emergent commitment to "competence" may rival sensual expressions of the pleasure principle in organizing the young organism's activities, as the child "sacrifices" immediate sensual gratification in order to develop and experience his or her own competence. See "Psychosexual Development and Competence," *The Nebraska Symposium on Motivation* (Lincoln, University of Nebraska Press, 1960).

18. Frank A. Beach, "Characteristics of Masculine 'Sex Drive'," *The Nebraska Symposium on Motivation* (Lincoln: University of Nebraska Press, 1956).

and social ways that we do not expect in other biologically rooted
behaviors. This assumption can be seen in the psychoanalytic literature, for example, in which the child who views the "primal scene"
is seen on some primitive level as intuiting its sexual character.
Also, the term *latency,* in its usage by psychoanalytic theorists,
suggests a period of integration by the child of prior intrinsically
sexual experiences and reactions; on this level, adolescence is reduced to little more than the management or organization on a
manifest level of the commitments and styles already prefigured, if
not preformed, in infancy and childhood experience.

In contradistinction to this tradition, we have adopted the view
that the point at which the individual begins to respond in intrinsically sexual ways, particularly in terms of socially available or defined outlets and objects, reflects a discontinuity with previous "sexual experience" (however that might be defined). Further, at this
point in the developmental process, both seemingly sexual and
seemingly nonsexual elements "contend" for influence in complex
ways that in no respect assure priority for experiences that are apparently sexual in character and occur earlier in the life cycle.

Essential to our perspective is the assumption that with the beginnings of adolescence—and with the increasing acknowledgement
by the surrounding social world of an individual's sexual capacity
—many novel factors come into play, and an overemphasis upon a
search for continuity with infant and childhood experiences may be
dangerously misleading. In particular, it may be a costly mistake to
be overimpressed with preadolescent behaviors that appear to be
manifestly sexual. In general, it is possible that much of the power
of sexuality may be a function of the fact that it has been defined as
powerful or dangerous. But this overenriched conception of sexual
behavior (to the degree that it is possessed by any individual) must
largely follow upon considerable training in an adult language that
includes an overdetermined conception of sexuality. Thus it does
not necessarily follow that the untrained infant or child will respond
as powerfully or as complexly to his own seemingly sexual behaviors as an adult observer.

We must also question the prevailing image of the sexual component in human experience as that of an intense drive stemming from
the biological substratum that constrains the individual to seek sex-

ual gratification either directly or indirectly. This is clearly present in the Freudian tradition. A similar position is observable in more sociological writings. This is apparent, for example, in the thinking of sociologists for whom sex is also a high intensity, societal constant that must be properly channeled lest it find expression in behaviors which threaten the maintenance of collective life.[19]

Our sense of the available data suggests a somewhat different picture of human sexuality, one of generally lower levels of intensity or, at least, greater variability in intensity. There are numerous social situations in which the reduction and even elimination of sexual activity is managed by greatly disparate populations of biologically normal males and females with little evidence of corollary or compensatory intensification in other spheres of life.[20] It is possible that, given the historical nature of human societies, we are victim to the needs of earlier social orders. For earlier societies it may not have been a need to constrain severely the powerful sexual impulse in order to maintain social stability or limit inherently antisocial force, but rather a matter of having to invent an importance for sexuality. This would not only assure a high level of reproductive activity but also provide socially available rewards unlimited by natural resources, rewards that promote conforming behavior in sectors of social life far more important than the sexual. Part of the legacy of Freud is that we have all become adept at seeking out the sexual ingredient in many forms of nonsexual behavior and symbolism. We are suggesting what is in essence the insight of Kenneth Burke: it is just as plausible to examine sexual behavior for its capacity to express and serve nonsexual motives as the reverse.[21]

A major flaw in the psychoanalytic tradition is that psychosexual development, while a universal component in the human experience, certainly does not occur with universal modalities. Even ignoring the striking forms of cross-cultural variability, we can observe striking differences within our own population, differences

19. E. Durkheim, *Suicide* (Glencoe, Ill. The Free Press, 1951).

20. J. H. Gagnon and W. Simon, "The Social Meaning of Prison Homosexuality," *Federal Probation*, 1968.

21. K. Burke, *Permanence and Change* (New York: New Republic, Inc., 1935).

that appear to require not a unitary description of psychosexual development but descriptions of different developmental processes characterizing different segments of the population.[22] The most evident of these are the large number of important differences between observable male and female patterns of sexual behavior.[23] This particular difference may in some respects be partly attributable to the role played by the biological substratum. We have to account not only for the gross physiological differences and the different roles in the reproductive process that follow from these physiological differences, but must also consider differences in hormone functions at particular ages.[24] However, while our knowledge of many of the salient physiological and physiochemical processes involved is far from complete, there is still little immediate justification for asserting a direct casual link between these processes and specific differential patterns of sexual development observed in our society. The work of Masters and Johnson, for example, clearly points to far greater orgasmic capacities on the part of females than males; however, their concept of orgasm as a physiological process would hardly be a basis for accurately predicting rates of sexual behavior.[25] Similarly, within each sex, important distinctions must be made for various socioeconomic status groups whose patterns of sexual development will vary considerably, more impressively for males than for females.[26] And with reference to socioeconomic status differences, the link to the biological level appears even more tenuous, unless one is willing to invoke the relatively unfashionable conceptual equipment of Social Darwinism. These differences, then, not only suggest the importance of sociocultural elements and social structure,

22. C. F. Ford and F. A. Beach, *Patterns of Sexual Behavior* (New York: Harper, 1951).

23. E. Maccoby, ed., *The Development of Sex Differences* (Stanford: Stanford University Press, 1966).

24. D. A. Hamburg and D. T. Lunde, "Sex Hormones in the Development of Sex Differences in Human Behavior," in Maccoby, *The Development of Sex Differences,* pp. 1–24; W. R. Young, R. Goy, and C. Phoenix, "Hormones and Sexual Behavior," *Science* 143 (1964): 212–18.

25. W. H. Masters and V. E. Johnson, *Human Sexual Response* (Boston: Little, Brown and Co., 1966).

26. A. C. Kinsey et al., *Sexual Behavior in the Human Male* (Philadelphia: W. B. Saunders Co., 1948).

but also stand as a warning against too uncritical an acceptance of unqualified generalizations about psychosexual development.

Scripts and the Attribution of Meaning

The term *script* might properly be invoked to describe virtually all human behavior in the sense that there is very little that can in a full measure be called spontaneous. Ironically, the current vogue of using "encounter groups" to facilitate "spontaneous" behavior can be defined as learning the appropriate script for spontaneous behavior. Indeed, the sense of the *internal rehearsal* consistent with both psychoanalytic and symbolic interactionist theory suggests just such scripting of all but the most routinized behavior.

It is the result of our collective blindness to or ineptitude in locating and defining these scripts that has allowed the prepotence of a biological mandate in the explanation of sexual behavior. (This possibly occurs precisely because the notion of such a biological mandate is a common element within the sexual scripts of Western societies.) Without the proper elements of a script that defines the situation, names the actors, and plots the behavior, nothing sexual is likely to happen. One can easily conceive of numerous social situations in which all or almost all of the ingredients of a sexual event are present but that remain nonsexual in that not even sexual arousal occurs. Thus, combining such elements as desire, privacy, and a physically attractive person of the appropriate sex, the probability of something sexual happening will, under normal circumstances, remain exceedingly small until either one or both actors organize these behaviors into an appropriate script.

Elements of such scripting occur across many aspects of the sexual situation. Scripts are involved in learning the meaning of internal states, organizing the sequences of specifically sexual acts, decoding novel situations, setting the limits on sexual responses, and linking meanings from nonsexual aspects of life to specifically sexual experience. These would at first seem only to be versions of the old sociological saw that nothing occurs internally that does not occur in the external social world. But it is more than this in two ways. Using this model the process of sexual learning can be specified without depending on nonbehavioral elements, and doing this reorders the sources of meaning for phenomena and the ways in which we think about the sexual experience.

This can be exemplified even more dramatically. Take an ordinary middle-class male, detach him from his regular social location, and place him for some business or professional reason in a large, relatively anonymous hotel. One might even endow him with an interest in sexual adventure. Upon returning to the hotel at night, he opens his hotel door and there in the shaft of light from the hallway, he observes a nearly nude, extremely attractive female. One may assume that his initial reaction will *not* be one of sexual arousal. A few men—the slightly more paranoid—might begin to cast about for signs of their wife's lawyer or a private detective. Most, however, would simply beat a hasty and profoundly embarrassed retreat. Even back in the hall and with a moment's reflection to establish the correctness of the room number, the next impulse would still *not* be one of sexual arousal or activity but most probably a trip to the lobby to seek clarification—via the affectively neutral telephone. What is lacking in this situation is an effective sexual script that would allow him to define the female as a potentially erotic actor (the mere fact of her being attractive or nearly nude is not sufficient) and the situation as potentially sexual. If these two definitional elements did exist, much of what might follow can be predicted with fair accuracy. But without such a script, little by way of sexual activity or even sexual arousal will transpire.

Our use of the term *script* with reference to the sexual has two major dimensions. One deals with the external, the interpersonal— the script as the organization of mutually shared conventions that allows two or more actors to participate in a complex act involving mutual dependence. The second deals with the internal, the intrapsychic, the motivational elements that produce arousal or at least a commitment to the activity.

At the level of convention is that large class of gestures, both verbal and nonverbal, that are mutually accessible. Routinized language, the sequence of petting behaviors among adolescents and adults, the conventional styles establishing sexual willingness are all parts of culturally shared, external routines. These are the strategies involved in the "doing" of sex, concrete and continuous elements of what a culture agrees is sexual. They are assembled, learned over time, reflecting—as will be clear in subsequent chapters—general patterns of stages of development. This relatively stylized behavior, however, tells us little of the meaning it has for its participants. The same sequence of acts may have different meanings for both different pairs of actors or the participants in the same act. This is the world where sexual activity can be expressive of love or rage, the will to power or the will to self-degradation, where the behavioral is experienced through the symbolic.

On the level of internal experience, it is apparent from the work of Schachter and others that the meaning attributed to many states of physiological arousal depends upon the situation in which they are experienced.[27] In this way, meaning is attributed to the interior of the body by many of the same rules as it is to an exterior experience, depending on a vocabulary of motives that makes the biological into a meaningful psychological experience. This phenomena is well understood in research in drug effects, with the meaning of the drug experience being dependent on mood, situation of use, prior history of the user, and the like, rather than what is spuriously referred to as the drug effect. This is apparent in the effects of all of the so-called mind-altering drugs including marijuana. The differing reports on the internal effects of LSD–25 lysergic acid (good trips, psychomimetic experiences, paranoid trips, art nouveau hallucinations, meetings with God) seem more attributable to the person-situation effect than to the drug. This is observable in young adolescents when they are required to learn what the feelings they have with reference to early post-pubertal sexual arousal "mean." Events variously categorized as anxiety, nausea, fear are reported which are later finally categorized as (or dismissed, even though they still occur) sexual excitement. A vast number of physiological events get reported to the central nervous system, but of

---

27. Stanley Schachter, "The Interaction of Cognitive and Emotional Determinants of Emotional State," in *Advances in Experimental Social Psychology,* vol. 1, ed. Leonard Berkowitz (New York: Academic Press, 1964), pp. 49–80. That similar processes of control over the autonomic nervous system also exist and can be operantly conditioned is demonstrated by Neal Miller, "Learning of Visceral and Glandular Responses," *Science* 163 (January 31, 1969): 434–45. Work on increasing "voluntary" control of sexual responses (e.g., penile erection) is beginning only at the present moment.

this number only a small proportion are attended to in any single moment. (How many persons, for instance, experience their toes curl or the anal sphincter twitch at the moment of orgasm?) It is this small proportion that is recognized as the internal correlates or internal "meanings" of the experience. In this case, the meaning is a consensual experience with various elements brought together to be the appropriate behaviors that will elicit the internal correlates or consequences of the external behaviors.

Scripting also occurs not only in the making of meaningful interior states, but in providing the ordering of bodily activities that will release these internal biological states. Here scripts are the mechanisms through which biological events can be potentiated. An example from the adult world is most apt in revealing this process. If one examines the assembly of events that are the physical elements of the current script in the United States for adolescent or adult heterosexual behavior that leads to coitus, it is clear that there is a progression from hugging and kissing, to petting above the waist, to hand-genital contacts (sometimes mouth-genital contacts) and finally to coitus. There is some variation about these acts in timing (both in order and duration), but roughly this is—at the physical level—what normal heterosexual activity is. Prior to or in the course of this sequence of physical acts, sexual arousal occurs, and in some cases orgasm results for one or both of the two persons involved. What is misleading in this physical description is that it sounds as if one were rubbing two sticks together to produce fire; that is, if only enough body heat is generated, orgasm occurs. However, orgasm is not only a physical event, but also the outcome of a combination of both biological and, more importantly, social psychological factors. Unless the two people involved recognize that the physical events outlined are sexual and are embedded in a sexual situation, there will not be the potentiation of the physiological concomitants that Masters and Johnson have demonstrated as necessary in the production of sexual excitement and the orgasmic cycle.[28] The social meaning given to the physical acts releases biological events. Most of the physical acts described in the foregoing sexual sequence occur in many other situations—the palpation of

28. Masters and Johnson, *Human Sexual Response.*

the breast for cancer, the gynecological examination, the insertion of tampons, mouth-to-mouth resuscitation—all involve homologous physical events. But the social situation and the actors are not defined as sexual or potentially sexual, and the introduction of a sexual element is seen as a violation of the expected social arrangements. The social-psychological meaning of sexual events must be learned because they supply the channels through which biology is expressed. In some cases, the system of naming must exist for the event to occur; in others, portions of the event that are biologically necessary are never observed in the psychological field of the participating persons.

The term *script* (or *scripted behavior)* immediately suggests the dramatic, which is appropriate; but it also suggests the conventional dramatic narrative form, which more often than not is inappropriate. The latter tendency is reinforced by our most general conception of the sex act itself, which is seen as a dramatic event with continuous cumulative action. This is suggested, for example, by the language of Masters and Johnson—"arousal, plateau, climax, and resolution"—a conception resembling somewhat an Aristotelian notion of the dramatic or the design for a nineteenth-century symphony. However, the sources of arousal, passion or excitement (the recognition of a sexual possibility), as well as the way the event is experienced (if, indeed, an event follows), derive from a complicated set of layered symbolic meanings that are not only difficult to comprehend from the observed behavior, but also may not be shared by the participants. Even where there is minimal sharing of elements of a script by persons acting toward each other (which, while not necessary, clearly facilitates execution of the acts with mutual satisfaction), they may be organized in different ways and invoked at different times.

The same overt gesture may have both a different meaning and/or play a different role in organizing the sexual "performance." The identical gesture undertaken during sexual activity may be read by one participant with a content that might resemble that of Sade or Sacher-Mosoch, while the other participant reads content from *Love Story*.

Elements entering into the performance may be both relatively remote to the erotic (or what is conventionally defined as remote to the erotic), as well as the immediately and intrinsically erotic. Moreover, the logic of organization may more closely follow the nonnarrative qualities of modern poetry, the surrealistic tradition, or the theater of the absurd than conventional narrative modes. The sexual provides us with a situation where the mere invocation of some powerfully organizing metaphor links behavior to whole universes of meaning; a situation where the power of a metaphorically enriched gesture, act, characteristic, object, or posture cannot be determined by the relative frequency with which it occurs; such organizing metaphors need only be suggested for their effects to be realized.

An example of this may be seen in Jerzy N. Kosinski's novel *Steps*,[29] where our nameless hero finds himself looking down upon a fellow office worker (female) whom he has long desired sexually and who is in a posture of unrestrained sexual accessibility. Though it is a moment he has long desired, he finds himself unable to become aroused. He then recalls the moment of his initial sexual interest; a moment in which, while watching her in the act of filing papers with uplifted arms, he catches a fleeing glimpse of her bra. This trivial image, originally arousing, remains arousing and our hero goes on to complete the act. It is that image (and what it links to) that both names her as an erotic object in terms of his sense of the erotic and names also what he is about to do to her. Though the image need only be briefly suggested (both in its origins and subsequent utilization), and though it may remain unknown to the behaviorist observer, it becomes critical to the performance. Its meanings could be multiple. For example, that the sexual becomes erotically enriched when it is hidden, latent, denied, or when it is essentially violative (deriving from unintended exposure). It also legitimates the appropriate name for the behavior. Consider the possible "labels" our hero could have invoked that could have been applied to the behavior, each with its own powerful and powerfully distinct associations—making love, making out, fucking, screwing, humping, doing, raping.

The erotic component we can assume is minimally necessary if sexual activity is to occur; that is its very importance. (A dramatic

29. Jerzy N. Kosinski, *Steps* (New York: Random House, 1968).

exception, of course, are many women whose participation in sexual activity has often—historically, possibly more often than not—had little to do with their own sense of the erotic.) On the other hand, a preoccupation with the erotic may reach obsessive proportions without overt sexual behavior necessarily following. Thus, like the biological component, it can be described as simultaneously being of critical importance and also insufficient by itself to be either fully descriptive or predictive of actual sexual careers.

While the importance of the erotic can be asserted, it may be the most difficult to elaborate, as a concern for the erotic—the acquisition of sexual culture—is possibly the least well understood or attended aspect of sexual behavior. We know very little about how it is acquired or, for that matter, the ways in which it influences both our sexual and nonsexual lives. Persistence of concepts such as libido or the sex drive obviate need for this knowledge. For those who hold these or comparable positions, the body is frequently seen as being both wise and articulate; recognizing and speaking a compelling language. Still others have assumed, in too unexamined a way, a direct link between collective sexual cultures and private sexual cultures, despite the fact that for many what is collectively defined as erotic may not be associated with sexual response or that much that the collectivity defines as non- or even anti-erotic may become part of the private sexual culture of a given individual; for example, various kinds of full and partial fetishisms. As a result, much of the research on responses to erotic materials often begins with the dubious assumption that experimental stimuli are recognizable in terms of a conventional social definition.[30]

One thing that is clear is that for contemporary society erotic imagery or metaphors are for the most part discontinuously or only latently a part of the images or metaphors of nonsexual identity or social life. (The exceptions are those social roles that are specifically assumed to have a "known" erotic aspect, such as the prostitute, the homosexual, the stewardess, or the divorcee, all of whom we tend to see as either fully erotic or unusually erotic to the point where we have difficulty seeing them in anything but erotic terms.) Thus, for conventional actors in relatively conventional settings, the

---

30. Masters and Johnson, *Human Sexual Response.*

invocation of the erotic, necessary for sexual arousal, frequently requires a series of rituals of transformation before the participants or the setting license (as it were) the sexual moment. For example, much of precoital petting or foreplay may serve less as facilitators of a physiological process, than as elements in a ritual drama that allow one or both actors to rename themselves, their partners, as well as various parts of the body in terms of the "special" purpose. The intrusion of nonerotic, manifest meanings to images—that is, parts of the body or other role commitments of one or another of the actors is experienced as disruptive of sexual interest or capacity, if only because such commitments are rarely predictive of sexual role needs. For most, as a consequence, the sexual flourishes best in a sheltered and, in some sense, isolated universe, a landscape denuded of all but the most relevant aspects of identity.

At the same time, the larger part of identity and sense of the rest of social life frequently intrude in an indirect way. The elaboration of the erotic or its direct expression is often constrained by an anticipation of an anticipated return to that larger social role, that more continuous sense of self. For some this may involve merely the insulation of silence; for others, symbolic reinterpretation and condensation—for example, an intensity of pressure that allows the actor to represent by that gesture either passion (or the message that uncharacteristic behavior is thereby explained), or love and affection (that the actor is the same as he or she is in their more conventional mode of relating), or sadistic aggression (illuminating a complicated fantasy rehearsed and experienced sufficiently that the gesture successfully evokes most of the emotional density generated by a long and frequently complicated scenario).

Beyond the very general level, however, little can be said. Important questions dealing not only with origins but careers have yet to be even examined provisionally. Where do such images come from? In terms of what sexual and nonsexual experiences do their meanings change? Is there need for elaboration? These, and many more, are the questions that we may have to examine before sexual activity, which all too often can be described as a "dumb-show" for its participants, becomes something other than a dumb-show for behavioral science.

2

Childhood and Adolescence

Infancy and Childhood

Obviously, Erikson was correct in agreeing with Freud: we do not become sexual all at once at puberty; there is a significant level of continuity with the past. Nevertheless, continuity is not a dominating causality, nor are the elements of continuity necessarily sexual in the psychoanalytic sense. In infancy, prior to the development of language, experiences occur that will influence the development of sexuality. Such experiences, however, will be influential not because of their essential sexual character, but because of their general influential character; that is, they will influence many more things than just sexual development. Our understanding from the work on mother-deprived infants and infra-human research is that in humans one would have grave difficulty in conceiving of situations in infancy—or even early childhood—that could be linked to psychosexual development on a level more specific than that of potentiation.[1,2]

1. Rene A. Spitz, "Autoeroticism Reexamined: The Role of Early Sexual Behavior Patterns in Personality Foundation," *The Psychoanalytic Study of the Child* 17 (1962): 283–315.
2. See the following works by Harry F. Harlow: "The Nature of Love," *American Psychologist* 13 (1958): 673–85; "Love in Infant Monkeys," *Scientific American* 200 (1959): 68–74; "Sexual Behavior in the Rhesus Monkey (Paper presented to the Conference on Sex and Behavior, Berkeley, Calif., 1961, mimeographed); and Harry F. Harlow and M. K. Harlow, "Social Deprivation in Monkeys," *Scientific American* 207 (1962): 137–46.

It appears from the point of view of ultimate sexual adjustments that trauma or deformities in early socialization do not so much result in specific fixations or defects as much as the general blighting of the organism's development. A wide range of cognitive, emotional disturbances are apparent which include problems in sexual behavior in the mature organisms who survive these kinds of infant experiences.

There are in infancy, however, key processes that are central to the development of the organism and serve as the basis for the development of specifically sexual identity. In the interrelations that are part of child care we can locate many of the preverbal experiences that are preparations for the development of verbal capacities which in turn will bind the child to the social world. In this period we can locate some experiences—perhaps only sensations—that will help bring about a sense of the body and its capacities for pleasure and comfort, and we can also locate those experiences that will influence the child's ability to relate to other bodies.

One of the major debts we owe to Freud is the recognition of the full range of emotional responses that are occasioned by the early experiences of pleasure and comfort. To experience pleasure and comfort, even on the most primative levels, is to create the inevitable experience of a denial of pleasure and of discomfort. To experience attachment, the beginnings of love and identification, is also to create the inevitability of separation, the experiencing of anger, frustration, indeed, of rage. The connection between the sexual and the sentimental was easily made by conventional approaches; the second relationship, that of the sexual and rage, was a critical part of Freud's contribution. In this essentially dialectic relationship, giving rise to guilt, anxiety, and ambivalence, the groundwork for the potential complexity of the sexual is established.[3]

The key word for these experiences remains *potentiation:* it is possible that through these primitive experiences, ranges are being established, but these ranges are sufficiently broad and overlapping that little can follow by way of specification except through the dubious route of tortured reconstruction. Moreover, if there are pro-

3. Sigmund Freud, *A General Introduction to Psychoanalysis* (New York: Liveright, 1935).

foundly significant experiences to the child—and some may well be —they stand not as expressions of biological necessity nor the inherent wisdom of the body, but as the earliest expressions of the forms of social learning.[4]

A central support for the significance of social learning are the patterns through which gender identity is formed early in life. The decision whether to raise a child as male or female is probably based on the most significant labeling experience that the child will receive. Once a parent or doctor has identified a child, always by the anatomic conformation of his genitals (perhaps this is the meaning of "anatomy becomes destiny," anatomy in conjunction with social attribution) as male or female, there are released the separate cultural syndromes that are related to the rearing of male or female children. The work of Money and the Hampsons indicates clearly the social elements in the early development of gender role, which they describe as

> . . .all those things that a person says or does to disclose himself or herself as having the status of boy or man, girl or woman, respectively. . . . A gender role is not established at birth, but is built up cumulatively through experiences encountered and transacted—through casual and unplanned learning, through explicit instruction and inculcation, and through spontaneously putting two and two together to make sometimes four and sometimes, erroneously, five.[5]

These scientists demonstrated that in their cases gender role was usually set by a little after two years of age, and attempts after this time to change the orientation in children who had been placed in

4. J. L. Gewirtz, "A Learning Analysis of the Effect of Normal Stimulation, Privation, and Deprivation in the Acquisition of Social Motivation and Attachment," in *Determinants of Infant Behavior,* ed. B. M. Foss (New York: Wiley, 1961) pp. 213–90.

5. See the following papers by John Money, Joan G. Hampson, and John L. Hampson: "Hermaphroditism: Recommendations Concerning Assignment of Sex, Change of Sex, and Psychologic Management," *Bulletin, Johns Hopkins Hospital* 97 (1955): 284–300; "Sexual Incongruities and Psychopathology: The Evidence of Human Hermaphroditism," *Bulletin, Johns Hopkins Hospital* 98 (1956): 43–57. Joan G. Hampson, "Hermaphroditic Genital Appearance, Rearing and Eroticism in Hyperadrenocorticism," *Bulletin, Johns Hopkins Hospital* 96 (1955): 265–73. The quotation is from footnote 19, p. 285.

the incorrect sex category because of external genital ambiguity had various negative psychic consequences for the child. Other criteria —gonadal or chromosomal—for sex assignment were of minor importance even though they have been assumed to have biological priority.

It is possible to argue, as indeed Money and the Hampsons do, that their research is antithetical and in basic contradiction to theories of innate biological bisexuality such as those of Freud. There is a more modest middle ground, however, which will admit directionality based on prenatal potentiation of the organism through directional hormonal effects on the nervous system, and this seems to be the one to take at present.[6] It is possible, as has been pointed out by Diamond, that the genetically abnormal cases studied by Money and the Hampsons may have been less biologically directed toward maleness or femaleness because of lowered hormonal levels and therefore more liable to misprinting in the sense that the latter authors use the term.[7] The normal biological substrate produced by prenatal hormonal effects may differentially ready the organism to receive the definitions and inputs of masculinity and femininity from the parents. The gender role and its components will then be built on the bisexual biological character, and the gender role will be a resultant of these two kinds of forces rather than the unique product of either.

Since many of these inputs of gender-forming information to the child occur without thought upon the part of the parent, it is clear that the actions that are involved even in the development of gender role are quite obscure; however, the fact that the parents are clear in their belief that the infant is either male or female has permanent consequences for the child.[8] Thus the vigor of play, the frequency of father-child as opposed to mother-child interaction, and the tolerance for aggression in the male as opposed to the female infant

6. William C. Young, Robert W. Goy, and Charles H. Phoenix, "Hormones and Sexual Behavior," *Science* 143 (1964): 212–18.

7. Milton Diamond, "A Critical Evaluation on the Ontogeny of Human Sexual Behavior," *Quarterly Review Biology* (in press).

8. John L. Hampson and Joan G. Hampson, "The Ontogenesis of Sexual Behavior in Man," in *Sex and Internal Secretions,* ed. William C. Young (Baltimore: Williams and Wilkins, 1961) pp. 1401–32.

and child all contribute to the development of the self defined as masculine or feminine.

It is after infancy, when the developing child is acquiring language, that we begin to recognize cognitive and verbal processes that go beyond the universe of unnamed gestures. None of these processes are completed instantly, and cognitive and moral development both show stages of organization more culture-bound than the ahistorical scientist would admit, stages that change and grow more complex as the child approaches adulthood. It is during this period that the child comes under the control of the communicative process, no matter how primitively at first, for it is in the naming and organizing of experience in scripts that the child begins to organize his plans for dealing with the world. Two salient experiences dominate the post-verbal years until puberty, all of which are influential in the development of an ultimate sexual identity. The first of these is the pattern of naming the child's behaviors in general and the specific adult reaction to behaviors that are conceived to be sexual. The second is the continued building of conventional gender identities based on preverbal social decision about the maleness or femaleness of the child.

When one examines the interaction of parents and young children, one is struck by the frequency of both negative injunctions and what appear to be—at least to adults—unambiguous instructions given to children in their early years. A simple household item such as the stove is an excellent example: the toddler is taught that the stove is hot, and whether it is hot or cold at any given moment he is told not to touch it, since a single failure in learning may well be disastrous. As the child grows older, more flexible information and attitudes about the use of fire and the stove are learned. The stove may be touched when there is no fire, cooking can be experimented with, and finally a series of complex and fine discriminations are learned in order to deal with a common household object. The new information comes in many forms and from many sources with both positive and negative components. This is the usual form of training given to a child in teaching him how to negotiate a complex environment where risk is high. From an original set of negative injunctions excluding all activity, a series of explanations

emerge that are based more and more frequently on rational calcu-
lations. The infant who is greeted with the shout "hot" when he first
approaches the stove, is later informed about the dangers of burn-
ing himself or of getting hurt and finally offered a complex set of
instructions about fire, temperature, cooking, and how to treat minor burns, all as part of dealing with the stove.

What is apparent about this process is that it follows, at least
crudely, the increasing levels of skill, both motor and cognitive, that
characterize the developing child, and while the final script emerges
only fragmentarily, knowledge is linked to developmental process,
and information becomes more than moral injunction. It is in the
area of emerging behaviors, both verbal and nonverbal, that appear
to be sexual to adults that very different strategies for learning of
behavior are applied. While some adults do attempt to engage in
formal sex instruction with their children, by and large parents are
reactive in terms of supplying information about what appear to
them to be the sexual interests and activity of their children.

Adult activity with reference to children's sexual development is
usually a result of the use of words or the display of activities by the
child that the adult defines as sexual. The adult may engage in a series of strategies of response to the behavior: he may describe the
behavior as sexual and say that it is wrong, he may mislabel the behavior, describing it as something it may not be, or he may nonlabel
the behavior by ignoring or providing a judgment without a specific
label. The first strategy is least frequent, the latter two the most, but
what is most apparent is that both the behavior that elicits the adult
response and the adult response itself mean something different to
the child than they do to the adult. Indeed, when the parent thinks
that he has given an adequate explanation of the behavior in conventional moral terms it is very unlikely that the child has internalized or maintained the message that the parent thought he was giving. The mis- and nonlabeling of behavior has a major consequence
for children's responses to parents in terms of the fragmentary elements of what will become sexual attitudes, values, and performances.[9]

9. Robert R. Sears, Eleanor E. Maccoby, and Harry Levin, *Patterns of
Child Rearing* (Evanston, Ill.: Row, Peterson, 1957), pp. 176–217. See pp.
215–16 for the origin of the term *nonlabeling*.

The primarily negative and dichotomous informational inputs of parents to the child are rarely revised by parents. The primitive form of moral conditioning which constructs only black and white labels for behavior maintains itself independently, since the parental figures, who create these early labels for the protosexual experiences of the child through direct action as well as indirection, are rarely reassessed or newly judged until quite late in adolescence, if at all.

It is possible for the child to reevaluate his parents' attitudes toward politics, vocations, and religion, for in these areas the parents have at times (it is to be hoped, at least) interacted with the child not only in a primitive injunctive manner, but also in a more complex and ambiguous manner. The child, as he matures, construes the parent as a religious, political, vocational being, and therefore the original inputs to the child are modified by consequent experience. This is not to say that even such reevaluations, especially if negative, are not accompanied by pain and grief and that in many cases they never take place; however, there is little doubt that most children and most adults are unable to consciously conceive of their parents as sexual creatures. Even those persons who remember having observed the primal scene—as well as the larger numbers who have repressed all such memories—should be included in this class. This observation of parental coitus, even if it occurs more than once—which is more likely to happen to those living in poor and crowded circumstances—is not sufficient to create an articulated sexual image of the mother or the father, whatever else it might do.[10] It is very difficult for children to believe that their parents even existed prior to their birth, and this primacy of mother as only mother and father as only father continues long into adolescence. Even after the experience of coitus, it is extremely difficult for a young man or woman to conceive of his parents in the same roles.

---

10. The chronic use of the term *motherfucker* by Afro-American slum dwellers is a case in point. Rather than being directed toward anyone's "real" mother or calling to mind coitus with her, it has an extremely abstract referent. In its use in verbal games which function as outlets for aggression and therefore social ranking among males it is clear that the reference is to womankind. See Roger D. Abrahams, *Deep Down in the Jungle* (Chicago: Aldine, 1970). This book provides examples and discussions of urban Afro-American folklore: see especially pp. 259–62 for the meaning of obscenities.

It is of great significance that the original organization of adult responses to protosexual learning and attitudes are never challenged in any major way, and it is not easy for the growing child to revise these early conceptions. This, in part, explains the general lack of parental capacity to engage in the larger sexual education of children.

Central to these early forms of social learning is the application even to the preverbal child of the sexual scripts for adult experience. We have to ask: In what sense can a young child fondling his or her genitalia be described as engaging in masturbation? Is there any basis for assuming that the physical event gives rise to, or exists in response to, a set of internal states at all equivalent to those of adults for whom the label, with its cluster of meanings and implied judgments, intervenes between the external act and internal responses? Surely not. But there does seem to be something communicated to the child by the response of the observer: it is a sense of judgment for acts or sets of states that have no name—for events that may have no meanings except those created by the sense of judgment.

The emergent forms of sexual commitment are extensively shaped by applying to the behavior of the very young the vocabulary of motives of fully formed sexuality; that is, the very young are provided with responses that are a function of adult sexual scripts, without providing the scripts. Such communication can only be extraordinarily gross, and the manner in which adult communications, verbal and nonverbal, are encoded by the preverbal child is one of the fundamental problems of behavioral science, for such encoding is clearly the substrate on which future learning develops. One's sense is that this pattern of communication of complex judgments made by adults on the behavior of the child is similar across all areas of learning, not only sexual. Perhaps the only variant is that the sexual judgments may contain higher levels of affect. What effect, however, this has on the child is unclear.

This process of application of judgment without naming continues with the older child and this may, in fact, be one of the two major hallmarks of communication processes in sexual training. While the adult activity of judging behavior without naming it tends to decline in other areas of learning, it retains its potency in the sexual area almost all the way into adulthood.

The most important preadolescent experience that children have with this process of judgment without naming occurs during a period of collective activity that appears to be sexual exploration: preadolescent children playing games that involve the exploration or exhibition of one anothers' bodies.[11] These occur most significantly in social scripts that are manifestly not sexual (doctor-nurse). Such "sex play," perhaps in this case it should be seen as "vocational play" as well, is not uncommon in the society of the United States. From the data on adults in the United States gathered in the samples of the Institute for Sex Research, about 57 percent of the males and 48 percent of the females who were interviewed as adults remembered sociosexual play prior to puberty, with most of it occurring between ages eight and thirteen.[12] Of a small sample of males interviewed before puberty, about 70 percent reported such sex play, suggesting that it is an even more widespread phenomenon, and that the memory of it is apparently often repressed by adult respondents.[13] Most of the play was sporadic and similar to children's other patterns of behavior, and the learning situation was usually initiated by a child slightly older, either in age or experience, and most commonly the behavior did not continue. The crucial and almost impossible question remains even for these postverbal children: What does it mean to the child? It is likely that some part of the adult definition of the activity is realized by the participants, but one suspects—as in much of childhood role playing of all kinds—that their sense of the adult meaning is fragmentary and ill-formed. It is clear that some learning about the adult world's judgments of the sexual occurs, as is indicated by the fact that a high proportion of adults recall that they were concerned, while engaging in childhood sex play, over the possibility of being found out. But it is apparent that the behavior does not derive

---

11. A. C. Kinsey et al., *Sexual Behavior in the Human Male* (Philadelphia: Saunders, 1948), pp. 157–92.

12. Kinsey et al., *Sexual Behavior in the Human Female* (Philadelphia: Saunders, 1953), p. 107.

13. Kinsey et al., *Sexual Behavior in the Human Male,* pp. 165–67.

from the intrinsic or internal capacity of the child for sexual experience but as a part of the process that creates such a capacity. The real attractiveness of the behavior, and almost all children know that it is something that "they should not be doing," will not derive from anything that resembles sexual pleasure, but from the mysterious and unnamed qualities that are ascribed to the behavior by the adult world.[14] Such behavior as it is noted by adults (and little of it is) will be described not in sexual terms, but in moral terms ("dirty," "bad," "good boys and girls don't," and the like), endowing the behavior with moral importance that will indirectly shape its sexual meaning. Such talk about sex begins to affect the child by creating partial responses that are appropriate to the structure of adult scripts.

For some small number of persons, sexual activity which appears to be adult sexual scripting does occur during preadolescence. Probably the largest number of these are those who become involved as objects of adult-initiated behavior. While adult-child contacts (either in fact or in fantasy) were central to Freud's early theories of the development of mental disorders, in fact, little seemingly follows from actual contacts. The provocation of childhood sexual development by adults or its existence as a universal childhood fantasy was part of the first intellectual crisis of psychoanalytic theory and still retains a significant, if confused, status.[15] Unfortunately, the theory depended on the capacity of the child to read the experience for what it seemed to be to adults; however, for the child who com-

14. It is these naming procedures that contribute to the mysterious quality attributed to sexuality by children. See Sigmund Freud, "Analysis, Terminable and Interminable," in *Standard Edition of the Complete Psychological Works, vol.* 23 (London: Hogarth Press, 1964), pp. 216–53.

15. Bernard C. Glueck, Jr., "Early Sexual Experiences in Schizophrenia," in *Advances in Sex Research,* ed. Hugo G. Beigel (New York: Harper & Row, 1963). pp. 248–55. Karl Abraham, "The Experiencing of Sexual Traumas as a Form of Sexual Activity," in *Selected Papers of Karl Abraham, M.D.* (London: Hogarth, 1927) pp. 47–63. Sandor Ferenczi, "Confusion of Tongues Between the Adult and the Child," *International Journal of Psycho-Analysis* 30 (1949): 225–30. Adelaide M. Johnson and S. A. Szurek, "The Genesis of Antisocial Acting Out in Children and Adults," *Psychoanalytic Quarterly* 21 (1952): 323–43. Edward M. Litin, Mary E. Griffin, and Adelaide M. Johnson, "Parental Influence in Unusual Sexual Behavior in Children," *Psychoanalytic Quarterly* 25 (1956): 37–55.

monly lacks the appropriate sexual scripts, the experience remains unassimilated, except perhaps for those who derive a "meaning" from a subsequent clinical experience. For some children it is clear that a severe reaction does occur as a result of falling victim to the sexuality of some adult figure, but here it is debatable whether this reaction follows from the sexual act itself or from the tone and the intensity of the reactions by others who learn of the experience.[16] In short, relatively few preadolescents become sexually active in accordance with an adult sexual script—that is, truly sexually active. When there is continuity in sexual contact with the adults and this occurs in both homosexual and heterosexual contacts (the former for males, the latter for females), the gratification or motivations of the child may develop a sexual component (or adult content), but more likely the sexual element in the relationship is exchanged by the child for a wanted emotional or other gratification that the adult provides. For preadolescent females more often than males, this sexual activity is not immediately related to internal states—capacities for sexual arousal or gratification—but to an instrumental use of sexuality to achieve nonsexual goals and gratifications. The "seductive" preadolescent female, for all her statistical rarity may represent a significant adumbration of a more general pattern of psychosexual development: a process, especially among females, wherein there is commitment to sociosexuality that precedes a commitment to the gratifications of the sexual performance itself. Among sexually active preadolescent males, behavior comes to be more closely linked to adult males scripting, at least in terms of its linkage to internal states, and is often associated with a high frequency of subsequent deviant adaptations, most often homosexual.[17]

The second major form of communicating the sexual, and hence creating it, is the reverse of a response to what appears to be sexual activity on the part of the child. In this former case the young are exposed to judgments and responses that follow from the application of a sexual vocabulary that they do not know—but there is

---

16. J. H. Gagnon, "Female Child Victims of Sex Offenses," *Social Problems* 13 (1965): 176–92.
17. P. H. Gebhard et al., *Sex Offenders* (New York: Harper & Row, 1965).

also the process by which the young are trained, more often informally than formally, in the sexual vocabulary without associating it with sexual activity, allowing the words to develop a complexity of meanings and associations long before they are ultimately applied to the realm of sexual behavior. In the vernacular there is a whole host of essentially sexual terms that are widely used in nonsexual situations and that are frequently learned first in terms of their nonsexual applications. The commonly used English vulgar terms for coitus ("fuck" or "screw") or those used for mouth-genital contact or homosexuality ("cocksucker," "muff-diver" or "queer") are frequently learned and employed by children and adolescents without a sense of their sexual meaning or the physical activities that they indicate. Thus words are learned that are powerfully loaded with emotion but are applied to the world in imperfect ways and, in these nonsexual and often aggressive and hostile applications, become another shaping force when they are applied to the sexual experience itself.[18]

The two processes most directly related to appearance of sexuality are thus imperfect complements. Activities that are physically homologous to adult behaviors are performed by children with a set of motives that are appropriate to their level of development in this society. Adults then judge these behaviors, bringing to them the affect and meanings that they associate with them. The child understands some elements of the cognitive scheme that the adult possesses and understands more clearly the anxiety, anger, and moral opprobrium that is presented. How this emotional display links to the child's behavior is unclear to the child, but he learns that things of this class result in a potent response by adults, whatever specific events this class of acts may contain. (Perhaps it is only the class of events that produces potent responses from adults.) On the other hand, words (including informational words) are being learned that have complex sets of sexual meanings to adults and fit into sexual scripts. The words are provided without their sexual content and denotations, to be used, sorted, and examined, but without experience to go with them. The child possesses two

18. W. Simon and J. H. Gagnon, "Sex Talk: Public and Private," *ETC* 25: 173–91.

tapes (to use the computer metaphor), one containing experiences, judged in certain ways; the other, words without experiences. His dilemma is to sort and merge them, attaching the proper words to the proper acts. The possession of words, experiences, and judgments, all unassembled, leaves the young child without a vocabulary with which to describe his emerging physical or psychic experiences.[19]

This specific absence of order has two major consequences. The first is the tendency for fantasy to overrun the sexual life of the child. The mysterious penis that must exist behind the female pubic hair, the feeling that females have been castrated, and other childhood fantasies are common because there has been no system of naming which will adequately control the child's nascent interest in his own or others' bodies.[20] The second consequence of the lack of a controlling set of symbols is probably related to the tendency for children to identify their sexual organs with excretory functions, and many psychoanalysts have noted that the emphasis on the dirtiness of the excretory function utilized to enforce sphincter control surely has consequences for the child's perception of the cleanliness of his own genitalia and of their sexual function. This may also be related to some of the sexual differences between girls and boys; since boys may get dirty—therefore dirt is not so bad—and girls may not, the association may be more firmly entrenched among the latter.

Given this framework of avoidance and, more rarely, imprecise and ineffective repression of misunderstood events by parents, it is not surprising that the child gets most of his sexual information, though not his attitudes, through peer relationships. Though the parents are not providing cognitive information about sexuality for

19. This has also been discussed by Albert Bandura and Richard H. Walters in *Adolescent Aggression: A Study of the Influence of Child-Training Practices and Family Interrelationships* (New York: Ronald, 1959), pp. 184–87.

20. We have already noted the lack of consensus about sexuality among adults who have at least had some sexual experience; how much more mysterious must sexual functions appear to the inexperienced child. The role of language as imposing order on the external world may be found explicitly in the works of Kenneth Burke and George Herbert Mead and implicitly in those of Erving Goffman.

the child, they are creating postures and orientations through which information from other children will be filtered. In the peer relationships, since no children—or, at most, few—have accurate information about even reproductive functions, they will systematically misinform each other just as they are systematically misinformed by their parents about being brought by the stork, being brought in the doctor's bag, or having been found in a cabbage patch. Unfortunately, these belief systems and their origins among children have not been systematically studied, and the most likely reason for this is that the research itself must be a form of sex education. In the exchanges between child and interlocutor the child will not remain unchanged, and even if he is asked only the meaning of certain terms, he will be in that moment informed or made curious. In this case there can be nothing but action research.

There is nothing in this peer-peer learning process which suggests that the children have any integrated body of sexual knowledge. The young boy with experience in sex play may not associate his first-hand knowledge of the anatomical differences between boys and girls with the fact that babies grow inside of his mother, and the biological facts of fertilization may never dawn on him at all (as they did not on mankind until the end of the nineteenth century). It would seem safe to speculate that, except for menstruation, females are unlikely to have learned the facts in any more logical or coherent order. In the case of females it is clear that the mother may often play a more decisive role because it is more appropriate that she inform her daughter of the dangers of sexuality and the possibility of menstruation. This is certainly not always the case, since a fair number of females report that they first learned of menstruation when it occurred for them the first time.

What is learned is important; however, the context in which it is learned is *more* important. The exchange of sexual information among children is clandestine and subversive, and the manner in which parents attempt to teach their children reinforces this learning structure. The admonitions of parents, since they are general and diffuse, do not result so much in cessation of either interest or behavior, but in their concealment and the provoking of guilt. It is clear that few males have been deterred by the horror stories attached to masturbation. Madness, degeneration, and physical stigmata have all at various times been attributed to this behavior in the face of the evidence that the majority of males, especially in adolescence, have masturbated and that they have suffered none of these consequences. Those they have affected have been related to the anxiety produced by worrying about the nonexistent consequences.

Thus children interact and exchange information on a sporadic and unconnected basis, usually but not always with some guilt. The novelist Richard Wright recalled in his autobiography that in his early childhood he repeated an obscenity to his grandmother and received a ferocious beating for it but did not know at the time why he had been beaten.[21] This seems to happen fairly often—that the child behaves in a manner an adult perceives as sexual, and the child is punished without being able to make a connection between stimulus and response. The punitive action of the parent may have little inhibitory power since it is nonspecific to the child's behavior, but it may provoke intense anxiety.

The development of guilty knowledge occurs extremely quickly, and the children's world resembles a secret society keeping the information from parents.[22] This secret society is under enormous strain from two sources, both of them pointed out by Simmel. One is the tendency of children to express spontaneously what they know or feel, and the second is the difficulty of keeping a secret in a "small and narrow circle."[23] There is a positive value set on the ability of adults to talk to children about their problems, and the quality of child-rearing is often judged by whether the child will go to the parents with his difficulties. Even with all of these tensions organized to force the communication of sexual attitudes and information between the parents and the child, the barriers of mutual distrust and anxiety are too high. Thus the sexual learning process

21. Richard Wright, *Black Boy* (New York: Signet, 1963), pp. 49–53.
22. This also has been pointed out by Freud. "We are shown . . . above all, how the secret of sexual life begins to dawn on her indistinctly and then takes complete possession of the child's mind; how, in the consciousness of her secret knowledge, she at first suffers hurt, but little by little overcomes it." Sigmund Freud, *Standard Edition of the Complete Psychologocal Works,* vol. 14 (London: Hogarth, 1963), p. 341.
23. Kurt H. Wolff, ed., *The Sociology of Georg Simmel* (Glencoe, Ill.: Free Press, 1950), pp. 330–35.

contributes another element to the child's future character structure —the capacity and need to keep sexuality secret, especially from those one loves.

Of major significance is the internalization of these values—or the images that powerfully stand for values—that are not directly or exclusively referential to sexual matters. For, in addition to these at least implicitly sexual sources of the creation of a sense of the sexual, more important numerically and perhaps in significance, are the nonsexual sources of the organization and shaping of sexual scripts. Too often, scientific thinking, like pornographic thinking, denudes the sexual landscape of social actors and social meanings, leaving only minor cues that sexual activity is social activity and occurs within social frameworks and is linked to men and women, not to undifferentiated bodies or organs lost in pornotopic or scientific space. These nonsexual values or value images will constitute aspects in the construction of sexual scripts giving rise to senses of the evil, the extraordinary, and the erotic. Despite our present capacity as a society to generate high levels of public discourse about sexual matters, it is probably not unreasonable to assert that learning about sex in our society is learning about guilt; conversely, learning how to manage sexuality constitutes learning how to manage guilt. An important source of guilt is the imputation by adults of sexual capacities, or qualities in children that the children may not have but that result in—however imperfectly—children learning to act as if they had such capacities or qualities. For example, at what age do girls learn to sit with their knees together, and when do they learn that the upper part of the torso must be hidden, and how does this learning get ultimately linked to sexual activity? Childhood learning of major themes that establish sex or gender role identities is of critical importance. Much of what appears under the heading of sex-role learning involves elements that are remote to sexual experience or that become involved with sexuality only after the latter has become salient.[24] Here the meanings and postures of masculinity and femininity are rehearsed and assimilated in many nonsexual ways. Here, also, the qualities of aggression, deference, and domi-

---

24. R. R. Sears, "Development of Gender Role," in *Sex and Behavior,* ed. F. A. Beach (New York: Wiley, 1965), pp. 133–63.

nance needs, which Maslow—however imperfect his data—persuasively argues are strongly implicated in the organization of sexual styles, are initially rehearsed, experimented with, and assimilated.[25]

Kagan and Moss report similar findings: aggressive behavior is a relatively stable aspect of male development, and dependency is a similar characteristic in female development.[26] Significant appearances of aggressive behavior by females tended to occur most often among females from well-educated families, families that tended to be more tolerant of deviation from sex-role standards. Of particular interest, they also find that ". . . interest in masculine activities for age six to ten was a better predictor of adult sexuality than was heterosexual activity between six and fourteen." Curiously, they also report that "it was impossible to predict the character of adult sexuality in women from their preadolescent and early adolescent behavior." This the authors attribute to a random factor, that of an imbalance of sex ratios in the local high school and, more significantly, to the fact that "erotic activity is more anxiety-arousing for females than for males" and that "the traditional ego ideal of women dictates inhibition of sexual impulses."

This concept of the importance of early sex-role learning for male children may be viewed in two ways. From one perspective, elements of masculine-role learning may be seen as immediately responsive to—if not expressive of—an internal sexual capacity. From another perspective, we might consider elements of masculine identification merely as a more appropriate context within which the physical sexual activities—which become salient with puberty —and the socially available sexual scripts can be mediated and coordinated. Our bias, of course, is toward the latter.

The failure of sex-role learning to be effectively predictive of adult sexual activities for females, noted by Kagan and Moss, may also lead to alternative interpretations. Again, from one perspective, where sexuality is viewed as a biological constant for both women

25. A. H. Maslow, "Dominance, Personality and Social Behavior in Women," *Journal of Social Psychology* 10 (1939): 3–39. A. H. Maslow, "Self-Esteem (dominance feeling) and Sexuality in Women," *Journal of Social Psychology* 16 (1942): 259–94.

26. J. Kagan and H. A. Moss, *Birth to Maturity* (New York: Wiley, 1962).

and men, one can point to the components of female-role learning that facilitate the successful repression of sexual impulses. The other perspective or interpretation suggests differences in the process not of handling sexuality but of learning how to be sexual, differences between men and women that will have consequences for both what is done sexually as well as when it is done. Our thinking, once again, tends toward the latter. This position is supported by some recent work of the present authors (see chap. 6) with female homosexuals, where it is observed that patterns of sexual career management (e.g., the timing of entry into actual sexual behavior, entry into forms of sociosexual behavior, onset and frequency of masturbation, number of partners, reports of feelings of sexual deprivation, etc.) were for lesbians almost identical with those of heterosexual women. Considering what was assumed to be the greater salience of sexuality for the lesbian—her commitment to sexuality being the basis for her entry into a highly alienative role—this seemed to be a surprising outcome. What was concluded was that the crucial operating factor was something that both heterosexual and homosexual women share: the components of sex-role learning that occur before sexuality itself becomes significant.

Social class differences also appear to be significant, although both in the work of Kinsey and that of Kagan and Moss they appear as more important factors for males than for females. Some part of this is due to aspects of sex-role learning which vary by social class. Differences in the legitimacy of expressing aggression or perhaps merely differences in modes of expressing aggression come immediately to mind.[27] Another difference is the degree to which sex-role models display a capacity for *heterosociality*. The frequently noted pattern of the sexual segregation of social life among working-class and lower-class populations may make the structuring of later sexual activity, particularly during adolescence, actually less complicated.[28] Another aspect of social class differences is the tol-

27. R. R. Sears, "Development of Gender Role," in *Sex and Behavior,* ed. F. A. Beach (New York: Wiley, 1965), pp. 133–63. H. B. Biller and L. J. Borstelmann, "Masculine Development: An Integrative Review," *Merrill Palmer Quarterly* 13 (1967): 253–94.
28. L. Rainwater, "The Crucible of Identity: The Negro Lower Class Family," *Daedalus* 95 (1966): 172–216. W. Simon and J. H. Gagnon, "Het-

erance for deviation from traditional attitudes regarding appropriate sex-role performances. Clearly, tolerance for such deviance is positively associated with social class position, and it may well stand in a highly complex and interactive relationship to capacities for heterosocial activities.

We have touched here upon only a few of the potentially large number of factors that should be related to important social class differences and to the processes of psychosexual development. In general, even during this relatively early period of life, complex elements of the ego begin to take form, including the crude outlines of what might be called a repertoire of gratifications. It seems rather naive to conceive of sexuality as a constant pressure upon this process, a pressure that has particular necessity all its own. For us, this crucial period of childhood has significance not because of what happens of a sexual nature, but because of the nonsexual developments that play a profound role in the establishment of sexual patterns in our society, and—given the structure of expectations of a society at a particular point in sociocultural time and space—produce what is observed as balanced and harmonious sexual relationships. Implicit here is the assumption that social roles are not vehicles for the expression of sexual impulse but that sexuality becomes a vehicle for expressing the needs of social roles.

Adolescence

Adolescence in Western societies remains a period with ill-defined beginning and end points. Unlike smaller and technologically simpler societies studied by anthropologists, where the events of biological puberty were celebrated as a transition into a wide variety of adult roles, including the sexual and the reproductive, modern Western societies have tended to operate more independently of these biological events as necessary signals for transitions into adult roles. The conventional mandates of most modern societies place

---

erosexuality and Homosociality: A Dilemma of the Lower Class Family," mimeographed (1966). W. Simon, J. H. Gagnon, S. A. Buff, "Son of Joe: Change and Continuity Among White Working Class Adolescents," *Journal of Youth and Adolescence* 1: 1334.

the moments for entry into sociosexual activities at a time (depending on culture and social class) from four to ten years after the onset of puberty and in the case of those who never enter those statuses that confer legitimacy on sexual activity the delay (on legitimacy
at least) can be permanent.

Regardless of the conventions of legitimacy and the ill-defined
character of the beginnings of socially defined period of adolescence,
it is at this moment that the society as such first acknowledges the
sexual character of the individual. Conventionally, this response of
the society is believed to be a necessary reaction to biological mandate of growing sexuality exhibited as a consequence of hormonal
shifts. While hormonal shifts do exist, it is our contention that their
consequences are not immanent in their occurence but that they
find their meaning in the way in which a society provides the individual with ways of interpreting both his new internal experiences
as well as his new presentations to the world around him.

In the particular cultural conditions of Western societies, the period of adolescence is largely a break with the past in terms of psychosexual development and the outcome of the changes associated
with this period in no respect assures a priority or special importance to those elements that previously appeared to be sexual. Even
positing this discontinuity between childhood and adolescence, it is
clear that we do not become sexual all at once; continuity with the
prior experience, however, does not give it causal priority. Often
when historical experience is combined with novel experience in a
major period of change, only the slightest lineaments of the past
may still be discerned. From this point of view the early years
around puberty, say from eleven to fourteen, are of major significance in the development of a sexual component in character structure. The past influences this period, but most profoundly through
forms of gender training that have minmal sexual character. Indeed, behaviors that seem to be sexual to adult observers are
probably of least importance in determining adult sexual character.

A version of this point of view has been partially expressed by
Kohlberg and Gilligan. They still use the phrase "drive," which is
incongruous, and are also committed to a limited structuralist point
of view with reference to moral development, but they have cap-

tured, at least with reference to sexual conduct, an alternative to a fixed developmental order.

If there is anything which can be safely said about what is new in the minds of adolescents, it is that they, like their elders, have sex on their minds. These changes, of course, have been the focus of Freudian thinking about adolescence as a stage. If anything, however, Freudian thinking has underestimated the novel elements of sexual experience in adolescence. For the Freudian, early adolescent sexuality is the reawakening of early childhood sexuality previously latent, with a consequent resurrection of oedipal feeling. Although it is true that adolescent sexuality bears the stamp of earlier experience, it is not the resurrection of earlier sexual feelings. Adolescent sexual drive is a qualitatively new phenomenon.

While sexual drives are awakened at puberty, there vast individual and cultural variations in the extent to which they determine the adolescent's behavior and experience. Sexuality is a central concern for the self of some fourteen year olds: it is something deferred to the future for others.[29]

As has already been indicated, for a number of individuals sexual activity begins prior to adolescence, or some portion of children begin engaging in adolescent sexual behavior before they are de-

29. Lawrence Kohlberg and Carol Gilligan, "The Adolescent as Philosopher," *Daedalus* 100 (1971). Also significant is Kohlberg and Gilligan's citation of Ellinwood's observations of the beginning of attributing to the self feelings formerly associated with external events which immediately follows the quotation above: "What is common for all, however, is an intensified emotionality, that is now experienced as a part of the self, rather than as a correlate of objective events in the world. C. Ellinwood studied the age of development of the verbal experiencing and expression of emotion in projective tests and in free self-descriptions. She found that prior to adolescence (aged twelve or so), emotions were experienced as objective concomitants of activities and objects. The child experienced anger because events or persons were bad; he experienced affection because persons were good or giving; he felt excitement because activities were exciting or fun. At adolescence, however, emotions are experienced as the result of states of the self rather than as the direct correlate of external events." These processes of change through which heightened emotional states are interpreted as having their sources internally probably involve an epistemiological error on the part of the adolescent (the demand characteristics of the situation and the responses of the self continue to exist only in interaction), but they are part of an error that allows the individual to experience himself as sexually needy, driven, or impulsive.

fined as adolescents. Thus, Kinsey reports that by age twelve about
a tenth of his female sample and a fifth of his male sample had already experienced orgasm through masturbation. (There is some
evidence that early entry into sexual activity is associated with alienative adjustments in later life, but this may not be a function of
sexual experience per se so much as the consequence of having fall-
en out of the more modal socialization patterns and, as a result,
having to run greater risks of not receiving appropriate forms of social support.) But this is still an atypical preface to adolescence.
For the vast majority, aside from relatively casual childhood sex
play and the behaviors that post-Freudians view as masked sexuality, movement into sexual experience which the actor defines and
accepts as such begins with the passage into adolescence. Even for
persons with prior sexual experience, the newly acquired definition
of their social status as adolescents qualitatively alters the meaning
of both current and prior sexual activity; they must now integrate
such meanings in more complex ways, ways that are related to both
larger spheres of social life and differing senses of self. For example, it is not uncommon during the transitional period between
childhood and adolescence for both males and females to report
arousal and orgasm while engaging in many kinds of physical activity
that are not manifestly sexual—climbing trees, sliding down bannis-
ters, or other forms of activity where there is genital contact—without it being defined as sexual by the adolescent.[30] Indeed, in many
such cases there may not even follow subsequent self-explorations
in order to achieve some repetition of what was, in all likelihood a
pleasurable experience.

The onset of adolescent sexual development, which really represents the beginning of what will be an adult commitment to sexuality, will be relatively disjunctive with past experience in most cases.
As we have suggested, not only are future experiences to occur in
much more complex situations, but also for the first time the more
explicit social implications of sexual activity will further complicate
matters. The need to manage sexuality, following from a growing
sense of having a sexual status, will derive not only from the intrinsic attractions of the sexual experiences for some but from the in-

30. Kinsey et al., *Sexual Behavior in the Human Male.*

creasingly important role sexuality will play in the conduct of both heterosocial and homosocial relationships.

Self-Definition and Physical Change

In the early years of adolescence there is the beginning of a major series of changes in the conformation of the bodies of males and females as a result of the hormonal changes. Menstruation in the female, ejaculation in the male, pubic and other axillary hair, breast development, voice change in the male and a general shift in body shape make apparent to both the developing child and adults around him that significant and (more important) collectively visible changes are going on. As far as can currently be told, the hormonal changes that are occurring at this time are not directional in terms of a necessary outcome in developing masculine or feminine personality structure but are rather activational in character. There is no evidence that differing androgen levels in the two sexes will account for differing rates of overt sexual behavior either within or between genders and no evidence that these same biological events produce variations in meanings attributed to these behaviors.

These years represent a difficult and inchoate period, from physical, psychological, and social points of view. While the varying developments or status changes involved in puberty are relatively invariant in sequence, they begin remarkably unevenly and are completed remarkably unevenly in individual cases.[31] From the recall data in the Kinsey volumes (which in the aggregate conform to those observational data collected at the same ages) women reported the median appearance of pubic hair at 12.3 years (varying from 8 to 18 years), the median appearance of breasts at 12.4 (varying from 8 to 24 years), menses at 13.0 years, and completion of growth in height at about a median age of 16. The cumulative incidence of menses is that 21 percent menstruate at age 11.9 or before, 29 percent in their twelfth year, 29 percent in their thirteenth year, and 21 percent in their fourteenth year and after.[32] In con-

31. J. M. Tanner, "Sequence, Tempo, and Individual Variation in the Growth and Development of Boys and Girls Aged Twelve to Sixteen," *Daedalus* 100 (1971): pp. 908, 917.

32. Kinsey et al., *Sexual Behavior in the Human Female*, pp. 122–25.

trast, males recall pubic hair at a median age of 13.4, growth completion at a median of 17.5 and, probably most significantly, first ejaculation at a median age of 13.9. The cumulative percentage of first ejaculation was 8 at age 11.9 and before, 19 percent at age 12, 29 percent at age 13, 25 percent at age 14, and 18 percent thereafter.[33]

While the aggregate figures seem orderly, young people of the same age and same year in school often appear extremely different in terms of their physical development.[34] Some twelve-year-old girls will have moderately complete breast development and will be taller than boys their own age, while other girls will not menstruate until fourteen and may, in consequence, feel that they are somehow deficient in a womanly characteristic. Early completion of general bodily growth in a boy can lead to adults believing that he is more psychologically advanced than he might be or to patterns of masturbatory behavior that are far in advance of his peer group. A grammar or middle school teacher who is facing a classroom of children in the fifth, sixth, seventh, and eighth grades is often teaching children with vastly different levels of physical development and with extremely varied levels of private experience.[35] The sex education course in the sixth grade will be speaking to girls who have been menstruating for a year and a half and others who will not menstruate for two years, and to some boys who have been masturbating to orgasm a number of times a week while others are still involved in games and other boyish pursuits.

This wide variety of available experiences within a limited age grading, an age grading whose members are often kept in close social-psychological interaction by the schools, is quite problematic for the child. The external physical signs of adolescence are differentially available to different sets of judges within the local environment. Inevitably, problems of comparison emerge between children which relate to physical strength and size and masturbatory

33. Kinsey et al., *Sexual Behavior in the Human Male,* pp. 182–87, especially Table 35.
34. J. M. Tanner, "Growth and Development of Boys and Girls," *Daedalus* 100 (1971): 919 and chart on p. 915.
35. An exemplary description of this period from a teacher's point of view is James Herndon, *Surviving in Your Native Land* (New York: Simon and Schuster, 1971).

prowess among boys or the appearance of breasts and menses among girls. The more public changes require judgment by the self, peers of the same sex, peers of the opposite sex, parents, and teachers. Some changes are (or seem) only apparent to the self, others to narrow or wide publics.

However variable the physical changes that mark the beginning and middle of early adolescence, it has meaning as a period of development because it is at this time that society at large (and, more approximately, parents, peers, schools, and media) recognizes and, in part, imposes on and invents the conventional sexual capacity of the individual. Even though the capacity for orgasm (as distinguished from ejaculation in the male) is available far earlier in life and even experienced by some infants and children, there is no sense in which the society promotes the utilization of or organization of this capacity into preadolescent experience.[36] Even though some few young people enter into adolescent sexual behavior before they are publicly defined as adolescents, for the majority this passage into overt sexual behavior is linked with the social transition as either defined by peers or by parents. Other than prepubertal sex play (and "play" is the appropriate word for the behavior), it is the entry into the new social status that triggers an increase in the rates of overt sexual behavior and the attribution and integration of new meanings for the behavior. In these earliest stages of the transition, extensively mixed modes of behavior occur, and hence it is possible for young boys to be both playing games of tag and using *Playboy* to masturbate. At this same moment physically precocious young girls will be covertly admired by older males and a generous amount of seductive behavior may be engaged in by such females without any conception of the mental constructs that it produces in the sexually experienced of either gender.

The sexually nonspecific character of the biological change and its minimal identification as being sexual by the experiencing child is evidenced by the numbers of children who report erection or orgasm from physical activities that were formerly only generally arousal producing—for example, tree climbing or fright—without their being defined as sexual. Only in a few cases prior to adolescence

---

36. Kinsey et al., *Sexual Behavior in the Human Female,* pp. 104–5.

is there evidence that attempts were made to repeat this behavior, even though it might have been experienced as pleasurable. While the child is unaware of the mechanics of making orgasm occur again (erections from the fear, anxiety, and excitement of climbing trees do not automatically translate into manual masturbatory repertoires), more significantly the event occurs without being bound into an organized set of behaviors which insure its reproducibility (except by climbing more trees, perhaps). This suggests the limitations of pure stimulus response interpretations of sexual activity, since the single pleasurable act requires an integration into a large and more complex structure of organized activities. As Kinsey states:

> The record suggests that the physiologic mechanism of any emotional response (anger, fright, pain, etc.) may be the basic mechanism of sexual response. Originally, the preadolescent boy erects indiscriminately to the whole array of emotional situations, whether they be sexual or nonsexual in nature. By his late teens the male has been so conditioned that he rarely responds to anything except a direct physical stimulation of genitalia or to psychic situations that are specifically sexual. In the still older male even physical stimulation is rarely effective unless accompanied by such a psychologic atmosphere. The picture is that of the psychosexual emerging from a much more generalized and basic physiologic capacity *which becomes sexual as an adult knows it,* through experience and conditioning.[37]

As is common in the Kinsey volumes, there is a limited understanding of the psychological or social explanations of the processes of development, but the observations themselves are most accurate.

The Emergence of Sexual Conduct

The phrase "which becomes sexual as an adult knows it" is the critical element in the transition between the general disorder of the beginnings of adolescence and participating in sexual activity with all of the social and psychological elements that adults attribute to it. The tentative sexual-like behaviors and the physical signs of adolescence are enriched by differential adult and peer imputations of

37. Kinsey et al., *Sexual Behavior in the Human Male,* p. 165.

motives, desires, and needs, which through their very imputation become the occasion for the child's learning them. Sexual behavior and the very desire for sexual activity become the occasion for attributing both old and new meanings to a novel and unexplored domain. Previously learned moral categories and oppositions (good and evil, purity and degradation, modesty) and gender role activities (aggression and submission, control and freedom, needs for achievement and affiliation) are integrated into new scripts, at first private and then collective, which contain new meanings to be applied to organs, orifices, activities, and people which make up the conventional sociosexual drama. It is the very artificiality (in an older sense) of the cultural conventions that at first elicit and then integrate sexual activity into social life that provides its fundamental interest and sustains our concern. Even the most sophisticated of developmental psychologists can fall into a belief in an orderly connection between earlier and later behaviors, assuming that there are ways in which the younger can "know" his own future. Even as Kagan denies the final power of biology, he still finds a place for a developmental "knowingness:"

> Although the known physiological changes at puberty are not necessary antecedents to the increased sexuality, it is likely that they contribute to the ascendancy of sexual thoughts, feelings, and actions. The adolescent must deal with the temptations of masturbation, petting, intercourse, and homosexuality. The statistics unambiguously indicate that the frequent sexual behavior of the seventeen year old is not yet manifesct in the eleven year old, who may be informed, but not yet active. One reason is that he is afraid; afraid of incompetence, parental discovery, and guilt. It is also likely that the sheer intensity of passion that is so urgent in the older adolescent is attenuated at this earlier age. The tension that is so overpowering in a seventeen year old is more like a tickle at eleven and, hence, more easily put aside. However, the eleven year old knows that his time is coming and he must prepare for it.[38]

A continuing commitment to the idea of the sexual seventeen year old existing as a seed in the informed, but the inactive eleven

---

38. Jerome Kagan, "A Conception of Early Adolescence," *Daedalus* 100 (1971).

year old fails to locate cause and effect. It is the very process
through which sexual activity becomes experienced as a temptation
that develops the capacity of the seventeen year old to experience
passion. There is no mystical procedure by which the eleven year
old "knows that his time is coming."

Masturbation, Gender, and Fantasy

Both in the onset and in the culmination of early adolescence it is
required that the developmental process as it takes place in the
male and female be distinguished. The two genders share the experience of transition from childhood, but the early outcomes of these
transitions serve to estrange each gender further from the existential
character of the other's sexual experience. For males this early adolescence is commonly characterized by the onset of overt sexual activity which is conducted in the context of secrecy experienced in
tension with the public masculine striving associated with homosociality. In contrast, among females overt sexual activity is infrequent; however, they, like males, live in a world dominated by their
own gender, but it is a more public world designed to promote future heterosociality. Within two years after puberty, most males
have had their commitment to sexuality reinforced by orgasm,
commonly through masturbation, though there is some social class
variation in the early onset of heterosexual contacts to orgasm.
These sexual experiences occur nearly universally in situations of
secrecy, with their most public affirmation in the context of male
peers, the secret society of the male alliance.[39] As part of this secrecy and the inability to share except in indirect and anxious ways
what is a powerful and novel experience, an experience for which
there is no social provision either in terms of adult instruction or lo-
calized places for performance, feelings of guilt and anxiety are en-
gendered. The available social world is composed of peers with the
same feelings of separation and fearfulness, but this peer group
world does provide a set of meanings that can be applied to both
masturbation and heterosexuality.

39. Evelyn Hooker has suggested that the beginning of sexual activity for
males in the social context where only other males are socially valued could
have potentials for producing at least some homosexual experience, if not
homosexual careers.

Unlike males, either during this period or later in life, few females masturbate to orgasm (only about two-thirds ever do so), and they do so at far lower frequencies. Not only are the rates of behavior different, it appears that as a result of a differing surrounding context, the experience of masturbation is far more idiosyncratic for women. The existence of male-male discussions, aspersions, and comparisons serves to regularize and order and further motivate the behavior, while among women the experience of early masturbation seems often unconnected with any other domain of behavior. The crucial difference seems to be the lack of collective or social sources to provide a larger set of social meanings.

The differences in rates can only in part indicate these psychological processes; however, the major break between men and women is expressed in the Kinsey data collected between 1938 and 1948, as shown in table 2.1.[40]

TABLE 2.1 *Accumulative Incidence of Masturbation to Orgasm*

	By Age	12	15	20
Percent Male		21	82	92
Percent Female		12	20	33

A more recent set of figures (table 2.2) taken from a 1967 national sample of college students (ages ranging between 17 and 23) indicates a remarkable continuity and stability for these figures on gender differences in masturbation:[41]

TABLE 2.2 *Frequency of Masturbation in High School*

	Twice a Week or More	Once to Once a Month	Never	N
Percent Male	77	12	11	586
Percent Female	17	23	60	581

40. Table constructed from percentages on p. 173, Kinsey et al., *Sexual Behavior in the Human Female.*
41. Table taken from J. H. Gagnon, W. Simon, and A. J. Berger, "Some Aspects of Sexual Adjustment in Early and Late Adolescence," in *Psychopathology of Adolescence,* eds. Joseph Zubin and Alfred N. Freedman (New York: Grune & Stratton, 1970), p. 278.

The key difference between males and females is that for the latter the organizing experience of puberty is the encouraging and furthering of the reality of marriage rather than, as for the former, the reality of sexual activity. Females live in a homosocial world as do males, but it is a homosocial world composed of both adult women and peers who primarily value the girl for her ultimate status as wife and mother. In this sense the girl is prepared for heterosociality, if not for heterosexuality. It is a world of women and girls training a girl for behavior with reference to men without a concomitant understanding of the diverging pattern of sexual development being experienced by men. This linkage of the young girl with the woman's role and the publically valued institution of marriage means that the female lives most of her life as preadult in a public status where the coercive forces of normal socialization are present.

The key role of the presence or absence of early sexual activity, either in terms of masturbation or early heterosexual involvement, cannot be underestimated in the reinforcing of a divergence in gender development. Nearly universally for males, even though the majority find masturbation pleasing, there is guilt and anxiety attached to the masturbatory experience.[42] While we no longer believe that there is a connection between insanity and the expenditure of these vital bodily essences, there is little evidence that there has been any reduction in the anxiety associated with masturbatory practices by the young who are beginning their sexual lives. Indeed, it is possible to hypothesize that it is the existence of this anxiety about masturbation that supports our experiential belief that the sexual drive is one of extreme potency. We presume that we are experiencing a biologically powerful experience when in fact it is the guilt and the anxiety associated with arousal identified as sexual which is provoking our sense of intensity. We mislocate the source of the intensity, attaching it to a bodily state rather than to the psychological states that accompany the physical experience.

This guilt and anxiety is not a simple consequence of the fact that society disapproves of the behavior. It rather derives from a

---

42. Ibid, pp. 275–95, reported that among college-going males who masturbated during high school 22% felt guilt often, while 39% felt guilt some of the time when they masturbated.

number of sources. Masturbation is performed in secret, not because of specific sexual prohibitions, but because most things connected with the genitals are performed in private. Here earlier training in modesty comes into play, a training that children do not experience as having sexual implications, though their parents may, in which the genitals become part of the excluded and private zone. Most early acts involving the genitals are involved with excretion, and privacy is part of this exclusion. The beginning manipulation of the genitals for purposes of pleasure retains this exclusion and is further intensified by the beginnings of fantasies of doing sexual things with oneself and with others. These fantasies are the preliminary rehearsals and the vicarious organization of sociosexual dramas using the primitive symbolic resources that are available at various stages of development. This activity in the private zone increases the breach between male child and parents (and other members of the immediate family) where the sentimental and the erotic are complexly intertwined. Often the utilization of available affectively bonded figures (sisters, relatives) in sexual fantasy creates an attachment between sexual performance and normative violation. Further anxiety is generated by the ambivalent attitudes of peers toward masturbation and sexual activity in general. While the male peer group is supportive of predatory, achievement-oriented, and aggressive styles of sexual performance (once again deriving from general gender-role training and not a hunting instinct), masturbation is treated with great suspicion unless performed in the context of heroic sexual contest.

Viewed from this perspective, which shares many of the concerns for the symbolic meaning of behavior generated by the psychoanalytic perspective without a concept of drive or unilinear biological causality, masturbation becomes a complex and ambiguous event in socialization. The age at onset, its frequency, its absence if it does not occur, its embeddedness in peer and parent relations, its relation to past socialization, are all interactively tied to other dimensions of social and psychological life.

If one is prepared to abandon the idea that masturbation is an activity performed in response to the increasing power of the sexual impulse resulting from the biological changes of puberty (and further that nocturnal emissions are not ways to reduce the pressure of seminal output), one can begin to examine the behavior as it emerges in early adolescence and link it to a variety of extra-sexual sources that have occurred earlier and to behavior and meanings that will occur later.

In its earliest phases masturbation seems shrouded by its diffuse origins. Clearly the capacity for orgasm in the female and erection and orgasm in the male exist far earlier than puberty, and while some children do masturbate to orgasm or handle their genitals prior to puberty, the upsurge of interest especially among males matches the shift from childhood into adolescence. Part of this development may well be partly linked to the upsurge of hormones that may increase the sensitivity of the penis to touch and produce a more frequent base for erection. What is apparent, however, is the diffuseness of this response. Males can come to orgasm or ejaculation the first time in nonsexual circumstances, under conditions that in terms of physical excitement or tension induction parallel only slightly the later patterns of directing induced sexual pleasure. Few males remember this period clearly when interviewed, reporting, often vaguely, only the year when first orgasm or ejaculation occurred. This is very much unlike females who remember with great precision the first menses. Part of this is surely that the latter is a public act that requires the response of others, while the male often begins his own experimentation with sexuality detached from an adult public world and adult public definitions.

The general absence of masturbation among women is, when contrasted with the male experience, commonly explained in one of three ways. It is assumed that masturbation is universal and that females repress their memories of it, or it is assumed that women's sexual drive is more inhibited or repressed than that of men, or it is assumed that the sexual drive itself is biologically weaker among women. These kinds of interpretations seem ill-founded, and they lead to endless confusions and misunderstandings about female sexuality. As has been argued, the assumption of a universal biological mandate for any sexual activity or for a gender variation in the strength of biological impulse is not supported by any body of data on humans. Further, the psychoanalytic model which imposes on women a male history of development makes the development of female sexuality far more mysterious than it need be, though as an existential experience, men can still see it only through a glass darkly. Explanations for this low level of female sexual activity or interest are numerous on both functional and historical grounds. The basic element in all of these is the idea that females in our society are not encouraged to be sexual and, indeed, it is possible that they are strongly discouraged from being sexual. As Rheingold describes this where men have only to fear sexual failure, women have to fear failure and success simultaneously.[43] Or, as several people have observed, while the category "bad boy" has many descriptive subcategories, the category "bad girl" tends almost exclusively to describe sexual delinquencies. Clearly, it is both difficult and dangerous for a female to become too committed or too sexually active during adolescence.

Whether this extended period of relative sexual inactivity represents the outcome of successful repression of an elementary sexual urge or merely represents a failure to have an opportunity to learn how to be sexual is an important question for consideration. The alternative answers have different implications for how we view the later development of a sexual commitment during late adolescence or postadolescence. The "repression" answer suggests that we approach later activity in terms of processes of de-inhibition by which the female learns to find, in varying degrees, modes of more direct expression of internally experienced feelings. It also requires a quest for the sexually determined aspects of nonsexual behavior. The "learning" answer suggests that women and men create or invent a capacity for sexual behavior, learning how to be aroused and learning how to be responsive. The latter approach also implies greater flexibility in overall adjustments; unlike the repression view, it makes sexuality something other than a constant that is likely to "break loose" at any point in strange or costly ways. In addition, the learning approach lessens the power of the sexual component as a variable; all at once, there is no necessarily healthy or pathological component to a particular style of sexual activity. Lastly, an ad-

43. J. C. Rheingold, *The Fear of Being a Woman* (New York: Grune & Stratton, 1964).

ditional appeal for us of this approach is somewhat subjective: it tends to seem less like a projection of male sexuality.

The lack of an upsurge in sexual activity at adolescence among females indicates that there is less of a break between the nonsexual training experiences of childhood and the experiences of early adolescence for females than for males. The future valued status of womanhood, with its relatively narrow commitments to wifedom and childrearing, seems relatively continuous with earlier experiences in gender training. Gender-linked training in submissiveness and lack of aggression toward parents link to similar roles that are expected of female adults with reference to husbands. Girls are trained to occupy essentially reactive roles, roles in which they are to be scheduled by the behavior of others, including their future children.

Similar to boys, girls are trained in notions of modesty, are not trained in sexual performances, and their quasi-sexual behavior is not defined in a directly sexual manner for them. It is not women's sexual drive that is inhibited, for the language of "drive" and "inhibition" are both faulty; it is that women receive little training in sexual activity that is not prohibitory, while at the same time being positively trained in docility.

During this period of sexual "training," females are offered a wide range of other nonsexual experiences that link to conventional gender role performance and that are coordinated with it. Menstruation is fundamentally linked to the capacity for pregnancy rather than sex (properly so, in most senses). The desire for the social occasions of romance, love, and marriage are universally reinforced by the conventional social order composed of both peers and parents. Parents are more protective in terms of controlling a girl's time and likelihood of sexual involvement, though this is not specifically inhibitory but rather limits the occasions in which she might fall into sexual encounters. Since masturbation among females is linked to so few other important social experiences, it rarely becomes organized into other patterns of behavior. For boys there is achievement, fear, aggression, and normative violation to attach to bodily manipulation; for the girls only a modest sense of anxiety unlinked to more powerful motivations. It remains until a later period for women to experience overt sexual behavior in concordance

with the powerful collective dimensions of romance, violation of taboos, and consequent emotional feelings that enhance sexual acts. It
is important to note that in the Kinsey data nearly half of the females in the sample who masturbated did so only after the first orgasm in sociosexual experience.

Even among woman who have masturbated to orgasm as adolescents (or even as adults) there does not seem to be a major shift to
describe gentialia themselves as sources of pleasure. It is possible
for some women to have masturbated to orgasm as adolescents and
in the sexual isolation that is common still among most women not
to have identified the experience of orgasm with specifically sexual
pleasure, only noting its significance to sexual conduct when it occurs in heterosexual relationships. Even the techniques of masturbation are less directly linked to heterosexual coitus. Rather than
masturbation being by insertion, it is commonly through rubbing
the clitoris and the labia with the fingers and tensing the legs and
thighs against another object such as a pillow. A significant element
in the physical activities of females during masturbation is that they
do not insert anything into the vagina. It and its liquids remain a
terra inconita except for those females who lubricate a great deal
during sexual excitement. Unlike a male, who leaves evidence in
the form of the ejaculate and its odors, the female is inexperienced
with her own nonmenstrual fluids. Masturbation that occurs prior
to extensive heterosexual contact seems far less often accompanied
by fantasies of sexual activity, and the genitals—even when orgasm
occurs—remain something that is "down there." Females do not
seem to experience masturbation as something that heightens sexual
autonomy, though there is evidence that females who masturbate to
orgasm do experience orgasm in heterosexual contact more easily.
There seem to be two significant elements here. The first is that the
masturbatory activity itself among females does not build on the
same kinds of gender commitments and therefore has less consequence in terms of developing sexual commitments. Secondly, the
absence of masturbation leaves women open to more diffuse and
less genital orientations in their future sexual contacts. The absence
of masturbation leaves a nonsexual period in the lives before the
genitals are defined as sources of sexual pleasure of girls; this conception does not occur until serious heterosexual genital contact.

Once again, as with many other behaviors among women, pleasure becomes reactive rather than proactive, leading not to autonomy but to continued heteronomy in the sexual domain.

In one sense during this period, biology in the guise of anatomy does have some importance. It is possible for the erect penis to become a sign of masculine prowess and masculine identity through its obvious erectile capacities. The ejaculation can be a visible measure of successful physical effort for the male. The availability of the anatomical sign is clearly some advantage in terms of the integration of bodily experiences and psychological states. At the same time, it is important not to attribute prepotency to this phenomena. Some 10 percent of the males in the Kinsey sample and an equal proportion in our own research report never having masturbated, even though they report being perfectly adequate sexually in other ways. A dilemma of the use of this physical sign for demonstration of masculinity is the production of severe anxiety when the sign fails to appear.

One of the key socialization effects of the differences in masturbatory behavior between men and women is the differential specification of the central loci of sexual response on the body. It is clear from cross-cultural evidence that the sequence of sexual foreplay that is seen as necessary to the production of orgasm in the West is a cultural invention rather than a biological necessity. The erogenous zones of the body are in large measure learned locations rather than special congeries of nerve endings that have built-in sexual meaning. Masturbation tends to focus the male sense of feeling of sexual desire in the penis, giving the genitals centrality in the physical and symbolic domains.

The physical activity required in male masturbation seems relatively simple. Most commonly the male learns to take the penis in hand while it is flaccid or partially erect and strokes it, usually while maintaining some fantasy in his head. In the earliest stages the fantasy may well not be specifically sexual but only up to the margin of the activities associated with sex that the boy knows about. The capacity for erection is an important sign element of masculinity and control for the male who is able in these moments to produce a behavior that is linked both to pleasure and fear. The linkage of the ejaculation and the culmination of the act produces an important beginning for a belief in what the normal sequence of sexual contact will be in the future. He comes to believe that all sexual contacts should result in orgasm, since it does so in masturbation which, at least in this society, is a prototype for the future. These first attempts are relatively fumbling, with the sources of when and why to perform the behavior, the fantasies involved, and the physical manipulation of the penis relatively uncoordinated.

A shift to genital priority occurs for women at a far later date if it occurs at all. Genital localization of erotic response is a function of reactive sexual contacts with males rather than through masturbatory sexual experience. It is this diffuse character of responsiveness that results from a differential staging of sexual socialization that has created the false dichotomy between the clitoral and vaginal orgasm. It is only through believing that the vagina is the "natural" place to feel response (since coitus involves intromission and this is the "natural" form of sexual behavior) that we have misunderstood the sociopsychological sources of bodily eroticism. In some measure, females may well be more flexible sexually than males in this matter and be able to respond with a wider definition of the parts of the body as participating in sexual performances. This contention that these matters are learned is also applicable to the breasts, where external definition of them as primary erotic signs is learned by women through their contact with men and the later autonomous erotic pleasure they take in them is commonly created by a prior male reading of the erotic possibilities of the female body.

Another distinction which must be made in terms of the significance of masturbation as an early form of overt sexual behavior is its provision of an arena for the acting out of specifically sexual fantasies which are tied to other social motives. Here there are differences not only between the genders but also between males of various social classes. Once the tension release aspects or the physiological dimensions of the masturbation are de-emphasized, what is observable is that there is a complex feedback loop between what is defined as a physically pleasurable act and the reinforcement of newly organized sexual scripts. In the most conventional learning theory terms, the masturbatory act reinforces a good deal of symbol manipulation, and this symbolic commitment tends to take on an independent life of its own later in life.

The differences between the symbolic commitments of males and females in sexuality, and expecially as they accompany masturbation, are only partially known. As we have noted, not many females masturbate and those who do, do so at rates that are much below those of males. Further, the fantasies that we know about (and the information is both retrospective in most cases and sparse) among females tend to support the belief that their fantasies on the level of specific sexual acts are commonly limited to the sexual things that they have done, and further, that the context of social arrangements that surround the thoughts of sexual acts are those which emphasize love, marriage, social attachment, and in some cases, mild forms of masochism. The participants in the act are either known or actors with the kind of social status that would be appropriate for marriage. In contrast, the male sexual fantasy, which can appear to the naive observer to be denuded of social factors (as with pornography, there are explicit social elements) is rich in specifically sexual behavior.

At the core of this behavior for many males, however, is the development of the capacity to link sociocultural elements to sexual activity. In part, masturbation offers the male (and some females) a series of alternative sexual selves. Secret masturbation which others are not to observe is the first analog of the secret sexual self, a self that can be innovative or conservative, but a self that requires a private dimension for sexual expression. At the same time, the boy must learn to synchronize his fantasy with his physical behavior, with the sequence of imagined steps in the fantasy regulated to come to orgasm as the physical stimulation itself comes to climax. He must learn to focus on the interior fantasy, while excluding the intrusive stroking of the penis. (After all, is he not participating in behavior with someone else who is providing the excitement or the stroking?) We quickly forget these fumbling origins because the masturbatory activity rapidly becomes self-reinforcing. The fantasy targets of sexual activity are the notorious (hence the erotic) and local females who have high status in the peer structures that surround the male. The fantasies commonly involve themes of sexual aggression, the use of transgressive sexual techniques (mouth gential contact and the like), and fantasies of sexual cornucopias (the harem). The more complex sexual fantasies develop later in this period, say from fourteen to sixteen. The sexual acts are often suggestive of needs for achievement (the making of the unattainable), the acting out of moral transgression, and reduction of anxiety through fantasies of omnipotence. What is central here is that the sexual act is being tied to nonsexual motives that pre-exist in gender-role training. The masturbatory fantasy prefigures ultimate male attitudes and in the cases where it occurs among females suggests the degree to which gender-role training is coercive in ultimate development.

While the incidence of masturbation across social class among males is quite similar, there is substantial variation across social class in its use and meaning.[44] From the Kinsey data and other studies, it appears that middle-class boys tend to masturbate most frequently and accompany it with relatively complex fantasies. Often for the middle-class boy masturbation becomes that behavior through which he can autonomously control his sources of pleasure. It proclaims his independence from others in this matter, and only in others approving it as less pleasurable than coitus is he moved away from it. The continued masturbation of men after marriage, not only when their wives are absent, is a measure of the continuing autonomy of the fantasy developed in early adolescence. In the fantasy world a male is less constrained by the mundane character of the sexual life that he normally finds around him. The cast of fantasy characters is not infinite, since it is restricted by the culture, but it is certainly more wide ranging than in actual practice. At the same time, he is familiar with his own body (no one else's hand on the penis is ever so skilled), and with the sequence of fantasy that attracts him. The finding by Masters and Johnson that the orgasm that results from masturbation is more intense physiologically may result from the fact that the masturbator does not have to regulate his or her own sexual pleasure to the sequence or routines of another person and thus inhibit the power of self-gratification.

44. Kinsey et al., *Sexual Behavior in the Human Male*, pp. 374–77 and pp. 506–16.

Masturbation on the part of males builds on prior gender training focusing on autonomy and initiative in sexual gratification.
While it is clear that there are substantial social-class variations
among males, these variations themselves seem to be linked to ultimate class adjustments. Masturbation in private with its accompanying fantasy, allows the middle-class male a location inside of
which to engage in unjudged (by others) sexual performances.
Lower-class males who move more quickly into heterosexual contacts have their sexual performances more strongly linked to peer
group judgments and allow the peer group attitudes toward women
and marriage to more extensively penetrate their later lives. Rather
than masturbation being a single-minded act, it is multipotential,
with its broadest origins located in gender-role training and with its
outcomes linked to a wide range of sexual performances.

The problem of managing a fairly elaborate and exotic fantasy
life is most typically a problem for higher social-class levels. On
lower-class levels there is a less frequent use of fantasy during masturbation, and this in turn may be linked to a generalized lack of
training and competence in the manipulation of symbolic materials.
Higher social-class male adolescents are presumably trained for
such competence. Masturbation accompanied by fantasy should in
turn reinforce the manipulation of symbolic materials. If we de-em-
phasize the physical component in the masturbatory act, it can be
conceptualized as an activity in which the actor is, in effect, training himself to invest symbols with affect and to derive gratification
from the manipulation of symbols.

It may well be that this behavior—which is something females
tend not to engage in—plays a role in the processes by which middle-class males catch up with females in measures of achievement
and creativity and then, by the end of adolescence, move out in
front. This is, of course, merely a wild hypothesis—the Dr. Krank-
eit (sic) hypothesis.[45] This primary reliance upon masturbation
with fantasy should also have a number of consequences beyond the
capacity for a relatively detached sexual performance. One such

45. M. Kenton (pseud. of T. Southern and M. Hoffenburg), *Candy* (Paris: The Olympia Press, 1958). That this view has a wider literary base is indicated by the line of dialogue from Christopher Hampton's play *The
Philanthropist:* "Masturbation is the thinking man's television."

consequence is a tendency to eroticize large parts of the world, as well as an ability to respond to a wide array of visual and auditory stimuli. Moreover, to the extent that Wilhelm Reich is correct in his assertion that the scripting for masturbatory fantasies has a non- and possibly anti-coital character, we might also expect both a capacity and a need for fairly elaborate forms of sexual activity.[46] Further, insofar as the masturbatory fantasy focuses upon relationships and activities essentially preparatory to the coital act, the masturbatory experience should also reinforce an already developing capacity for sustaining heterosocial activity. The ultimate effect, however, may be to engender a critical ambivalence about coital activity.

A major source of guilt and anxiety—the unmanliness of masturbation—should be more typically a concern of lower-class male adolescents. Among them the general pattern of sexual segregation of social life and the relatively narrower range of rewarding social experiences available to them should combine to constrain the adolescent to move into heterosexual relationships sooner than his middle-class counterpart. The first condition, the sexual segregation of social life, should make it easier for him to gravitate toward a world of casual, if not exploitative, sexual relations; it is easier for him than for the middle-class adolescent to learn that he does not have to love everything he desires. The second condition—the more limited available social rewards and, particularly, rewards deriving from activities that will be validated by his peers—should lead to an exaggerated concern for masculinity-enhancing behavior leading, in turn, to displays of physical prowess, successful staging of aggressive behaviors, and visible sexual success. The three—physical prowess, aggresive behavior, and sexual success—are, of course, not unrelated and frequently are mutually reinforcing.

Heterosexuality and Homosociality

It is this phasing of the movement into heterosexual experience, either directly or as a fundamentally valued experience that can re-

46. W. Reich, "The Function of the Orgasm," in *The Discovery of the Orgone, 1* (New York: Orgone Institute Press, 1942).

place masturbation distinguishes between males of various social classes. It is apparent that there are pre- and early pubertal entries into coitus in all social groups, but these are quite exceptional in the middle classes and only slightly more frequent in working- and lower-class communities. At age thirteen there are very few boys who are capable of handling the relatively complex social skills required to perform the social manipulations necessary to have coitus with a female of the same age. That it does happen is not doubted, but it does not represent the main drift of sexual socialization during this period. The proportion of white males in the Kinsey college educated group who had intercourse in the sequence of years during this period were: by age 12, 1 percent, by age 14, 6 percent, and by age 16, 16 percent.[47] In contrast, the percentages for the same ages for white working-class males were: 9 percent, 20 percent, and 40 percent.[48] In a sense, the lower-class male is the first to reach "sexual maturity" as defined by those working in an essentially Freudian tradition, that is, these lower-class males are generally the first to become exclusively heterosexual and exclusively genital in orientation.

What is significant about these acts of coitus is not the specific acts themselves, which are relatively sporadic and infrequent even for the most successful male, but rather the milieu in which they are performed. This period is dominated by *homosociality,* that is, a period in life when valuation of the self is more keyed to those of like gender than it is to those of opposite gender. This male world, full of rather primitive predatory sexual values focusing on the moral differences between "good" girls and "bad" girls, and acting out achievement motives involved in seeing "how far one can get," uses sexual contacts with females as a device for confirming social status among males. What is critical is not the act, but to whom the act is referential. The higher incidence of coitus among working-class males and the value system of sexual predation often means that such early sexual experience essentially limits (though it does not have to in other social milieus) the capacity for heterosocial commitments later in life. By *heterosocial* is meant the development of

47. Kinsey et al., *Sexual Behavior in the Human Male,* Table 136, p. 550.
48. P. H. Gebhard, J. H. Gagnon, W. B. Pomeroy, and C. V. Christensen, *Sex Offenders* (New York: Harper & Row, 1965), Table 55, p. 564.

the capacity to perform sexual acts that value the women and bind together males and females, in contrast to those sexual performances with females that bind together males.

Homosocial values exist among middle-class males at this time, but there is far more interpenetration of male social life by females (mothers and peers) in middle-class than in working-class environments. The efflorescence of early dating patterns in middle-class contexts, which are so worrisome to many parents because they seemingly increase the risk of early sexual experience, may well serve to increase male commitments to heterosociality. Much of the sexual contact during this period is petting above the waist, with some genital contact, but such contacts do not commonly easily proceed to coitus. These steady dating experiences may well serve to increase the young male's investment in the rhetoric of love and emotional commitment which seem so necessary a part of the marriage pattern of this society. Even when the young male's protestations of affection are cynical affectations to achieve greater sexual access, what must be kept in mind is that we often become what we thought we were only pretending to be.

Since coitus requires that males have a partner, there clearly must be at least some females in this age period who have these extensive sexual contacts. The Kinsey percentages for sexual intercourse among white nondelinquent females for this period are as shown in table 2.3.[49]

TABLE 2.3   *Accumulative Incidence of Coitus for Females*

	Percentage	
Educational Level	Age 13	Age 15
0–8	9	18
9–12	1	5
13–16	–	2
17+	1	1

What is most apparent is that there is little difference between educational levels (except for educational level 0–8) and from data

49. Kinsey et al., *Sexual Behavior in the Human Female,* Table 75, p. 337.

gathered by the authors in 1967, there is little difference for these ages between the Kinsey data gathered on college women from 1938 to 1950 and for females presently in college.[50] What seems to occur during this period is that a limited number of females become the targets for the sexual interests of a larger number of males. The "easy lay," "the bad girl," the "peg board," reinforce the male imagery of purity and corruption that is one of central symbolic dimensions of sexuality. These females, for whatever reasons, become that relatively small pool who are involved in sexual experience early in life. While they are the targets of male sexual interest, they are also the targets of female rejection.

The relative absence of overt sexual activity by females during this period does not preclude the fact that they are receiving training experience which will link to sexual activity later. In the homosocial world in which females live, during this period there are sets of informing goals that link to competition, not in the sexual marketplace, but in the marriage marketplace. Competition requires learning to present the self to males as a marketable commodity, in some sense as a potentially sexual object. On the cosmetic level, nearly all young females, especially in the more recent past, have begun to learn these skills relatively early. This process has been described as learning all of the postures of sex except pleasure, but this pattern may have aided in the development of females' attitudes toward attractiveness that has some sexual overtones. The content of the sexual role for the female retains its essential commitment to service for the male, a service that is to be provided for in the future and in the context of love and marriage.

While this period of life is filled with moral injunctions about the behavior of young girls, it does not appear to us that much of this instruction is directed toward specifically sexual prohibitions. Few parents tell their daughters not to copulate in so many words (and given the limited existential link between the usual imprecise "so many words" and copulation, one wonders what messages such injunctions do contain). Rather they hedge in girls' lives with notions of good behavior, good companions, early hours, and restricted dat-

---

50. W. Simon, A. S. Berger, and J. H. Gagnon, "Beyond Anxiety and Fantasy: The Coital Experience of College Youth," *Journal of Youth and Adolescence* 1: 203–22.

ing. As a consequence, certain forms of sexual behavior in this period are linked to testing these injunctions of control rather than to the ambiguous pleasure that exists in the sexual act itself.

In this period, the male and the female are being trained in essentially opposite modalities, though there is more interconnection between boys and girls in the middle class than in other social locations. The central themes for females are commitment to affect-laden relationships and to the rhetoric of romantic love. It is not so much that their sexual development is inhibited, though it is policed, but that it exists as a vacuity and can only be experienced as an absence. The male themes are more complex; there is a growing and developing commitment to sexual acts, in part for themselves and in part as acts as they relate to other main patterns in male gender role training—autonomy, aggression, control, achievement, normative transgression. What most males, except for those in the middle class, are not learning are socioemotional skills directed toward females. Both through masturbation and hetersexual contact, males can be committed to directly sexual activities and, in some part, to gratification from them. Females, even when they report sexual arousal, do so in the haze of romantic as opposed to erotic illusions.

Adolescent Homosexuality

The other major form of sexual activity during this period is homosexuality. By major we do not mean that it is especially frequent or even that it has a very great incidence. It does appear that for many adult males who become homosexual, first experiences can and do occur during this period; however, of the vast majority of males who have a single homosexual encounter at this time, few carry it on into adulthood. In a reanalysis of the incidence figures from the Kinsey research, it was noted that among the college educated about 30 percent of the males reported a single homosexual experience. Fifteen percent of the total males (50% of those experienced) had only experiences during the period 12–16 with no later experience, and some 10 percent of total males (33% of those experienced) had experiences during this period with some experiences at 17 and 18, but nothing after that (see chap. 5).

The meaning of these experiences is difficult to determine, as are all phenomena that are transient and seemingly without consequence. Most of the homosexual contacts that occur between males early in the period (say ages 11, 12, 13) are more like prepubertal sex play in their motives, even though they may be accompanied by ejaculation. Curiosity, mutual instruction, the influence of slightly older males result in physical exploration. What is risky for the youth is that the uninstructed adult will impose on this behavior the complex meanings which adult homosexuality has for the adult and behave accordingly toward the young people. This can only be demoralizing and disrupting. Homosexuality in the latter part of early adolescence has a number of meanings depending on the social location and the prior social and sexual experiences of the actors. It can be the transient response to opportunity where there is arousal in private situations, or it can have more emotional depth between an admired older boy and a follower. In a sense, adolescent homosexual acts are not usually integrated into the mainstream of development, though some homosexual activity may result from the existence of a male alliance (a *homosocial* world) in early puberty in which strong dyadic affective relations between boys can occur. In other cases, young boys may be victimized, or a marginally delinquent boy may perform as a prostitute. While these latter events are relatively rare, they are instructive in that they provide another instance of the way in which a sexual act can be symbolically transformed. The exterior view is that such contacts are homosexual, while the young male defines himself and his act, because of his role, as continuously heterosexual or, at least, not queer.[51]

Evidence on early homosexual relations among females is extremely sparse, perhaps more sparse than the behavior. There is a good deal of body contact among females during this period, hand holding, sleeping together, or being partially nude. Except for the rare girl, none of this is found to be erotic or sexual. It has been argued elsewhere that the development of female homosexuality is directly linked to the development of normal femininity and gender role in the society. During this period (and, for most women,

51. Albert J. Reiss, "The Social Integration of Queers and Peers," *Social Problems* 9 (1961): 102–20.

throughout the life cycle) the feminine gender-role training excludes and disavows the sexual component in homosexuality as powerfully and in the same fashion as it does in heterosexuality (see chap. 6).

Early Adolescence: Summary

The period from twelve to sixteen is probably the period of priority in developing and integrating the sexual into general patterns of gender development in Western societies. The beginning signs of physical changes are cues to parents and youth themselves to begin to conceive of a young person as potentially eligible to occupy what are conventional sexual roles in the society. The specific sexual acts themselves are then linked to prior gender-role categories (not prior sexual commitments) and it is through this integration that meanings can be attributed to newly developed physical capacities and bodily conformations. The very experience of the body, however, must be translated through meanings that are drawn from nonsexual domains. The experience of sexual activity as achievement on the part of young men or as a form of social service on the part of females does not derive from immanent meanings derived from biology, but from the invented and created role categories that are available to members of a society.

The increased salience of sex as a moral category is also significant during this period. Sexual behavior in the West has been inextricably linked to dramas of good and evil as part of the phenomena of excess and restraint. The imagery of the moral value of restraint (virginity) and the moral failure of excess (the orgy) take their symbolic roots from scarcity societies that have transmuted their values through a secularized Protestantism. Children during this period are learning some of the primitive elements of what is an ultimately sophisticated and complex dramatistic conception of the sexual.

The development of the sexual comes relatively late in character development and rather than being the engine of change, it takes its meaning primarily from other sources of personality development. It rarely becomes an autonomous area of behavior and retains its dependent status for nearly all persons. If there is a strain toward moral autonomy during this period, it occurs relatively late and rather more frequently with males than with females. Because sex is at the service of so many other motives, the rules that constrain it seem more external and less flexible than in other domains.

The boundaries of early adolescence are diffuse and variable, especially across cultures (and even within subsectors of a society), but in the West it seems to be a critical moment for people in terms of psychosexual and sociosexual development. One's identity as a sexual being gains much of its shape during this period as society and—quite secondarily—biology combine to mark the end of childhood. The movement into later adolescence and the concomitant increase in opportunities for sociosexual activity can be described as a situation in which males—committed to sexuality and less trained in the rhetoric of romantic love—interact with females who are committed to romantic love and relatively untrained in sexuality. Dating and courtship may well be considered processes in which persons train members of the opposite sex in the meaning and content of their respective commitments. And while data in this area are deficient in many regards, the data that are available suggest this system of exchange often does not work smoothly. Thus, as is partly suggested by Ehrmann's work and partly by our own present studies of college students, it is not uncommon to find, ironically, that the male suitor frequently becomes emotionally involved with his partner and correspondingly less interested in engaging in sexual activity with her and that the female, whose appreciation of the genuineness of her suitor's affection allows her to feel that sexual activity is now both legitimate and desirable, becomes *more* interested in engaging in sexual activity with him.[52] This difference in commitment is exemplified in several ways. One such item, deal-

---

52. Zeitgeists are largely out of fashion among the more empirical sociologists, however, the current model of sexuality before marriage seems at least formally related to Adam Smith. In its crassest form " . . . the division of labor . . . is an incentive system (normatively regulated) through which goods are produced and exchanged. Since sexual desirability is itself a goal, sexual access can be exchanged for economic or political advantage." Kingsley Davis, "Sexual Behavior," in *Contemporary Social Problems,* eds. R. K. Merton and R. Nisbet (New York: Harcourt Brace Jovanovich, 1971), p. 320.

ing with the number of times individual respondents had intercourse with their first partner, shows the mode for males around one to three times, while the mode for females is at ten times or more. Clearly, for females, initial intercourse becomes possible only in relatively stable relationships or relationships involving rather strong bonds.

On a theoretical level, we find the male experience conforming to the general Freudian expectation, with males moving from a predominantly sexual commitment to an ability to form cathectic attachments in loving relationships. In effect, this movement is reversed for females, with cathectic attachments being, in many cases, a necessary precondition for coital activity. It is not surprising, perhaps, that Freud had great difficulty approaching female sexuality. This "error" in conceptualizing female sexuality—of seeing it either as being similar to male sexuality or as a mirrored image—may derive from the fact that so much of the theory construction in this area was done by males. In Freud's case, we also have to consider the very conception of sexuality that was essential to most of Victorian Europe—it was an elemental beast that had to be curbed.

Later Adolescence: Summary

Young people are thrust together in the beginnings of a dating and mating game in which far more than sexual outlet is involved and that will extend until marriage. In this game there are tests of competence, victories and losses, a confrontation with sexuality that requires not only the management of the self but also the management of others. It is also a sexuality where the content of the societal norms in terms of regulatory content is more apparent and more specific. The rating and dating game is presently a U.S. institution, but it seems to be as exportable as Coca Cola. In modern and modernizing societies where there is a gap between marriage and puberty, where the adolescent is defined as sexual, where access between the sexes is allowed, and where an ideology of puritanism is eroded both by a romantic ethic and an increased secularism, this kind of premarital game or some variant of it will characterize most social locations.

The script for the physical elements of this relationship is apparent to all who participate in it. First there is kissing, then tongue kissing, then touching of the breasts through the clothing (perhaps here a break in sequence), touching of the breasts under the clothing or the genitals through the skirt or outside the underwear, then finally genital contact with either a branch to mouth-genital contact (in some few cases) or coitus. Most frequently the culmination is in coitus. Two things are apparent from this description: the first is that the description is one of male as subject (active, controlling) and female as object (passive, controlled). Males in this kind of world do, females react or gate keep. The physical exchanges are surrounded by other exchanges of words and gifts that affirm the increasing accessibility of the female's body. Relationships are described in terms of the level of affection offered (from girls to their friends) or the degree of sexual access achieved (from males to their friends). It is an achievement-oriented activity blunted only by the universality of love and caring that is endemic among both sexes.

The second element in the description is its apparent naturalness; one progresses from lips to genitals and with increasing levels of palpitation and excitement. It is this apparent natural developmental physical script that is most deceiving. In their earliest experience with the physical contact (kissing, holding hands), males will feel very high levels of excitement that will be nearly the same as that they will feel later when coitus occurs. This high level of physiological excitement accompanies the entire cycle and sequence of physical contacts for males in the early stages of sexual learning and often can lead to premature ejaculation or ejaculation even when coitus is not going to occur. It is only with practice that the excitement and plateau phases prior to orgasm become more extended and closer to the time cycle presented by females who just are learning the script for the excitement and plateau phases that occur before orgasm. This earliest experience with high levels of excitement for the male are commonly derived from a sense of conquest, achievement, anxiety, and norm violation. It is quickly apparent that there is no special connection between the specific physical acts (kissing, the taste of lipstick, touching genitals through clothing) and sexual excitement. Kissing was defined only a few years earlier as sissified by most boys (and desirable, but not sexual, by girls), but during the period of dating the same physical act is defined as sexually meaningful and accompanied by a sense of physical excitement. There is no change in the physical acts, only in the meanings attributed to them.

This active role for the male is accompanied by preexisting fantasies from masturbation, potential descriptions of intercourse and its delights ("hitting a home run"), and a physical sense of the pleasure of orgasm that give his behavior a goal-directed character. In contrast, the female who has rarely conceived of the pleasures to which she is to be introduced and whose body itself is only vaguely eroticized (that is, had its parts given meanings such that when they are touched in appropriate circumstances she is able to report to herself that she is feeling pleasure or ecstasy), is most consciously engaging in preventing further access to her body. She is being touched, not touching; she is allowing access, not being responsive. The script is sufficiently well known so that petting above the waist may well occur for the female without much sexual arousal. While the breasts are defined publically as sexual objects, they vary in sensitivity among females not because of differences in the number of nerve endings but because of the differing feelings that females think they should have from the breasts being touched. It is only in reaction to the definition of arousal and response that females now begin to do things that appear to be specifically responsive to intended sexual stimuli.

When the contact goes below the waistline and becomes genital, the young men and women have to begin to come to grips systematically to with odors and liquids that they have not previously experienced. Such odors that remain on the fingers, hands, genitals, or clothing become evidence of ambivalent prowess for males (the odors that remain on his hands can be called "stinkfinger") or submission for females. Throughout all of this the female remains except for submissive gestures the object of attention. Indeed, most other fondlings or clutchings can be defined as being overwhelmed by passion. She may comply, but until she begins to touch the male's penis herself, definition remains less than openly sexual. In contrast, touching the penis begins to define her in specifically sexual ways. There is now between the two participants a minimal definition of the female beginning to be linked, perhaps for the first time, to the initiation of sexual performance. Unlike the erect penis during dancing or in passive petting, the act of touching the penis indicates a movement both in terms of the interpersonal relationship and in terms of her self-definition. It is important to note however that this act of touching the penis can also be seen as a "service" to the male, facilitating his pleasure without directly implicating the female as being sexual herself. She is doing something for him rather than for herself. Her gratification is in his gratification.

The script until touching below the waist is public; below the waist and with female complicity is private. The couples who engage in this behavior do so in private dyads (except for the curious *menage a quatre* that is the American double date) and learn about each others' bodies through the screen of this script. Girl's breasts are erogenous, tongue kissing is exciting, her clitoris is sensitive (once again the descriptive content of sexuality is nearly all male in origin), but the actual playing out of the script only approximates the outline that is available. Sometimes contact on the clitoris hurts, the breasts may not be sensitive, his fingers are crude, their clothing becomes disarrayed; she worries about being caught and if he is going to use a condom. At the same time, the couple is insulated in a silent world where it is not really possible to know what the other is feeling except through inarticulate gestures and sounds. At no point is there assurance that what one is doing is in fact having the effects that one would wish (a characteristic of more than sexual behavior), and indeed one can only marginally observe what these effects should be.

Once the couple have proceeded to coitus, they are confronted for the first time with integrating their sexual behavior into another series of meanings. Petting and necking can be defined as those behaviors that go along with dating. A boy picks the girl up in the early evening, they go some place defined as fun or appropriate to the premarital couple, engage in some time-passing activities (eating or drinking), and then they begin the sexual component of the evening. This is short or long depending on the age, experience, prior knowledge of each other, and residential linkages to the family of origin. It can range from a goodnight kiss to intercourse at one's own or another person's apartment. The necking and petting component may be integrated into the dating system by locating it in the home of either partner (usually the girl's) or just before leaving her off at home.

Coitus involves more extensive commitments of (outside of one-night stands) time and energy and learning of etiquette. The script has many of the same elements, but clothing must be taken off and if they are going to be presented to judging others later that night must be arranged in ways that they will not wrinkle. This inhibits the sense of passion. Arousal (an erection or lubrication) must be maintained while disrobing in front of someone who has never seen one undressed before. One begins to expose portions of the anatomy that are commonly only privy to the self and others who may share certain housing or bathroom accommodations. The penis has a size, the breasts look a certain way, one is now being compared with the relatively wide range of others who, at least in fantasy, might be available for sexual contact. Images of beauty and virility come into question. For the male, with his strong, unpracticed achievement motivation, there are questions of potency, premature ejaculation, unsatisfactory performance. There is the arrangement of an unfamiliar body—where are the legs to go? what signals she will make to assure me that I'm doing well? During this stage of the experience the female may well relax; the test is really his rather than hers. But at this point one must notice and accommodate to the fact that there are unfamiliar odors, that sheets might be stained by vaginal or seminal fluids.

During the build-up and the physical act itself one may mask worry through excitement. It is when the two actors return to the world of speech that they must now begin to integrate the sexual performance into their other expectations of each other. The first words that they exchange must be assuring of continued pleasure and linked to further desire. What does one say when returning to the conventional world? There are phrases that are routinely used: "That was good," "Hello," or some other reestablishment of conventional realities. There are the problems of getting up and going to the bathroom after sex, and whether the bathroom door should be open or closed.[53] Should one wash one's genitals? Each of these tiny hurdles must be leaped and done so in silence, for the perform-

---

53. For at least one of the authors the fundamental radicalism of Jane Fonda became manifest when she made the public observation that getting up from the bed after first coitus with a man and having him watch her walk to the bathroom was a trying moment. Her (and our) dilemma is, of course, the return to "normal" functioning after the social regression involved in participation in the erotic.

ance of sex requires that the staging remain within the limits of the script. Cigarette smoking after coitus (remembering 1940s movies) may be one of the major ways of reestablishing social contact after coitus has occurred. Only after coitus has happened with more regular frequency can these become matters of less significance to the partners involved. Commonly these are problems that must be resolved again when new partners are found, since there are substantial individual variations on the specific script. The significance of literary models for the managing of these relationships must not be overlooked, since they can provide symbolic rehearsals.

Coitus is perhaps the easiest of the sexual acts to manage, for this has the greatest societal support and the greatest amount of regularity attached to its various components. Having learned it in a few relationships, one can in a limited way apply prior experience to new contacts. There are new touches, tastes, and smells, but these fall within the regularized orbit of the sexual experience. In a sense, coitus is something that can be done with lessened conflict, since it is the appropriate culmination of all of the other elements in the script. Once a person is defined in specific ways and previous exchanges have defined him or her appropriate for coitus, the body can manage (no matter how poorly, in a technical sense). At the same time, it must be recognized that the normality of the script is culture-bound.

It is not necessary that for either sexual excitement or orgasm to occur that the movement be from the lips to the genitals, nor is it necessary that orgasm culminate from these acts. In other cultures, coitus occurs first and then what we consider precoital behavior occurs after coitus. We move from the relatively clean deodorized state to the sweaty, odoriferous state, the odors and fluids now defining the sexual state of the individuals. Satiation is the detumesced penis. In other cultures coitus may occur with any of these "precoital" elements or in some rearrangement of them. The erogenous zones that we consider requisite may be avoided or not thought of as erogenous. The orgasm itself may be seen as having other meaning than culmination. The successful internalization of the social script allows us to proceed in behavior as if there were no questions to be asked. Perhaps this is the definition of successful internalization: it is that behavior for which the participants have strong attachment (or aversion) but without accessible explanations.

For both males and females, progressively greater involvement with sociosexuality may be one of the factors that marks the end of adolescence. This is a transition about which little is really known, particularly with reference to noncollege-going populations. Our present feeling about the place of sexuality in the management of this transition is that it plays a significant role. First, on a somewhat superficial level, progressive involvement in sociosexuality is important in family formation or in the entry into roles and role obligations that are more explicitly adult in character. But, perhaps on a more fundamental level, it is possible that sociosexual activity is the one aspect of identity experimentation that we associate particularly with later adolescence, a period in which the psychosocial moratorium that Erikson describes as protecting the adolescent during this period of crises and experimentation fails to operate.[54] This may be partly due to the fact that the society has some difficulty protecting the adolescent from the consequences of that part of his behavior it is not prepared to admit he or she is engaging in. More importantly, it may be due to the fact that we have, at all age levels, great problems in talking about sexual feelings and experiences in personal terms which, in turn, makes it extremely difficult to get social support for our experiments with our sexual selves. (The term *pluralistic ignorance* is perhaps nowhere more applicable than in the sexual area.) It may be that these experiments with sexual capacities and identities rank among the first unprotected tests of competence and the quest for a basis for self-acceptance. We suspect that success or failure in the management of sexual identity may have consequences in many more areas of personality development than merely the sexual sphere.

54. E. H. Erikson, *Childhood and Society* (2nd ed.,) (New York: Norton, 1963); A. J. Reiss, Jr., "Sex Offenses: The Marginal Status of the Adolescent," *Law and Contemporary Problems* 25 (1960).

3

Postadolescent Sexual Development

Young Adulthood and Later

For most persons in U.S. society the movement into adulthood that is linked to occupational life is accompanied by a movement into marriage. An extensive involvement in overt heterosexual behavior generally emerges either just prior to marriage or within the marital state. This is true for both men and women, though obviously is more characteristic of women. Indeed, the management of sexual commitments within a marital relationship characterizes the largest part of postadolescent sexual experience in our society. As with other aspects of sex behavior, it is important to underscore the real poverty of data on this topic. We presume that sexual adjustment plays an important role in overall adjustment, but this judgement is derived largely from studies of broken marriages or marriages that are in trouble. We really have very little sense of the degree to which sexual problems in troubled or dissolved marriages exceed those found in marriages that remain intact. It is possible that we have assumed an important role for sexuality and the management of sexuality in the maintenance of marital bonds because we have assumed that sex itself is an important part of most people's lives. This may not be true. Particularly after the formation of the marital unit, it is quite possible that sex—both as a psychological reward and a physical outlet—declines in salience. It may become less im-

82

portant than alternative modes of gratification (work, children, security, constant affection—any or all may become more significant), or the weight of these alternative gratifications may minimize the effects of any sexual dissatisfaction. It is also true that individuals learn to derive equivalent levels of gratification from non- or only partially sexual activities. This is not to offer support for the concept of sublimation but rather to point out that in the processes that follow marriage, newly learned alternative patterns of gratification may be substituted for the sexual (which may well have had only situational significance due to its salience during mate selection).

At the present time the main determinant of adult rates of heterosexual activity in our society is the level of male commitment. While interest in intercourse is highest for males and females during the early years of marriage, the peak in orgasmic responsiveness occurs much later in marriage for females (who require longer periods of time to either become de-inhibited or to learn to be sexual—depending upon your point of view). Nonetheless, coital rates in marriage decline steadily through marriage.[1] This decline, it should be noted, can only be partly attributed to declines in biological capacity on the part of the male. The decrease may derive from many things. In many cases the problem is one of relating sexually to a person whose roles have been complicated by the addition of maternal functions.[2] For lower-class males, there is a problem of not receiving homosocial support for marital intercourse, to which we might also add the disadvantage of being less trained in the use of auxiliary materials to heighten sexual interest.[3] For middle-class males, the decline is less steep, owing perhaps to their ability to find sexual stimulation from auxiliary sources—literature, movies, and the like. A greater capacity for invoking and responding to fantasy is also operative. It should be noted that for about 30 percent of college-educated males, masturbation continues

1. A. C. Kinsey et al., *Sexual Behavior in the Human Female,* (Philadelphia: W. B. Saunders Co., 1953).

2. S. Freud, "The Most Prevalent Form of Degradation in Erotic Life," *Collected Papers,* vol. 4 (London: Hogarth, 1949).

3. W. Simon and J. H. Gagnon, "Heterosexuality and Homosociality: A Dilemma of the Lower-class Family," mimeographed, 1966.

as a regular source of sexual outlet in marriage and during periods when a wife is available.[4] To this we might add an additional, but unknown, proportion who do not physically engage in masturbation but for whom the source of sexual excitement is not coital activity alone but also the fantasy elements which accompany coital activity. But even for the middle-class male, sexual activity declines in amounts that cannot exclusively be accounted for by changes in the organism. Perhaps it is simply that the conditions under which we learn to be sexual in our society make it extremely difficult to maintain high levels of sexual performance with a single partner over long periods of time. This may remain relatively unimportant in the maintenance of the family unit, however, or even with respect to the individual's sense of his own well-being because of the relative unimportance of sexual dissatisfaction or the relatively greater significance of other areas of life.[5]

Given the achievement orientation of males toward sexual activity learned in adolescence and the capacity of sexual activity to be put to a wide range of uses in human relationships, there is a tendency on the part of many males (and fewer females) to seek variety in their sexual experiences, especially after marriage and even during the period of more extensive experimentation that precedes it. This search for variation can be managed in a number of ways, all of which transgress some normative constraints on sexual behavior. The search for variety can occur within a single relationship through the expansion of the number of sexual things that people do with each other. Anal intercourse, mouth-genital contact or variety in coital positions are the most common physical techniques.[6] It is also possible to role play other social arrangements, either openly with the cooperation of the spouse or through the individual use of fantasy during coitus. In contrast, one may seek variety through

4. Kinsey, et al., *Sexual Behavior in the Human Female;* Kinsey, et al., *Sexual Behavior in the Human Male* (Philadelphia: W. B. Saunders Co., 1948).

5. With our increased mental health commitment to the significance of sexual activity in old age, frequent tests of sexual competence are likely with concurrent increases in dissatisfaction.

6. Extrasexual activities should be included as well, ranging from physical activity (massage, Yoga, biofeedback) to the creation of elaborate stage settings for sexual performances (water beds, vibrators, pillows, fireplaces).

contact with partners outside of marriage. It is in the violation of normative boundaries that elements of domination-submission, good and evil, enhancement of other forms of striving, or compensations or reparations for losses may be managed. The search for variety is more commonly experienced among men, though it may occur among women (either through extramarital coitus or through coitus with the spouse under new circumstances or on vacation). There are also class variations among males, with variety in technique more common in middle-class males and variety in partners among lower-class males. Even the staging of extramarital coitus may vary with class, occurring earlier in marriage for lower-status males and later in marriage for middle-class males.

It is these activities that are at the margin of conformity which introduce new elements into the marital or premarital state. Positional variation in coitus is perhaps the most frequently practiced variant. While the conventional social script for coitus has the male above and female below, a postural affirmation of the symbolic dominance of men and submission of women, this is one of the more easily eroded of all sexual taboos.[7] The problem here, as it is in initiating or maintaining nearly all forms of sexual variety, is that the novel behaviors must normally be accomplished without speaking. The female must roll over (or be rolled over) in order to gain coital entrance from the rear; she must get or be placed on top for coitus to take place with the female above. In order for this to be successfully managed, the female must usually give signs that the change in position is a source of pleasure. Commonly this is done through either having orgasm occur or making the noises that are conventionally associated with sexual excitement. Textual legitimation of these positional variations (as well as other techniques) may be found in marriage manuals (or the mass women's magazines) that are more often available to women than to men, especially at lower social levels in the society.

7. This ease of transgression is probably most true for middle-class persons with a wider conception of the social and sexual capacities of a woman. Working-class men or even middle-class men with a highly restricted sense of the appropriateness of a wife's (Madonna's) sexual activity may find it more difficult to have intercourse with her on top than to have fellatio with a prostitute or even extramarital coitus. The activities and actors are differently valued in each script.

The success of attempts to introduce positional variety depends on the flexibility of the sexual script possessed by the two partners. If the male or the female finds that the conventional position is the one in which orgasm can be achieved (not because it is more erotic or technically better, but because it is "normal"), there will be powerful constraints to return to this position. However, the constraints on the male or female to return to this position will be quite different. The male may feel that the female above is dominating or that rear entry is degrading to a person who is to be loved. In many cases there is constraint against experimentation with the wife since she is the object of nonerotic love preventing her from occupying (either assuming or being attributed to her) the roles that are identified with women who are sexually degraded. At the same time, women may find the sequence of behaviors that lead to orgasm requires that she be underneath, sometimes to preserve a more limited sense of "letting go" that is part of the culturally prescribed experience of orgasm. Certain positions may be chosen since they symbolize dominance and submission or degradation which can serve to heighten sexual response through the introduction of components that either confirm or deny conventional nonsexual social postures. The sequence of physical activities (and the injunctions of the marriage manuals) is not the organizing factor in either sexual arousal or response, but it is the meaning that is attributed to the activities themselves.

Mouth-genital contact is perhaps the most tension-producing technique in sexual experimentation. The physical activity itself involves introducing the penis into the mouth of the female or the male putting his mouth on the female's vagina. Given the definitions that these organs have in terms of odor, taste, cleanliness, and excretion, putting the mouth and genitals together in an act that can be defined as pleasurable is extremely complex. Indeed, in much of conventional sexuality the genitals are out of sight or at least at arms' length, and in consequence the penis or vagina are experienced as objects of sensation, but only marginally significant in terms of manipulation. Given the strongly initiatory role that men have in sexual activity, the instigator for the largest proportion of mouth-genital activity is the male. Central to male sexual culture are a series of myths about mouth-genital contact and one of the sources of its power and significance is the desire to place the penis in a forbidden location. Since there is no meaning immanent in the activity and nothing intrinsic to the mouth that makes it better orifice for stimulation of the penis, the meaning of the act and its capacity to arouse must be sought in extrasexual and extraphysical areas. One element in the physical character of fellatio that suggests its physical component is not central to its enjoyment is that there is a considerable constriction of the degree of freedom of movement on the part of the male—and actually only a limited number of females who could be described (from a male point of view) as technically proficient at fellatio. These two constraints suggest that it is the psychological inputs that serve to heighten arousal and not the value of the physical stimulation.

A series of symbolic meanings can be cited that heighten the significance of fellatio as a form of sexual contact. The images of filling up, choking, dominating, controlling, degrading are all immediately available, not only from pornography but from the sexual and nonsexual fantasies of males who are engaged in the behavior. Complementary elements are the expression of affection and bonding that women feel when they find that in the act they give greater pleasure to the male. The couple may act out conventional gender role models, he dominating, she submitting, while the transgression of the taboo gives both persons a heightened sense of erotic power. The etiquette of introducing mouth-genital contact into the sexual repetoire of a relationship (at least in most conventional circumstances) is commonly nonverbal, though the ubiquitous marriage manual may serve as justification. To perform the act the female must learn that the penis may be defined as an appropriate object to put into her mouth (in middle-class groups, cleanliness wars with sexual service), and she must deal with the problem of texture and taste. Even though the female is more physically active and dominating and the male more passive, the act of fellatio is symbolically constructed in terms of male dominance and female submission. This is part of the common practice found in sexual activity of relabeling physical acts to fit social definitions. Whether the male can ejaculate in the female's mouth at the culmination of fellatio remains at the edge of the taboo. The taste of semen and its consistency are not quite within the range of normal sexual stimuli and whether the semen is swallowed or not increases the psychological complexity of the relationship.

The historical nature of the male-female relationship in terms of duration is complexly related to the activity of fellatio and its etiquette. It is possible in some relationships for it to become part of the regular repetoire of sexual conduct between a couple, but this is only possible when the relationship is not narrowly conceived as being nonerotic or purely maternal. If the relationship, however, is narrowly conceived, then there will be a tendency to restrict the range of sexual activity and have what are defined as more erotic contacts with females with whom there is an only a short-term relationship.

The act of cunnilingus is not physically symmetric to fellatio, though its practice may be physically reciprocal and psychologically symmetric in terms of the exchanges and of intimacy. This is frequently true in middle-class circumstances where principles of reciprocity and equality between the genders is more developed, but the normative constraints on the behavior are sufficiently powerful to require symbolic manipulation to allow normative violation. In nearly all male youth cultures, cunnilingus is viewed either ambivalently or negatively. There is a powerful component in male humor which avers to the uncleanliness of the vagina, its odors, and its peculiar (often described as fish-like) tastes. Concurrently there is the imagery that cunnilingus is somehow a homosexual act. (A version of this same belief occurs in some psychoanalytic treatises.)

At the same time, the behavior has powerful symbolic components linking it to taboo violation. The use of certain ensignia by motorcycle groups to indicate that they have performed cunnilingus or, at a higher level of violation, cunnilingus with a menstruating female (whether the acts have in fact occurred or not) are techniques for the use of violations of sexual norms to stand for group solidarity and to outrage conventional onlookers. In this latter case a specific sexual act stands for male status enhancement and male collective solidarity, rather than for the bonding of two individuals as it can in a middle-class marriage. The physical activity is the same; the meanings attributed to it and the consequences are strikingly different. As with most other behavior, to search for universal meanings in the physical activity is to aim at an unknown target.

Cunnilingus is usually an activity initiated by the male, as is nearly all activity in dyadic heterosexual behavior. The female may want the behavior to occur, but private speech is their mechanism for this to occur. Thus, Neil Eddington reports that "giving head" (an argot expression for mouth-genital contact in general) is commonly referred to and expected among the pimps and prostitutes of the bright lights areas that he studies.[8] Once again, the sexual act that can be requested by the female now surfaces only in locations where the role of the female is defined as deviant. Such requests for sexual variety can occur in middle-class populations, but some mechanisms such as love, expectations of marriage, or marriage must be utilized to neutralize the deviant character that such a request might have.

The male in this case must manage the aversion that he might have to taste vaginal fluids and odors, and his touching the genitals with his tongue or mouth must be rewarded by evidence from the female that what he is doing is powerfully arousing for her. If orgasm does not ensue either during the contact or during coitus that follows, there is minimal reinforcement available for the continuation of the behavior. The act of cunnilingus is nearly always begun (and often sustained) in the context of masculine striving for the enhancement of the capacity to produce sexual pleasure in the female. The introduction of cunnilingus into the sexual repertoire of a couple once again depends on the stage of development that the relationship has. Some males introduce it with all females with whom they have intercourse as part of their regular repertoire of sexual activity. In many ongoing relationships there may well be inhibitions of the sort that we observed in fellatio; the act itself may be defined as too degrading or too excessively erotic for the definition that the nonsexual portion of the relationship maintains.

As in fellatio, there are the problems of introducing cunnilingus into the normal sequence of expected sexual behavior. Nonverbal cues are developed between the couple (often stereotyped between the pair) to indicate a desire for this kind of contact. At the same time, ending cues are required to indicate whether the act will continue to orgasm or whether it will move to intercourse. These cues

8. Neil Eddington, personal communication.

can either be verbal or nonverbal, but they must not intrude on what is defined as the normal sequencing of sexual excitement. Whether the act continues to orgasm or does not, there is the problem of how to manage the oral kissing behavior that often follows mouth-genital contact of any sort. Vaginal fluids or semen have meanings that are partially rooted in feelings about excretion, and for both partners such kissing frequently becomes an act of reassurance and denial. The act of oral kissing also returns the behavior to a more conventional sequence, coincidentally returning the bodies to immediately pre-coital positions. Unless previous activity has brought the male to orgasm, the sequence will typically end with coitus, since a taboo against mouth-genital contact after intromission persists among many who are otherwise committed to oral sex. Anxieties about the excremental and the homosexual combine to make postcoital mouth-genital contact fairly rare, except as it serves to celebrate a more diffuse commitment to the sexually unconventional.

Though the combining of fellatio and cunnilingus appears as a kind of sexual justice, the internal scripts that support both the additional complexity and anxieties about the violative aspects of the behavior need not have the same symmetry. For most females it may be experienced, at least initially, as a transcendent intimacy, an intimacy that licenses a right to "indulgent" sensuality. The male, who often experiences fellatio through the metaphors of dominance, tends to experience cunnilingus through the identical modalities, seeing it as control rather than submission. Thus it is not uncommon for many men to find the performance of cunnilingus either maintaining or increasing levels of sexual arousal, despite the fact that their own genitals are not concurrently being stimulated. At the same time, moreover, a more superficial script organizes the activity as an apology for (if not a denial of) the degraded view of fellatio.

Beyond mouth-genital contact, anal intercourse becomes an additional source of elaboration. Though far less common than mouth-genital activity, its occurrence tends to be facilitated by its essential resemblance to coitus, as well as the fact that male and female continue to occupy a conventional social-psychological relationship to each other in terms of dominance. This resemblance to coitus and coital positions allows for a view of anal intercourse as an extension of coital activity, rather than as "unnatural" or abberational. As we note in chapter 8, even more complex transformations of the meaning of anal intercourse can be found in the more extreme circumstance of homosexuality in prison. In terms of complexity, the act itself may well intrude on the sequencing of sexual excitement since it often requires the use of artificial lubricants. This preparatory pause also exists when a diaphragm is used for birth control and is experienced by many females as reducing the spontaneity that is necessary in sexual activity. This suggests some of the problems for females in either avoidance of thinking about the mechanics of sex or lack of learning about how to integrate novel elements into the sexual sequence. This reflects other gender differences of the same kind—while males may wish to include more "fetish" or "thing" elements in sexual contacts (special clothing, objects, new roles), females tend to respond with the apparatus of the body.

Anal intercourse also involves the mastery of older symbolic forms about body odors that are strongly tabooed in Western societies. Fecal odors are to be restricted to the bathroom (notice the strong taboos on flatulence) and they must be combined with a sexual sequence that is defined quite differently. Digital manipulation of the anus may require that the odors will later be smelled during nonanal contacts, insertion of the penis into the anus commonly creates the sense of a need to defecate, and the penis should be washed for hygienic reasons after anal intercourse. Each of these activities becomes more problematic in situations where the anal intercourse is not a terminal behavior, but must be linked to further sexual activity. These problems are much more apparent in middle-class populations where cleanliness rules are powerfully learned and reinforced.

In situations where the anal intercourse is not merely a substitution for genital coitus, a transcendant set of meanings is required to legitimate the behavior. In Norman Mailer's *An American Dream,* buggery is practiced by the Jewish hero on a German female who stands for the Nazi domination of the Jews. Into the "death hole" the hero plunges, chosing to ejaculate there rather than in the vagina in order to avoid placing his own life forces symbolized by the

semen in her "life hole."[9] Even though such a modestly complex
symbolic rendering does not commonly occur as the accompani-
ment of anal intercourse, among those more symbolically committed to sexual activity, anal intercourse is commonly an expression
of male dominance, with strong sadomasochistic overtones, at least
in its originating phases. In order to breach the taboo and introduce
the behavior to the female, the male must have sufficient investment
in the activity to risk being turned down. The behavior is normally
initiated through the use of digital contact and then later in terms of
attempts to enter, at first subtly and then more insistently. The
standard initiator/gate-keeper roles are assigned to the male and
female, just as they are in the majority of sexual contact in the society, with the female's passive response being read as acceptance.
The meaning of the act to the female in the beginning has strong elements of submission in which the normative violation can be read
as an affirmation of the submissive component in femininity.
Among those females with higher levels of dominance needs, such
symbolic investment of specific sexual acts with submissiveness may
serve as reaffirmations of femininity which is not available to them
in occupational or other spheres of life.

Orgasm in this activity is more common in the male, though it
does occur in many women. The capacity for orgasm in this circumstance is evidence for our contention that specific physical sequences (the myth, for example, of the necessity of clitorial stimulation for orgasm to occur) are not necessary for the experience of
orgasm on the part of females. This capacity to invest a behavior
with meaning that allows it to be part of the orgasm-producing cycle is less socially supported than that sequence that invests the
breasts with the same sensitivity, but while the specific ways in
which sensitivity is produced are different, the outcomes are remarkably similar. What we here observe is the difference in the ways in
which the body parts are put to use in the creation of ordered sequences of sexual excitement that result in sexual climax.

In addition to that between spouses in the marital state, there are
three situations in which heterosexual activity may occur during
adulthood. It may occur prior to, during, or after marriages have

9. Norman Mailer, *An American Dream* (New York: Dial Press, 1964).

terminated. During marriage it may occur with persons other than spouses. It is this period during marriage that is of most interest here, for that which occurs after or between marriages has many of the same attributes as that which occurred prior to marriage except that sexual access seems to be more easily gained. Extramarital intercourse, adultery, or infidelity as it is variously termed by science, the law, and the participants is one of the single largest domains of normal sexual deviance.

About half of all ever-married males and a quarter of all ever-married females will engage in extramarital sexual activity at one time or another. For females there is some suggestion of a secular trend toward increases in extramarital activity from the beginning of this century to the early 1950s. This is linked to a corresponding generational rise in rates of female orgasm during this same period.[10] It is possible that these changes represent basic changes in the very nature of female sexuality. For males there are strong social class differences, with lower-class males accounting for most of the extramarital activity, particularly during the early years of marriage. This may be a direct reflection of their earlier mode of assimilation of the sexual commitment. As we previously observed, it is difficult for lower-class males to receive homosocial validation from marital sexual activity (unless, of course, it culminates in conception). This is not the case for extramarital activity, for which there is abundant homosocial validation.

In an important sense we have exhausted most of the bodily possibilities that are available (except the adding of additional bodies, which we will discuss later) and in consequence, except in some rare instances of narrow sexual scripts within marriage, nothing is done physically in extramarital coitus that is not done inside of the marriage. The body remains a physical constant, explaining little by its conformation or shape. The sources of sexual experimentation outside of marriage must be sought, then, in the social and psychological domain, rather than in the specifically sexual.

As we have noted before, there are strong class variations among men in the staging of extramarital coitus. It occurs earlier in the

10. Kinsey et al., *Sexual Behavior in the Human Female* and *Sexual Behavior in the Human Male.*

lives of lower-class men and later in the lives of middle-class men. Regardless of staging, however, the cumulative number of contacts always remains higher among men in lower-class locations, partially because of prostitute contacts (which we will disregard) and partially because of the continuity between sexual practices prior to marriage and during marriage. Regardless of these differences, male extramarital coitus in all classes serves to enhance and promote feelings of masculinity and continues to create a sense of personal competence. For lower-class men much of this derives from the male peer group, declining when the peer group itself ceases to reward sexual experimentation. (In those societies where the male peer group remains the major source of masculine endorsement, the public affirmation of male extramarital coitus will support such practices into a much later period in life, for example, in Sicily and Southern Italy.) Among middle-class men, sexual experimentation outside of marriage begins both as reparation and as opportunity. With rising incomes, the occupationally successful man can seek outside of marriage that sexual experience of which he often feels that he was cheated by his low rates of sexual activity prior to marriage, while those feeling the tremors of occupational failure or demotion by lack of promotion find in it reparations for losses sustained in the larger world. The motives are simple in outline but moderately complex when put to use. In most cases when the relationships have an extended duration they seem almost overdetermined in character. (For an interesting particularistic description of longer-term relationships, see Morton Hunt's *The Affair*.[11])

For females the interest in extramarital sexual contacts is more obscure in origin and less frequent in occurrence. Here one must deal with the complexities of marital status. Extramarital coitus occurs whenever one of the partners in the sexual activity is married. It does not seem unreasonable to suggest that the majority of married females who have extramarital coitus do so with married men, while for married men there might be a tendency, at least, for unmarried females to represent a larger proportion of their partners. These beliefs derive not from data (none, in fact, exist), but rather

---

11. Morton Hunt, *The Affair* (New York: New American Library, 1971).

from the character of sexual and nonsexual role behavior in the society. In general, the married female has greater access to (unless
she is working, and even in that case this supposition may well exist)
married males. Extramarital coitus in these cases is more likely to
occur among those who are known previously to the familial circle
rather than to those who are known only to the female. When a
female works, contacts may well be made with males who are unmarried, but with the increasing age of the female this proportion would
tend to decline enormously. Given the initiatory character of the
male role in sexual performances, it is apparent that a wider range
of females in terms of marital status will be sought out and these
contacts will include women both known and unknown to the
family circle.

In large measure, most extramarital intercourse has a normal
character. For most men, no matter how much they are in search of
sexual adventure (and unless they make a serious pursuit of it), a
female outside of the home is someone who has to be pursued and
seduced. Few women ever move into a concern with sexuality that
matches that of males, and in consequence males are presented with
at least some of the problems (if not all, when they pursue younger
females who have never married) that they faced in pursuing females when the males were premarital. These pursuits require energy,
time, and money that few persons possess in great abundance. In
consequence, much of extramarital coitus for the male occurs away
from the home, in all-male situations (conventions of occupational
or all-male social groups) and on a single-instance basis. The male
may feel guilty, but the guilt can be managed by conceiving the act
as insulated from the life of the family. Even when such relationships expand beyond a single encounter, in large measure the normal response is to manage guilt through the same mechanism
through which most sexual guilt is generally managed: expressions
of mutual passion which insulate the behavior from moral condemnation.

It is to be expected that females will be more likely to use these
feelings of passion to insulate themselves from guilt than will males,
given the general greater tendency of females to associate the sexual
with a romantic commitment. However, in long-term relationships
there is a tendency on the part of both males and females to in-

creasingly characterize the relationship as one involving love. As the relationship becomes more intimate and more involved, there is a greater tendency for it to have consequences for a preexisting marital bond. Expressions of passion involve what Philip Slater has called "dyadic withdrawal or social regression" (an unhappy phrase, in our opinion, but an observable phenomena) and in the building an emotional base for the extramarital relationship there are consequences for the character of the marital relationship. In some cases such extramarital involvement decreases sexual involvement with the spouse, but there is probably an equal proportion of cases where the extramarital relationship—either through guilt or simply heightened levels of erotic involvement—increases the rates of sexual contact with the spouse. As the actor in the extramarital relationship sees himself or herself as sexually more proficient, the sexual character of the marital relationship becomes more significant as well. This is parallel to the fact that nocturnal emissions in adolescence as often occur after other acts of sexual activity as they do before. The expression of sexual activity is as likely to feed into the dreaming life as the dreaming life to respond to sexual abstinence.

What is significant here in terms of the doing of sexual things is that the extramarital relationship can once again be linked to the dynamics of sexual performances that existed before marriage. It is in the search for tension or novelty that the significance of extramarital coitus arises, not in the avoidance of tension or the commitment to the conventional. Sex outside of marriage can be put to many social purposes by either a man or woman. For the lower-class man, it affirms the sexual prowess that he had before marriage. For young married men going to a prostitute, it may increase the bonds of maledom. For the middle-class male who is moving toward new occupational success, it is opportunity to confirm achievement in nonoccupational rewards. For the woman, it is a desire for femininity to be reinforced in a way that marital coitus can rarely provide. For persons of both sexes, it is the boredom of conventional sexual or social activity transcended—the reentry into the world of risk and passion is treatment for the dailiness of regular sexual lives. The range of possibilities is wide open for those who can manage the necessary guilt that occurs with the behavior. Indeed, the search for guilt could be one of the reasons for the behavior itself. In an important sense, sex (as we note elsewhere) is part of those behaviors that represent environmental mastery, a mastery that provides at least the illusion of individuality and choice of an individuality and sense of control that is seriously eroded in a post-industrial society.

Among those involved in extramarital coitus, there are those who differ from its conventional practice. This is a domain that attracts and provokes the erotic fantasies of many in the society: wife-swapping and swinging. These represent interesting theoretical problems (they are not quite social problems), since they create conditions under which sexual behavior must become the topic of conversation between spouses and, indeed, topics that will require the creation of a new set of social and psychological categories to manage them.

Wife-swapping is that situation in which a pair (or more) of husbands and wives engage in the trading of sexual partners on an equal access, *quid pro quo* basis. In order for this to occur, there must be agreement between the husband and wife before the arrangement is made. This requires that the topic of infidelity (a more appropriate word in this context) has been the topic of conversation. It is possible to create a series of parodic conversations or situations in which such conversations might occur, but it seems to us that the anxiety and fear attending the beginning of such an enterprise deserve more than parody. Most commonly on the husband's initiative, sexual topics emerge in conversations with the spouse—for example, the topic of the sexual attractiveness of other men's wives. Such discussions normally follow a tentative and drifting course, a course sometimes influenced by knowledge on the part of the wife of the husband's previous extramarital behavior. In any case, the husband, for reasons of guilt (most likely), ideology (women's equality?), or ineptitude finds himself unable to manage or get access to affairs outside of the marriage. The problem for the male is how to make available to the female an opportunity that she perhaps may not want and to make it attractive to her. It is evident that most women enter into these relationships to please (as they have in the past) their husbands' own sexual needs. There occurs a series of inconclusive conversations that finally culminate in an attempt at sexual adventure.

What has occurred is a crucial change in the marital unit. Sexuality has been changed from an activity which previously only bound the couple together into an activity that may occur with others with mutual consent. The historical limitation on sexual access has now been breached and sexuality for the couple is now a dyadic form of deviance (they have a co-partner in crime) in which sex is now both more public and significant and more casual and private. It is public between the two and significant in organizing their nonmarital behavior and more private to the couple since it is wrong and must be limited to specific audiences. At the same time, the technology and performance components of the sexual act become more important. What happens to the wife-swapping couple is what rarely occurs to any couple in the society—there are now alters who may judge not only their physical attractiveness, but also their competence as sexual partners. Both the male and the female in these situations are confronted with the requirement that they please others sexually in order to maintain the marital unit. Sex in this case binds the unit through its provision of sex to others, rather than in its provision to each other. The very need to please creates a situation of legitimated eroticism and sexual experimentation.

An important element in this relationship (however it is initiated, through the mails or with neighbors) is that the husband now possesses an object which may be used in sexual trading. It regularizes the extramarital relationships by giving him a counter to use in obtaining females, a task—given limited female commitments to sexuality—that is often not easily solvable. Hence, there are powerful constraints against the couple engaging in an individual search for sexual partners. The male in this case is at a disadvantage in most instances, given the larger proportion of males in search of females than females in search of males. One of the critical junctures in this process is when the female decides that she can search on her own, thus depriving the male of his most important token in securing sexual partners.

The engagement in this "singling" behavior is more dangerous in terms of the development of psychopathology on the part of the female than on the part of the male. His activity falls within the limits of available social roles; males have a history and set of ideologies linked to sexual experimentation outside of marriage. The narrowness of the role sets available to women in the society suggests that when she falls outside of these narrowly limited roles there is both a greater possibility and need for role invention (a major problem for anyone) and a greater tendency for the expression of individual psychopathological behavior.

The increasingly public nature of the sexual performances increases not only the general level of sexual activity and the threats of compared sexual performance (a more difficult problem for males than females), but also serves to increase the level of eroticization of the female through degrading her. Sex with another man increases the erotic character of the wife, opposes her maternal role, and by violating the norms of sexual performance increases her desirability. At the same time, there is created a set of constraints that surrounds even the rule breaking itself in order to preserve the dyad.

The Pattern of Psychosexual Development

It is not a concern of these chapters to develop a general and universal stage model of psychological development in the tradition of Erikson, since these models are generally faulty, becoming time-bound and reified, and—by becoming objects of study in themselves—fail to draw our attention to model processes. The point of the descriptive process offered here is to delineate periods in the life cycle during which certain events commonly take place in this culture. It should be noted clearly that these periods are not seen as *necessary,* either within or across cultures, nor *necessary* in some psychodynamic sense. They are roughly what has happened in between the 1930s and 1970s in a complex Western society, largely to its white working- and middle-class populations and in large measure to those persons of most ethnic and racial minorities who are attached to these model schemes of development or who have not been entirely alienated from them. There can be vast reversals and changes in the design of human sexuality, from the feelings it evokes to the kinds of things that are appropriate to or included in its performance elements. The age and moment when specific behaviors can be introduced, performed, and lived with vary enormously, so that any biological fixity in the sequence of behavior is most likely to occur in infancy and very little after that.

The following charted presentation of the sequencing of conventional sexual development is primarily of hueristic value for examining the connections among the various agents and institutions involved. Persons are selected as participants in conventional, unconventional, deviant, or criminal sexual acts from various points in this cycle. The meaning of their conventionality, their deviance, or their criminality is largely drawn from their place in this sequential collection of socializing agents, institutions, and programs. Hence the meaning of heterosexuality for two fourteen year olds who are having intercourse emerges from their stage in sexual socialization. Their motivations for the act and its consequences must be understood in terms of where they are in the developmental process. This is equally true of the two fourteen-year-old males who are having sex together; the meaning of their homosexuality arises from a specific point in the life cycle, and its significance is embedded in both that life cycle moment and the local culture (or, in complex societies, in a subculture). Thus, the interaction of fathers and daughters in incest will be meaningful in terms not of some abstract violation of the incest taboo, but in terms of the character of the family in which they live and the ages of the two participants. This is equally true in terms of the child who is the victim or participant in prepubertal sexual behavior, since the meaning of the behavior for the child is drawn from its available intellectual and emotional resources for organizing experience. *The gender identity-sexual identity-family formation-reproduction pattern* in this society is the central informing process for the sexual life as it is lived here.

The chart that follows, then, contains a set of stages with flexible age boundaries, the social components that are significant in either sexual or nonsexual learning that takes place during them, and finally, a rough suggestion of what is being learned or assembled. The word *assembly* is used quite deliberately. It was selected to indicate the collage-like, constructed, put-together, indeed artificial, character of human development and to oppose an imagery of the natural flowering of an organic process.

Heuristic Stages of Conventional Stages of Sexual Development

Stage and Ages	Infancy (Ages: 0–2½ to 3)
Significant Agents	Mother to Family
Assemblies	Formation of base for conventional gender identity package

Stage and Ages   Childhood (Ages: 3–11)
Significant Agents   Family to Peers, Media increasing
Assemblies   Consolidation of conventional gender identity package;
                       modesty-shame learning; nonsexually motivated "sex"
                       play; learning of sex words without content; learning
                       of sex activities without naming; learning of general
                       moral categories; mass media through commercials
                       and programming content reinforcing conventional
                       gender, sex, and family roles; media also preparing for
                       participation in youth culture

Stage and Ages   Early adolescence (Ages: 11–15)
Significant Agents   Family, Same-sex Peers, Media
Assemblies   First societal identification as a conventional sexual
                       performer; first overt physical sexual activity with self
                       or others; development of sexual fantasy materials; be-
                       ginnings of male/female divergence in overt sexual ac-
                       tivity; application of gender package to sexual acts;
                       application of moral values to emergent sexual be-
                       havior; privatization of sexual activities; same-sex peers
                       reinforce homosocial values; family begins to lose
                       moral control; media reinforces conventional adult con-
                       tent of gender roles; media attaches consumer practices
                       to gender success; basic attachment to youth culture
                       formed

Stage and Ages   Later adolescence (Ages: 15–18)
Significant Agents   Same-sex Peers, Cross-sex Peers increasing, Media,
                       Family reducing
Assemblies   Increased practice of integrating of sexual acts with
                       nonsexual social relations; movement to heterosocial
                       values; increased frequency of sexual activity; declining
                       family controls; continuing media reinforcement of
                       sexual-gender roles, and consumer and youth culture
                       values; sexual experience with wider range of peers;
                       common completion of sexual fantasy content; con-
                       solidation of gender differences in sexual roles and
                       activity; good girl/bad girl-maternal/erotic distinctions
                       completed

Stage and Ages   Early adulthood (Ages: 18–23)
Significant Agents   Same-sex and Cross-sex Peers, Media, Minimum Family
                       of Origin

Assemblies   Mate selection, narrowing of mate choice; increased
                        amount of sexual practice; commitment to love by
                        male, sex by female; linkage of passion to love; dyadic
                        regressions; insulation from family judgment and peer
                        judgment; increasing pressure to marry; relief from
                        same-sex competition by stabilization of cross-sex con-
                        tacts; legitimization of sexual activity by peers and
                        romantic code; media reinforces youth culture values
                        of romance and virtues of marriage; experience with
                        falling in and out of love; termination of protected
                        school/student statuses

Stage and Ages   Final mate selection-Early marriage (Ages: 20–27)
Significant Agents   Fiancee(s), Spouse, Same-sex Peers, Family of Origin
                        increases
Assemblies   Regularizes and legitimizes sexual activity; stable rates
                        of sex activity; variation in kinds of sexual behavior;
                        children born in most cases; increasing sexual anxiety
                        about children; family values reinforced by children
                        and family of origin; declining eroticism, increased
                        maternalism; culmination of purchasing/consumer val-
                        ues in wedding gifts or buying new products; routini-
                        zation of sexual behavior; decreased contact with cross-
                        sex peers unless they are married; interaction in
                        multiple dyads; sexual activities restricted by pregnancy,
                        children, work

Stage and Ages   Middle marriage (Ages: 28–45)
Significant Agents   Spouse, Same-sex Peers, Family of Origin, Married
                        Peers
Assemblies   Declining sexual activity in marriage; some extra-
                        marital sexual experimentation; maturing children;
                        conflict of erotic with maternal; emergence of sexual
                        dissatisfactions; increase in occupational commitments;
                        declines in physical energy and physical beauty; fantasy
                        competition by youth culture; continual multiple dyadic
                        interactions and insulation from cross-sex peers; mar-
                        riage moving to nonsexual basis for stability and con-
                        tinuity

Stage and Ages   Post young Children (Ages: 45+)
Significant Agents   Spouse, Same-sex Peers, Married Peers
Assemblies   Further decline in sexual activity; some extramarital
                        sexual experimentation; substitution of nonsexual com-
                        mitments other than children as basis of marriage;

further decline in physical strength and beauty; further desexualization of gender identity; movement out of public sexual arena

This rough outline of a sexual career is the most common heterosexual pattern available in U.S. society and, even with the introduction of divorce and widowhood, the cycle does not vary except in small and minor ways. Similar modal career patterns with greater or lesser variability could be described for some of those sexual minorities who operate with alternative sexual patterns in the society. Indeed, this conventional heterosexual process is the modal sexual career that all alternative patterns must confront. The man who desires large numbers of females, the homosexual man or woman, and the sexually active women must live with the reality of this pattern, its values, and its links to the past and the future in a day-to-day way. This assembly designates the availability of sexual partners, their ages, their incomes, their point in the economic process, their time commitments, all of which shape their sexual careers far more than the minor influences of sexual desire.

Conclusion

In some places what we have been describing in terms of the integration of persons and acts into sexual scripts has been, perhaps, more dramatic than necessary. While a majority of persons might have had intercourse with the female above and the male below, only about half of the males and one-fourth of the females (even though there is some increase) engage in extramarital behavior. Mouth-genital contact is a majority experience only for the college-educated, and anal intercourse in heterosexual relations is somewhat of a rarity. By discussing the sexual at all, the sexual assumes a larger place on the stage than it deserves. What we have not noted enough are two dimensions: the first is that sex occupies very little of most people's time and energy (except those defined as sexual professionals), and the second is that most sexual behavior is accompanied by a great deal of silence.

In general, it is our feeling that sexuality and sexual activity are, by and large, derivative functions, even during adulthood. There are only a few periods in the life cycle at which there are high rates of sexual activity or sexual activity that is complicated by passion and high intensity of affective investment. These are usually adolescence in the male, the early and romantic years of marriage for both men and women, and the highly charged extramarital experiences that can be called affairs. Most of the time, sex is really a relatively docile beast, and it is only the rare individual who through the processes of self-invention or alienation from the normal course of socialization is prepared to risk occupation, present comfort, spouse and children, or the future for the chancy joys of sexual pleasure.

From this point of view it might be more proper to suggest—contrary to the Freudian point of view that sex manifests itself in other types of conduct or that other conduct is symbolic of sexual conflict —that reports of sexual conflict may in fact stand for difficulties in the more conventional zones of life. Thus, the married couple who come for counseling because of a sexual problem may be merely reporting the conventional rhetoric of the society about what they think the sources of a marital difficulty ought to be. Ovesey reports that homosexual dreams (overtly homosexual, not merely symbolic) of heterosexual men really relate to occupational problems and that the submissiveness required occupationally appears in the convenient symbolism of the "purported" femininity of homosexual relations.[12] Indeed, many forms of both heterosexual and homosexual acting-out seem to be related to stress reactions to other life situations, rather than having specifically sexual motivations. Thus, studies of sex offenders often are overly concerned with the sexual life of the offender when this may merely be the symptom of disorders of other kinds.

While the talk about sexuality is important (and it should be observed that in some cases people do sexual things in order to talk about them), what is impressive is the enormous control that silence retains in the sexual area. While one can find many locations in which the sexual is at the service with the rest of social life, it is rarely experienced as being continuous with other aspects of social life and is often, in fact, discontinuous with it.

12. L. Ovesey, "The Homosexual Conflict: An Adaptational Analysis," *Psychiatry* 17 (1950): 243–50.

While talk is significant in shaping behavior, it often does so through its imprecisions and its absences. In a very immediate and concrete way, most people remain untrained in the ability to talk about their own sexual activity or scripts, particularly with persons with whom they are having sex. There is even a major difficulty talking to the self about matters sexual when one is in the process of a fantasy or in the midst of sexual arousal. It is as if the aroused state were the only legitimate condition during which an internal dialogue about sexual matters could occur. Thinking about sexual activity in the abstract is extraordinarily difficult for most people, and the attempt to think about it at all may become in some cases, especially for males, the occasion for arousal. Much of the character of the early periods of psychoanalysis involves training the patient in how to talk without arousal about this aspect of his life. Even when this process is successful it creates the capacity to talk only in the context of the specialized therapeutic relationship and often with a highly abstract vocabulary that protects both the therapist and the patient from directly confronting sexual content. This is learning a capacity to neutralize the topic of sexuality, not learning to talk about it without concomitant anxiety or arousal. In an important sense even though language is the life of man, there is a tendency to move into the totalitarian land of silence when one moves into the sexual.

Such incapacities for speech often make the experiencing of sexual pleasure extremely difficult. Researchers have observed that with increasing sexual excitement and increase in general sensory thresholds there is a declining capacity for speech, creating in this society a seeming opposition between the physical activity of sex and the rational and intellective processes. There are those women who have so poorly learned the capacity to name the elements of sexual pleasure that orgasm itself is seen as a dangerous, ego-disintegrating experience, and the physical signs of arousal are read as promonitory symptoms of urination or defecation. The problem here is clearly an incapacity in assigning language to name and control the internal landscape.

One of the consequences of silence is that it produces a severe sense of discontinuity between experiencing the self in nonsexual circumstances and in sexual circumstances. It is awkward at both the transition from the conventional to sexual identity and from the sexual to the conventional, language-filled identities. A result of this discontinuity is that there are few ways of communicating to others the experience of sexual satisfaction or dissatisfaction. There seem to be no mechanisms by which the physical gestures can be converted into language so that gestures in the future can be altered or continued. For most persons the silence mounts, and with it a sense of guilt, frustration, and inadequacy. These, in turn, decline as sex itself declines in importance. And this decline is more easily managed than most would imagine. It is important to remember that people receive social recognition and support for many things, but —except for very special populations who pay different kinds of costs—there is no basis for this kind of recognition and support for sexual competence. Conversely, people may be judged failures for many things, but rarely for failing sexually, as only their partners really know, and they are equally committed to silence.

The doing of sex implies that there is some culmination to it, a moment of ecstasy or joy. Conventionally this has been identified with the moment of orgasm. Central to the work of Masters and Johnson is a description of the orgasmic cycle. Their focus is on the act (as it must be), a sequence of touching either alone or with someone else that can be described in four phases: excitement, plateau, orgasm, and resolution.[13] It is clear from much of their work that they know a good deal of the psychological component in this process, but their necessary focus is on the bounded character of the physical acts leading to orgasm. Yet even here this social and psychological component is as crucial. No one comes to age in this society with a prepared set of sociosexual repertoires that are immanent in their physical equipment. The capacity for erection or vaginal lubrication must be interpreted and linked to a suitable set of activities, people, and situations that will lead to intromission and orgasm on the part of the male and the female. The feelings that occur in the interior of the body have no immanent meaning attached to them, and they must as surely be learned and managed as is the information that is processed from the exterior of the body.

13. W. H. Masters and V. E. Johnson, *Human Sexual Response* (Boston: Little, Brown and Co., 1966).

Indeed, it may be that the confluence of internal sensations that is identified as orgasm is so identified because of the situation in which it occurs, rather than being a necessary connection between the sensory inputs and the central nervous system.

The problem that we have begun the tentative discussion of is the way in which physical activities that are identified as sexual by actors are integrated into sequences that are conceived to be exciting sexually and the way in which this information ultimately becomes linked to the capacity for orgasm. Much of this linkage clearly occurs earlier in life (the capacity to identify touch as pleasurable or not, for instance) and then becomes attached to sexual activities themselves. Because we live most of our lives unself-consciously, we tend to fail to note the amount of open-ended learning that occurs early in life that is put to other uses later in life.

A sexual performance that is to end in orgasm can be as narrowly experienced as tension release or as complexly as the ritual expiation of sin. The narrow construction of the sources of sexual excitement that are overtly supported in the society and the sequence of physical behaviors (from kissing to coitus) that are approved in the search for orgiastic pleasure (itself socially defined), are sufficient for most persons at least most of the time. The bodily postures assumed, the organs connected, and the timed sequences of behaviors involved appear to be intimately connected with internal sensation—these are the necessary and sufficient sequences of activity. It is only when the artificial quality of these performances is considered that it becomes apparent that they are constructions which are culturally created and normatively constrained and further built on earlier sequences of behavior that are reorganized in the performance of sexuality.

When we move beyond the physical activity and beyond the single orgasmic cycle, what becomes apparent is the inordinate complexity of the physical act of coitus as well as the integration into the act of coitus of variety in positions, variations in partners, changes in techniques or orifices of interest. The physical transitions or variations in this scripting of the arrangements is probably no more difficult (and perhaps less) than learning to ski or ride a bicycle. However, the management of bodies is also the management of meanings that are designed to constrain and organize expectations about behavior. Indeed, these expectations are the very basis for the experience of sexual excitement. We need only one further example to suggest this complexity. If one were to go further than having two in a bed and had to involve a third party in a sexual performance, what becomes apparent is that the etiquette of dyadic sexuality is totally different from the etiquette of the *ménage a trois,* regardless of the gender of the third person. Who does what to whom with what and in what order becomes a crucial question, a question that never occurs in the managing of two bodies, since it seems to us that there is not any problem of management (at least after we have had some practice). Yet, as we can see, there are problems of management of bodies, of attributing meaning to flaccid or tumescent penises, of managing strange fluids and odors, and of managing new and strange bodies, of managing entrances and exits so that the ordered process of increasing sexual excitement can be maintained. What enhances the limited repertoire of the body is the variety of meanings that may be attributed to those bodies, meanings that arise from the ordered and disordered connections of physical sexual activity to social life. In our present cultural state of affairs it is the possibility of transgression and normative violation that gives sex a status beyond gourmet cooking—it is the possibility of believing that one is controlling a powerful drive that allows a sense of virtue to arise from conformity and the observation of norms, and a sense of sin to arise from their violation. The wisdom of the body (at the risk of being metaphysical) is a consequence of consciousness and culture.

What is suggested here in an untentative way is that it is the sociocultural that gives sex its meaning and it is the myths of the society that give it its power. There is a sense of dismay when one makes the suggestion that sex is really just like everything else, and that there is no natural man struggling against the pressures of civilization. It tends to undermine the dramatic and powerful images of sex and leaves in its wake a sense of relatively simple and pleasant capacity that cannot fulfill the promises that have been made for it. Perhaps the last act of resistance to big brother and 1984 is properly an act of copulation—it can be allowed because it is of no danger to anyone.

Epilogue

It is only a fairly recent development in the history of man that he could begin to conceive of the possibility of social change, that he could begin to understand that his time and place did not represent the embodiment of some eternal principle or necessity but was only a point in an ongoing, dynamic process. For many it is still more difficult to conceive of the possibility of the psychological nature of man changing—and particularly changing in significant ways.[14] Much of this conservative view of man still permeates contemporary behavioral science. Thus, for many social theories, a view of man as a static bundle of universal needs supplies the necessary stability not available elsewhere in the flux of social life. A conception of man as having relatively constant sexual needs is a necessary part of this point of view. As a contrast to this conservative view, we attempt to offer a description of sexual development as a variable sociocultural invention, an invention that in itself explains little and requires much explanation.

14. J. H. Van Den Berg, *The Changing Nature of Man* (New York: Dell, 1964).

4

The Pedagogy of Sex

One of the most impressive social inventions of the late nineteenth and early twentieth centuries was the emergence of an exceptional concern with the life of the child. This is not to say that modern children are loved more intensely or that their loss is mourned more deeply than in previous times, but there is a special awareness of them as occupying some special social and psychological status as children. Only occasionally in pre-nineteenth century literature was a child depicted in present-day terms; rather, children were represented as smaller and physically weaker (though not always morally weaker) versions of the adults surrounding them. A reading of Geoffrey Chaucer and William Shakespeare fails to reveal a special internal or external world belonging to the child, and it was not until the nineteenth century that such writers as William Wordsworth, in poetry, and Charles Dickens, in the novel, showed a new and prepossessing concern for the unique experiences and perceptions of children.[1] They depicted childhood as a developmental stage

1. An analysis of this historical change, particularly in France, is the work by Phillipe Aries, *Centuries of Childhood* (New York: Alfred A. Knopf, 1962). For changes in attitudes toward sexuality, see especially pp. 100–127. A remarkably original work tracing from an existentialist point of view the general implications of this change in consciousness is J. H. Van Den Berg, *The Changing Nature of Man* (New York: Dell Publishing Co., 1964).

110

during which moral and intellectual categories were related to age as well as to station.

Prior to this emergent literary consciousness (the execution of the princess in Shakespeare's *Richard III*) and even contemporaneously with it (the labor of children in the mines and factories in the nineteenth century), children shared with adults the assets and dangers of their common social positions of nobility or proletariat. There was no universal dispensation for age independent of social status even in the nineteenth century, although a change of consciousness began to appear in the genius of the period.

This newfound early nineteenth-century concern with the child as a separate social and psychological entity presaged the understanding of the impact of a child's experience on his character as an adult, which was the basic contribution of Sigmund Freud. While much of the discussion of bourgeois childhood in the late nineteenth century was idyllic and asexual, this tendency should be read as being more complex than self-delusion or self-denial. It was in part a result of an honorable desire to protect the child from the approaching realities of adulthood. At the same time, however, the quality of protection given to any individual child often depended upon his presumed innocence. Concurrent with this increasingly prevalent image of the sexless child, which is often conceived to have been repressive and wrong-headed by modern scholars reacting to "Victorian prudery," was the writing about the sexual capacity of children in British and other national medical literature which focused upon its dangers and thus certainly did not deny its existence.[2] The shock of Freud's pronouncements upon adults was not that children might be involved in sexual activity but that this activity was not confined to a few "evil" children and was, in fact, an essential precursor and component of the development of the character structure of the adult. What superficially appeared to be an aspersion on the innocence of childhood was in reality an assault upon public anti-sexuality and asexuality of adults.

As an outcome of the artistic invention of the special character of childhood and the creation of its correlative, a special psychology of

2. Steven Marcus, "Mr. Acton of Queen Ann Street, or the Wisdom of Our Ancestors," *Partisan Review* 31 (1964): 201–30.

childhood, a new collective belief about the consciousness of children developed. While this new version of the special role of childhood in human development has not been universal, it has found a place in the United States and Western Europe. More than likely it will be the dominant orientation of the future.

One of the consequences of this belief in the special character of childhood and its impact on ultimate character structure (even without the special emphases on sex generated by psychoanalytic theory) is that adults now have a greater conscious concern with the processes by which children learn about sexuality. During the nineteenth century the popular method of dealing with childhood sexuality when it intruded upon adults was either to suppress the behavior or to deny its existence and to avoid thinking about it at all providing it was not a public issue. Until very recently these methods remained, for the majority of the population, the most popular ways of dealing not only with the sexuality of children, but also with that of adults. During the late 1940s and 1950s, as sexuality became more and more of a public concern in the United States and a growing desire was expressed for ways to instruct children appropriately in sexual matters, instruction was limited to that which imparted information without provoking either discussion or overt behavior. Through this ambivalent process it was hoped that the alleged traumas that were assumed to result either from incomplete or mislearning information could be avoided and, at the same time, the essentially nonsexual character of the child could be preserved. As part of this de-eroticized instructional repertoire, textbooks of sexual knowledge were developed to relieve parents of the anxieties and embarrassments of talking about sexuality to their children.[3]

3. An example of the confused thought that results from thinking constrained by this dilemma—that children should know about sex but not act out their knowledge—is provided by the following paragraph in a relatively sensible popular work on the sexual development of children: "Shielding children from the awareness of adult sex conduct goes without saying. Much more injurious than any play among themselves would by the observation of adult behavior and loose significant talk. As in the case of vulgarities—the greater the prudery, the greater the pornography—so the greater the freedom among adults, the greater the freedom among children. Also, the greater the denial of legitimate understanding among them, the greater

While this first approximation of sex education was being considered, other more profound changes were occurring that changed the kind of adult sexual environment for which the child was being prepared and challenged the very idea of this kind of sexual instruction. Largely as a function of increasing affluence, sexual lives are probably managed more adequately today than at any time since the processes of urbanization began to relax the overvalued and overrated controls of small town and rural morality. The society is really closer to eliminating syphilis than it is prepared to admit, and the epidemic of gonorrhea is as much a consequence of misplaced medical priorities as it is promiscuity. Knowledge about effective forms of brith control is considerably more widespread than ever before; and, while abortion remains an important problem, we can now see that any problems concerning it are the result of collective stupidity rather than the expression of a tragic individual decision to copulate. Perhaps more important than the erosion of risks is the growing belief that sex is a potentially positive, joyous, and enriching experience that no longer is the sole possession of an alienated and radical minority in the society.

As part of this wider acceptance of sex in the 1960s as at least a potential good, there exists a demand that some programmatic form of sex education be developed in order to facilitate sexual lives that fulfill this potential. This is an important transition, because most of the earlier concern for sex education focused on the necessity and unfortunate aspects of sexuality, treating it as a dangerous force requiring careful control. The concept of sex education classes was that the teacher was imparting safety precautions such as those used in handling highly explosive materials.

Some elements of this style remain part of the motivation for the growing interest in sex education, but few people today take seri-

---

the exploration. Far from being an abnormal or perverted or precocious entrance into heterosexuality, sex play in children is a normal, if socially unacceptable, instance of sex interest, an expression of a normal developmental need. If they are not to provide an answer to that need themselves, we must provide it for them, not only in knowledge of the life processes, but in legitimate though vicarious participation in those processes. Words alone do not satisfy." Francis Bruce Strain, *The Normal Sex Interests of Children* (New York: Appleton-Century-Crofts, 1948), p. 139.

ously the assumptions that sex education will lower rates of illegitimacy, venereal disease, or promiscuity (whatever that value-laden term might mean). Indeed, the disadvantaged and disorganized populations most vulnerable to these problems are precisely those populations for which education as a whole has failed. There is no reason to assume that those same educational systems can succeed in that area—sex education—where there is the smallest accumulation of skill and experience. The more viable assumption behind an interest in sex education is that it should work to make sex a more rewarding part of people's lives—to make sex education impart competence and not necessarily constraint.

Much of the rhetoric aiding and abetting this public and quasi-public interest in sex education is organized around the central image of a current or impending sexual revolution among the young. Since we are unable to assess with accuracy current sexual patterns, thus preventing us as a society from rising above both anxiety and fantasy, the recent increased capacity for public discussion about sex has been quickly translated into intuitions of impending social disaster. This illusion of revolution may be a necessary element in generating progress in this direction; before the conservative resistance to new and expanded programs of sex education can be overcome, the effects of a sexual equivalent to Sputnik may be required. The problem is that the usual response to the imagery of crisis tends to produce the most muddled and defensive kinds of thinking. And, as during the Sputnik-provoked crisis in American education, it becomes easy to begin thinking that increased amounts of education of any kind represent progress. In that defensive posture, it will not be understood that, in the case of sexual behavior, knowing *how* to teach may not be so difficult as knowing *what* to teach.

Complicating this picture is the additional fact that, unlike many content areas, if the schools do not provide sex education it does not follow that there will be no sexual learning. To the contrary, sex has special salience particularly from adolescence on. There has been and there will continue to be sex education among the youthful recruits *(enlistees* may be a more proper term) on the pleasures and risks of sexual experience. In no current survey are schools, parents, physicians, or religious institutions to be found playing a significant role in sex education except for a small minority of cases. Moreover, there is little evidence to suggest that this privileged group makes better sexual adjustments as adults, and there is some small evidence that they may actually make poorer adjustments. In this society, now as in the past, the modal sources of sex information are age-mates who manage to put together odd pieces of information—legend and first-, second-, and third-hand experience—frequently adding novel or innovative features that are purely distortions resulting from the rumor process.

That the primary source of sex information is the peer group has been a stable characteristic of most of the populations studied, beginning with the Max Exner study of 1915 (85% of 948 college men),[4] and continuing through Walter Hughes in 1926 (78% of 1,029 schoolboys),[5] Glenn Ramsey in 1943 (90% of 291 high school students, either from peers or by self-discovery),[6] Paul H. Gebhard and co-workers in 1965 (91% of 477 lower-class men, 89% of 888 incarcerated criminals, and 89% of 1,356 convicted sex offenders).[7]

In approximately one-half of the cases in all of the studies, neither parent contributed any information. In the Ramsey study of 1943, 60 percent of the mothers and 82 percent of the fathers had given no sexual information.[8] In the study by Gebhard and co-workers, approximately three-quarters of the parents of both sexes had failed to give any direct sexual information.[9]

The information that mothers give is usually related to menstruation and pregnancy; however, less than one boy in four in the Ramsey study received this information from his mother. Learning about contraceptives, prostitution, and coitus was practically re-

4. Cited in Glenn Ramsey, "The Sex Information of Younger Boys," *American Journal of Orthopsychiatry* 13 (1943): 347–52.
5. Ibid, p. 349.
6. Ibid., pp. 349–50.
7. Paul H. Gebhard, John H. Gagon, Wardell B. Pomeroy, and Cornelia V. Christenson, *Sex Offenders: An Analysis of Types* (New York: Harper & Row, Publishers, 1965).
8. Ramsey, "The Sex Information of Younger Boys," 350–51.
9. Gebhard et al., *Sex Offenders*. Also, the data for 5,000 college males is currently being analyzed at the Institute for Sex Research: This should provide some evidence about the experience at this social level.

stricted to peers (over 90% in each instance). The role of the father is most ambiguous in this whole area: the good heart-to-heart talk between father and son seems to be a myth. The father even less than the mother serves as a source of sexual information, surprisingly enough. Apparently the father either assumes the boy will learn in his own good time, or that he—the parent—has no real role to play in this area.[10] Unfortunately, the questions asked have not ascertained whether the typical father ever made an attempt to teach his children anything about sex and then found out he was too late.

The Ramsey study also focused upon the age at which learning took place, and it is clear that pregnancy was learned of first (69% by age ten), intercourse usually next (57% by age ten), and masturbation next (43% by age ten). By age fourteen, the point at which it is suggested that most sex education programs should start, nearly all (92 to 100%) of the boys had learned about the previous three categories, and as many had learned of female prostitution. They remained most ignorant of menstruation (38% by age fourteen) and venereal disease (57%).[11]

As we have observed earlier (chap. 2), there is nothing in this process of information acquisition to suggest that the children have an integrated body of sexual knowledge. The young boy with some experience in sex play may not at all associate his firsthand knowledge of the anatomical differences between boys and girls with the fact that babies grow inside the mother, and the pertinent biological facts of fertilization may not dawn on him at all. These very same confusions exist for girls, since there is ample evidence that the very event of menstruation was, for a larger proportion of an older

10. This has also been discussed by Albert Bandura and Richard H. Walters in *Adolescent Aggression: A Study of the Influence of Child-Training Practices and Family Interrelationships* (New York: Ronald Press Co., 1959), pp. 184–87.

11. All figures are from Ramsey, "The Sex Information of Younger Boys."

12. It may, in fact, be a myth of the intellectualizing classes that value consensus as an outcome of rational deliberation exists to any extent in most populations. There is a strong tendency among those to whom ideas and language are important to impute the same significance to others for whom words are inadequate or coherent ideologies unimportant.

generation, and is, for some few of the present, learned when it first occurs. For a long time to come, no matter what programming innovations are introduced on the school level, it is difficult to conceive of any school program that will be essentially supplemented to this basic source. The continued advantage of peer groups as sources of sex education is that they can do what very few schools can even begin to do—relate sexual learning to sexual experience.

Clearly, the peer group, the school program, and, to a lesser extent, the inadvertencies of mass culture will remain the major sources of learning about sex in our society. The other candidates for this role—the medical and religious professions and the parents —have not only been ineffective in the past, but might properly remain so in the future.

The medical profession, fortunately, does not have the time to cope with this kind of program—fortunately, because there is some indication that the medical profession as a whole does not possess the necessary information, that often its members are likely to have inappropriate attitudes, and that ignorance and prudery cloaked in authority are most dangerous. The religious organizations that command the affiliation of most of the young have, in one form or other, opted for this role and have been almost universally ineffective. Again, the word "fortunately" may be appropriate, because so many of our major religious organizations maintain positions of condemnation of what we know the young have done and will continue to do regardless of what the churches say.

Because of their acute concern and anxiety about having some societal agency take over this activity parents should not be charged with the responsibility. For parents to take on the serious responsibility for the sex education of their children—beyond a concern for technical minutiae or behavioral imperatives—would immediately involve having to present a sense of their own sexuality to their children and, at the same time, admit to themselves the sexual nature of their children. For the majority of adults it is difficult to conceive of a way in which this can be done without provoking the most profound ambivalences on the part of the child, and equally profound anxieties on the part of the parent.

One of the primary sources of this adult anxiety is that adults live in a sexual culture in which there is no coherent community of values that they can use in dealing with the child's questions. There is a cluster of negative values that represents the one salient component of the body of public sexual norms. But, as Lionel Trilling says in evaluating the larger cultural significance of the book *Sexual Behavior in the Human Male,*[13] "Nothing shows more clearly the extent to which modern society has atomized itself than the isolation in sexual ignorance which exists among us. . . . Many cultures, the most primitive and the most complex, have entertained sexual fears of an irrational sort, but probably our culture is unique in strictly isolating the individual in the fears that society has devised."[14]

This development of adult sexual consensus about acceptable overt behavior, which occurs through the interactions of pairs of individuals rather than among larger social groups in the community, has serious consequences for the nature of public discussion of sexuality, especially in times of controversy. The privatization of sexual consensus means that no one can be sure of the behavior of others, and this insecurity is accompanied by a belief that statements differing from the convention norms will be taken as evidence of sexual deviation. The system of values that is most frequently invoked in a time of sexual controversy about children is commonly the most conservative, and this often results in the most puritan segment of the community defining the content of public school sex education.[15]

This lack of public consensus makes it very difficult for a body of disinterested opinion about sexuality to exist. Any statement by an individual about sexuality is often presumed to be related to the sexual preferences and desires of that individual. In this sense, those sexual statements that are not assumed to be ideological in

13. Alfred C. Kinsey, Wardell B. Pomeroy, and Clyde E. Martin, *Sexual Behavior in the Human Male* (Philadelphia: W. B. Saunders Co., 1948).
14. Lionel Trilling, "The Kinsey Report," in *The Liberal Imagination* (New York: Anchor Books, Doubleday & Co., 1953), p. 216.
15. This is not always true, since in some communities sex education in schools has successfully weathered rather extreme conflicts. However, it is the fear of this situation that keeps most adults silent.

character are assumed to be biographical. Another consequence of this lack of knowledge and consensus is the degree to which fantasy may be projected into the sexual situation, ultimately helping to shape it. In most areas of social activity, a reality check upon individual fantasies is provided either by interaction with other persons or by contact with the mass media; but the sexual area lacks such checks, and the proportion of fantasy probably outweighs the proportion of reality. With these conditions prevalent in the adult sexual community, it is not difficult to see some of the difficulties inherent in parent-child interaction (out of which come the primary experiences that shape character structure and sexual behavior).

These confusions on the part of parents and the consequent disorderliness of the child's life are now commonly placed at the door of permissive child-rearing. It is now suggested by psychiatrists, as well as Dr. Benjamin S. Spock, that discipline—when not carried too far—is a good thing and that good discipline is needed for the child's own sense of security.[16] The sentiment of psychiatrists that parents should return to punishment—administered "wisely" is the usual codicil—is based on two disparate but mutually supporting experiences. The first is related to the stresses of the therapeutic life for the therapist, for whom treatment failure and changes in the syndromes of new patients have endlessly complicated the problems of traditional psychoanalysis. (In contrast to Freud, it is possible to argue that the success or failure of psychoanalytic therapy is unconnected to the explanatory value of the theory in reference to human behavior; however, since psychoanalysis has been primarily used as part of a treatment program, this distinction is usually not made.) As Freudian analytic techniques are rejected, so are the pronouncements about the processes of normal childhood development and the role of permissiveness. This reaction is especially notable among

---

16. The revision of Spock's classic in 1957 to include a greater concern with discipline is noted in Martha Weinman, "Now 'Dr. Spock' Goes to the White House," *The New York Times Magazine,* 4 December 1960, pp. 26, 120–21. The cause of the revision was "permissiveness running away with itself." The child-rearing column of the magazine section of *The New York Times* is increasingly running to titles such as, "Relearning What Permissiveness Means," or "When Discipline is Called For," The column usually translates psychiatric positions into laymen's language.

those therapists who deal with criminal or other deviant populations or mass groups such as school children.[17] The intractability of the case or the dimensions of the problem (often simply in terms of size) are enough to make people suggest a return to techniques which are applicable to the mass and by the number.

The second experience is the difficulty which parents have in applying the suggested methodology and the responsibility that it implies. The popular literature is replete with anxious parents unhinged by the dangerousness and difficulty of the child-rearing task, and much advice to parents is bent upon reducing parental anxiety. The opening pronouncement of Dr. Spock is the summation of all such reassurance: "You know more than you think you do."[18] The current mode is to tell parents to rely upon their common sense, whatever that might be. The import of these admonitions is to remove the onus from the parent of the terrifying (and rightly so) responsibility of rearing children. This responsibility is often too much for the consciousness of the parent; he cannot reconcile the seriousness of his task, the lack of accurate guide rules (as opposed to clichés) for his behavior, and his emotional involvement in the child who is demanding his attention. The new literature even deflects from parental responsibility by pointing out elements such as inherent differences between children, as if these provided an exclusionary clause. It is not that the techniques of permissive child-rearing are necessarily indicated by the failures of parents in using them, but rather that parental incapacities have made adherence to the principles so sporadic and of such uneven intensity that they resulted only in confusion for the child.

Of the three effective sex educational sources—peer groups, schools, and forms of mass culture—the schools, to judge from available data, are the least effective. But they do have the virtue of

17. Many of these impressions come from personal interaction with psychiatrists, but the *Journal of Offender Therapy,* which is directed toward dealing with criminal populations explicitly, says what many therapists feel when confronted with these kinds of problems. See Ernst Schmidhofer, "Acting Up or Acting Out," *Journal of Offender Therapy* 8 (1964): 1–4, or Mark D. Altschule, "The Alleged Value of Antisocial Self-Expression," *Journal of Offender Therapy* 7 (1963): 73–74.

18. Benjamin S. Spock, *The Pocket Book of Baby and Child Care* (New York: Pocket Books, 1946), p. 3.

being the only one of the three that in the immediate future might become the object of self-conscious programming. This is why recent trends toward increasing sex education in the school systems of the nation ought to be encouraged. Nevertheless, while receiving as much encouragement as possible, it is equally important that such programs be subjected to the most critical scrutiny. This is clearly an area where good intentions are not enough. Too quickly, programs can become the empty rituals that serve to lessen the anxieties of parents and educators (i.e., "something is being done") and, at the same time, only reinforce the children's and adolescents' already well-developed belief in the unhealthy and hypocritical posture of adults toward sex. Sex education as ritual becomes submerged in that rigidified structure known as "school system programming"—a structure that is nearly totally resistant to innovation or even the incorporation of new experience.

This demonstrated rigidity of the schools has provoked radical critics of the current educational process to resist the integration of sex education in the school curriculum. Their resistance derives from issues that transcend the question of sex education itself. With some cause, they suggest that, as a group, our public school educators tend to be unintelligent and cowardly. Those critics contend that the failure of the schools in so many areas of learning that require far less sensitivity and imagination than does sex education, raises the question of why it should be assumed that they, the schools, would make a meaningful contribution to a topic of such complexity and delicacy. Perhaps to this radical stance one can say no more than that the abandonment of any faith in the collective educational enterprise also implies the abandonment of hope for rationally planning the future.

If the school is the chosen site for sex education, the important questions, which few have approached directly, are: What should be taught? How and when should it be taught? Who should do the teaching? The answers to these substantive questions often reveal a fundamental retreat from many of the more important goals of a meaningful program of sex education. The first major commitment to what should be taught tends to make sex education a study of reproductive biology. The rationale in this focus, not totally unjustifiable, is that the understanding of the biology involved lessens the tendency for the child to become estranged from his or her own body. Too often, however, the desexualization of the experience through the use of a biological imagery, which helps the teacher control his or her own anxieties and also makes the program less politically vulnerable, produces a costly sense of estrangement between the biological events (particularly as they are never experienced) and the emotional and psychological events (which are experienced).

Sex education delivered in the guise of reproductive biology characteristically centers around a naturalistic but strongly nonhuman imagery. Sex is represented as something so natural that it can barely be linked to the human experience, which is by definition unnatural in the sense that it derives its real meaning from an emotional content that is not located in or produced by the biological functions. The most typical imagery is that of the noble sperm heroically swimming upstream to fulfill its destiny by meeting and fertilizing the egg. The sexual act is described in ways that either misrepresent or totally obscure the sources of pleasure and meaning in sex. The end result of this substitution of reproductive biology for sex education was summed up perfectly in the experience of a mother of two children. She responded to the question of how babies were made with what sounded like a reasonably accurate description of the joining of organs explained as part of a sequence of biological events. At the conclusion, her child responded by saying: "Then you've done it twice."

The evidence is quite clear. An amazing number of youngsters and adults in our society have either extremely vague or totally inaccurate ideas of the biological processes salient to the sexual component in their lives. In the name of the ultimate good that should follow from increasing knowledge, it might be well to ensure greater access to accurate knowledge of these processes. It is equally clear, however, that few of the problems young people have with managing sexuality (and they may be both numerous and difficult) derive directly from a lack of knowledge about the biological processes involved. The fact that entire societies have survived in ignorance of the technical biological facts is no reason ours should. The fact of their survival, however, suggests a different order of priorities in defining the content of sex education.

The other major content component of standard sex education

programs concerns the undeniable fact that a considerable part of managing sexuality also involves managing social relationships. But, following from an adult inability to cope with the fact of the sexual nature of one's own children, this component is often transformed into the more desexualized forms of social etiquette. When should boys and girls go steady? When is it proper to engage in petting? Even the masturbatory prohibition tends to appear not in the moral or physical or mental health context, but in one of nonsexual social relations: in excess it leads to or encourages social isolation. The language of this approach to sex education eliminates any sense of a phenomenological feeling; the young person is once again made aware of the fact that he or she is alone—or almost alone—in a series of important and dramatic experiences.

It would be naive to think it possible, or even desirable, given the nature of the schools, to create situations where students can openly talk about their own sexual experiences or feelings. This, for better or worse, is something that may have to be left to the peer group. Between these two extremes, however, we should be able to find some way of programming content in sex education so that the adult world does not appear determined to remain oblivious to or ignorant of what is being experienced by the young. The pretense should not be maintained, for example, that an adolescent boy of fourteen is Andy Hardy with all sexual discoveries still ahead of him, when it can be safely assumed that he is engaging in frequent masturbatory behavior accompanied by a fairly rich fantasy life. Of course, the pretense can be continued, but any discussions will have little relevance to the reality of the boy's sexual experiences.

In essence, then, the content of sex education too often represents sex as something that merely happens. It is almost never presented as something that is experienced, as something that is thought about. It is left to the mass media, whose representation of the sexual experience is least trustworthy, to provide the young with an imagery that is at all correlated with how they will experience their own sexual selves—that is, in terms of fear, passion, pleasure, and pain. The possible correlation between mass media representations of sexual activity turns out to be, of course, not accidental; much of the training in how to be sexual derives from this very source.

There should be realistic alternatives to the exaggerated and frequently self-frustrating training provided by the mass media and the overly bland "sex is fun, in its time and place, because it is the healthy way" approach that marks the few existing school sex education programs. There ought to be some way of allowing young people (and perhaps adults) a meaningful exposure to a realistic objectification of the range of behavior into which their own experiences, those of their peers, and those of the larger world around them, will fall.

This indication of the need for a sex education content that substantively allows for the approximately honest representation of the sexual experience clearly takes us into the realm of the utopian. After all, students are rarely offered an approximately honest representation of how political or economic affairs are run, which on the surface, at least, appear less emotionally charged. It must also be remembered, however, that the young are more likely to experience an earlier confrontation with our collective dishonesty on the sexual level than they are on the remote levels of politics and economics. But, once again, the guiding principle on this question might be: to be overly realistic is to leave the future to chance.

The "who," "how," and "when" questions of sex education are in one sense not so important as the content question; that is, settling for something less than a substantively honest program linked to what young people are experiencing makes of these questions interesting political problems, but they lose meaning as educational problems. This is simply because, without the content related to experience, sex education really will not make any significant difference.

To be sure, with a competent and sensitive teacher, student levels of anxiety about sex may decrease measurably; an untalented teacher may needlessly increase fears. But there is little indication that either will have a powerful effect on ultimate sexual adjustments. Almost all adult males grew up with the gym teacher's standard anti-masturbatory plea made in the name of sanity and good health. Few were seriously deterred for more than a week by those remarks. Positive or enlightened teachers of sex education (of the reproductive biology and social etiquette variety) are likely to be even less effective merely because they will be less relevant to actual experience. One reason that even inadequate improvement in the character of sex education programs ought universally to be encouraged is that, while the programs may continue to fail to help most young people in managing their own sexuality and in moving toward some kind of sexual maturity, they may encourage those who have eluded difficulty to be less intolerant of that minority of the young who fall into serious sexual troubles.

Once there is a commitment to a broad and honest content in these programs, the "who," "how," and "when" questions become of major importance. It is relatively obvious that a great deal of the positive effect that follows an exposure to information about sex has a great deal to do with the style in which it is presented. That sex can be talked about not clinically, but casually and nonjudgmentally, appears to be the significant factor. Nonjudgmental talk about sex does not mean that widely held negative social attitudes about sexual behavior are ignored, nor that the legal proscriptions against certain forms of sexual activity are played down. What other people have done, how they have felt about their own sexual activities, and the dichotomy between what people do and what people will say they do are all appropriate topics of discussion. The obvious connection between sex and what is considered to be moral behavior must come up as well; however, as part of the "how" there should be no attempt to convert the situation into one of character-building. The information has to be presented in a situation where the recipient does not feel that it is being provided for a predetermined "good" purpose, but rather, as an attempt to spell out the options that are available to him and the risks and joys that are likely consequences of his choice.

The "who" answer is derived from the "how" answer; that is, the person will be someone, regardless of professional status, who feels comfortable with young people and whose own burden of guilt about his sexual feelings is sufficiently low that he can talk in the service of the children's needs rather than in the service of his own. What one does not need is the aimless masochism that produces an attitude that the young people are all really right in their criticism of adult hypocrisy or the directive sadism that seeks to create a copy of the adults' image of the sexually free or the sexually moral.

As for the "when" question, the school should be able to do what the peer group can do; it should talk about something when there is need to talk about it. If the information comes too soon, the content is either meaningless or anxiety-provoking. When it comes too late, it can be of only limited significance. One of the real marks of the failure of many currently operating programs of sex education is that students more often than not report that they didn't learn anything they didn't already know and, moreover, that it was less than what they already knew.

The overwhelmingly unplanned and unplannable elements in the development of the sexual life of children make it extremely difficult to discuss the role that planning in sex education might play. It is possible, however, to suggest that information imparted to children in schools or in other educational contexts should be communicated in each grade as part of the general curriculum. While it may be too rapid for some children and too slow for others, in general—if there is a source of accurate information that the children may tap anonymously and which is presented in a nonpejorative manner—at least the methods of communicating the information to the children will not in themselves be particularly destructive.[19] The specific age at which a child receives this information as well as the specific items of information to be imparted are of less significance than the preparation of the child for receiving this knowledge. The child who is traumatized by the sight of a nude body, or by learning that intercourse occurs, or by learning that babies grow inside of the mother, has developed a background of experience that sooner or later, in one context or another, would leave him unable to cope with similar encounters with the sexual. The specific triggering event is less important than the accumulation of readying experiences that prepared the child for such responses.

Such answers as these to the "how," "who," and "when" questions may be more utopian than our answers to the content question. Unless there is a change in American school systems more radical than anyone is predicting, the chances of finding a system with a capacity for flexibility and a climate of genuine mutual trust are far less than the chances of finding a school system with a capacity for telling its students the truth about sex. If there is a capa-

---

19. E. C. Cumings, ed., *Symposium on Sex Education* (New York: American Social Hygiene Association, November, 1957).

bility for telling the truth, no matter when or how, the young people are ahead of the game; if the truth is permitted to be told without judging, when the child needs the information, and in a way that ties to his daily experience, then there is the opportunity for changing human sensibility.

Finally, real progress on any of these levels will continue to suffer simply because there is really not a great deal known about sex, particularly about sex as it falls into the normal or modal ranges. There is a great deal of talk, but the talk is based on very little information. There is little understanding of how a commitment to sexuality develops and the role it plays in general personality development. More is known in our society than any previous society about who does what to whom and how often, but little is known about the role it plays in organizing a life in which, even under the best of circumstances, sex tends to play a minor role. In many ways, the resistance to systematic research in the sexual area is greater than the resistance to sex education, which is possibly defined as less threatening or less subversive. Indeed, what may produce the bankruptcy of the sex education movement is that, even among the advance guard, there is a tendency to believe that education without knowledge is possible. Even the accumulation of scientific knowledge about human sexual behavior may not accelerate much the pace or direction of change, for in this area of behavior —as is probably true in others—the statement, "Ye shall know the truth, and the truth shall make you free," may not apply. In a society that is addicted to the ideology of limitless possibilities in human engineering, it is perhaps important to focus on some of the refractory elements in human development. While it is possible to be more hopeful about the human capacity for change than Freud was in his later years, his statement about the limited potentials of sex education should be kept in mind. This statement was made during his discussion of the purely intellectual consideration of instinctual conflicts and the reading of psychoanalytic writings and their limited effect on mental health. Freud said of these activities:

We have increased his knowledge, but altered nothing else in him. . . . We can have analogous experiences, I think, when we give children sexual enlightenment. I am far from maintaining that this is a harmful or unnecessary thing to do, but it is clear that the prophylactic effect of this liberal measure has been greatly overestimated. After such enlightenment, children know something they did not know before, but they make no use of the new knowledge that has been presented to them. We come to see that they are not even in so great a hurry to sacrifice for this new knowledge the sexual theories which might be described as a natural growth and which they have constructed in harmony with, and dependence on, their imperfect libidinal organization—theories about the part played by the stork, about the nature of sexual intercourse and about the way in which babies are made. For a long time after they have been given sexual enlightenment they behave like primitive races who have had Christianity thrust upon them and who continue to worship their old idols in secret.[20]

20. Sigmund Freud, "Analysis Terminable and Interminable," *Complete Psychological Works,* vol. 23 (London: The Hogarth, Press, 1964), pp. 223–24.

5

Male Homosexuality

Estimates and Theories

One aspect of any consideration of life styles that involve alternative or unconventional sexual adjustments is an estimate of the size of the population to be included. Unfortunately, the proscribed character of most sexual alternatives makes it unlikely that the conventional sources of social bookkeeping will offer the required statistics. This is the situation with reference to male homosexuality as well as most other aspects of sexual conduct in the society. However, the continued search for such estimates of the numbers of homosexuals indicates that the numbers question has a significance and a variety of functions in the public domains of homosexuals and nonhomosexuals as well.

For the scientist, an estimate of the size of a population is often an indication that there are measures of homogeneity or agreed-on definitions of the attributes that divide it from other populations. Unfortunately, this is not always the case, and only recently—when homosexuality ceased to be exclusively of concern to the criminologist, the abnormal psychologist, and other students of what is defined as the psychopathological—did it become possible to consider estimates of numbers of homosexuals greater than the number arrested or in therapy and at the same time to consider attributes that went beyond sexual organs in juxtaposition. More recent researchers, urged on by estimates emerging from the original Kinsey research, have begun to consider definitions based on life cycle stages and sociocultural definitions, leaving the boundaries between alternative sexual styles more flexible and permeable.

This same impact of varying estimates of populations with alternative sexual adjustments can be seen in the behavior of those who create or those who carry out public policy mandates. Regardless of moral caveats, there are points at which laws become unenforceable or behavior becomes redefined depending on how many members of the community are involved. The historical example of the failure of alcohol prohibition is now matched by the steady erosion of moral and legal prohibition against marijuana. This same slow process of de-criminalization of sexual conduct can now be observed partly because of newer estimates of the numbers of offenders. Indeed, as long as the numbers were assumed to be small, repressive policing practices could continue, providing they did not exceed limitations set by considerations of work load or involve high status members of the community.

The problem of estimates also affects the relation between conventional and unconventional sexual performers, since the status of the latter as deviant, criminal, or psychopathological is in part a function of numbers as well as the reigning cultural theories of behavior. When estimates are tiny or unknown and the behavior subject to sanctions, those who perform it do so in climates of suspicion and alienation, often driven together in self-defensive groups. The emergence of larger estimates often becomes the occasion for the political use of numbers, hence the overestimates of one male in six or one male in ten as homosexuals were essentially gestures to normalize the homosexuality by emphasizing its commonness. A parallel historical normalization strategy was the inversion of the psychoanalytic notion of latent homosexuality as a support for the argument that everyone was a little homosexual. This question of numbers is critical to those with unconventional commitments since it is a primary defense against the criminalizing or abnormalizing tendencies of the society. Estimates affect the lives of the conventional by putting them in possession of expectations of how likely they are to meet or have friends who possess the attribute. Indeed, the number supplies for them a measure of normality and increases the possibility that a person with an alternative sexual commitment will possess a close social relationship to them.

The only large-scale study in the United States in which systematic questions about the incidence of homosexuality were asked of a fairly general population was the research of the original Kinsey group at Indiana University between 1938 and 1953. Whatever the quarrels about the sampling methods of that research, it was the stimulus for reevaluation of homosexuality in the society and continues to provide the only extensive data pool for estimating the general incidence of homosexual behavior in American society. The figure from that research which gained the most attention was that 37 percent of the males interviewed had shared in at least one homosexual experience to the point of orgasm between adolescence and old age. This figure was based on populations that included a very large number of criminal and delinquent males, and when corrected to an overall national estimate, probably exceeded actual rates. A recent retabulation of the records of those persons interviewed by the Kinsey group while they were in college or graduate school provides some useful estimates to complement the 37 percent figure. It was among this college-educated population or attending populations that the effects of volunteer bias were minimized. Therefore they represent the best collection of cases from a sampling viewpoint. In a reanalysis of the cases of 2,900 young men who were in college between the years 1938 and 1950, the bulk of whom were under thirty at the time they were interviewed, 30 percent had undergone at least one homosexual experience in which either the interviewee *or* his male partner was stimulated to the point of orgasm (note that this varies from the Kinsey definition). Of these 30 percent, however, slightly more than one-half (16% of the total) had shared no such experiences since the age of fifteen, and an additional third (9% of the total) had experienced all of their homosexual acts during adolescence or only incidentally in the years before they reached the age of twenty. Thus, for 25 percent of all males who were interviewed, homosexual experience was confined predominantly to adolescence or to isolated experiences in the later adjacent years. The remaining 5 to 6 percent are divided into those men who had only homosexual experiences, comprising some 3 percent of the 2,900, and the remaining 3 percent who had substantial homosexual histories as well as heterosexual histories. These data are directly applicable only to male populations in college largely between 18 and 25. However, other data suggest there is no reason to suspect that these figures will differ a great deal for persons of other educational or occupational levels, except for those portions of the male population who have substantial criminal or delinquent careers or those who have had experience in reformatories or penitentiaries either as young people or as adults.[1]

These estimates are relatively low, particularly in contrast to the estimates of many of our social journalists. Despite these relatively low proportions, however, the actual number of persons with exclusive homosexual experience in a population as large as that of the United States is very large and apparently would run into millions. Given such numbers, it is appalling that there is so little in the way of systematic knowledge about the life of the homosexual. Perhaps more appalling is the fact that a great deal of the research which has been done in this area is of little value.

The study of homosexuality today, except for a few rare and relatively recent examples, suffers from two major defects. It is ruled by a simplistic and homogeneous view of the psychological and social contents of the category "homosexual," and at the same time it is nearly exclusively interested in the most difficult and least rewarding of all questions, that of etiology. While some small exceptions are allowed for adolescent homosexual experimentation, the person with a major to nearly exclusive sexual interest in persons of the same sex is perceived as belonging to a uniform category whose adult behavior is a necessary outcome and, in a sense, reenactment of certain early and determining experiences. This is the prevailing image of the homosexual and the substantive concern of the literature in psychiatry and psychology today.[2]

In addition to the fact that sexual contact with persons of the same sex, even if over the age of consent and in private, is against the law in forty-six of the fifty states, the homosexual labors under another burden that is commonly the lot of sexual minorities in any society.[3] The process of labeling and stigmatizing behavior as de-

1. In these latter populations the incidence of homosexual experience is larger, probably upward of one-half having had such experience either in or out of prison. However, the etiology and conditions of such homosexuality are basically quite different, relating in most cases to deprivation, aggression, and seduction.

2. Irving Bieber et al., *Homosexuality, A Psychoanalytic Study* (New York: Basic Books, 1962).

3. Sex law reform occurred in the state of Illinois as part of a general reform of the criminal code in 1961. For the manner in which the law's

viant not only facilitates the work of legal agencies in creating a bounded category of actors such as the "normal burglar" and the "normal child molester" as suggested by Sudnow, but it also creates an image of large classes of deviant actors who appear to be operating from the same motivations and for the same etiological reasons.[4] The homosexual, like most significantly labeled persons (whether the label be positive or negative), has all of his acts interpreted through the framework of his homosexuality. Thus the creative activity of the playwright or painter who happens to be homosexual is interpreted through the fact or rumor of his homosexuality rather than in terms of the artistic rules and conventions of the particular art form in which he works. The plays of the dramatist are scanned for the Albertine Ploy and the painter's paintings for an excessive use of phallic imagery or vaginal teeth.

It is this nearly obsessive concern with the ultimate causes of adult conditions that has played a major role in structuring our concerns about beliefs and attitudes toward the homosexual. Whatever the specific elements that make up an etiological theory, the search for etiology has its own consequence for research methodology and the construction of theories about behavior. In the case of homosexuality, if one moves beyond those explanations of homosexual behavior that are rooted in constitutional or biological characteristics—that is, something in the genes or in the hormonal system—one is left with etiological explanations located in the structure of the family and its malfunctions.[5] The most compelling of these theories are grounded ultimately in Freudian psychology, where the

---

reform was translated for police officials, see Claude Sowle, *A Concise Explanation of the Illinois Criminal Code of 1961* (Chicago: Burdette Smith Co., 1961).

4. David Sudnow, "Normal Crimes," *Social Problems* 12 (Winter 1965): 255–76.

5. A. C. Kinsey, "Criteria for the Hormonal Explanation of the Homosexual," *The Journal of Clinical Endocrinology* 1 (May 1941): 424–28; F. J. Kallman, "Comparative Twin Study on the Genetic Aspects of Male Homosexuality," *Journal of Nervous and Mental Disorders* 115 (1952): 283–98; F. J. Kallman, "Genetic Aspects of Sex Determination and Sexual Maturation Potentials in Man," in *Determinants of Human Sexual Behavior,* ed. George Winokur (Springfield, Ill.: Charles C. Thomas, 1963), pp. 5–18; and John Money, "Factors in the Genesis of Homosexuality," in *Determinants of Human Sexual Behavior,* pp. 19–43.

roots of this as well as the rest of human character structure is to be found in the pathological relationships between parents and their children.

The work of Irving Bieber is the most recent of these analytic explorations, the central finding of which is that in a highly selected group of male homosexuals (affluent and in psychoanalytic therapy) there was a larger proportion of males who had mothers who could be described as close-binding and intimate and fathers who were detached and hostile.[6] The argument proceeds that the mother has selected this child for special overprotection and seductive care. In the process of child-rearing, sexual interest is both elicited and then blocked by punishing its behavioral manifestations. As a result of the mother's special ties to the child, the father is alienated from familial interaction, is hostile to the child, and fails to become a source of masculine attachment.

Regardless of the rather engaging and persuasive character of the theory, there are substantial complications. It assumes that there is a necessary relationship between the development of masculinity and femininity and heterosexuality and homosexuality. There is the assumption that homosexuals play sexual roles which are explicitly modeled upon those of the heterosexual and that these roles are well-defined and widespread. This confusion of the dimensions of sexual object choice with masculinity and femininity is based on two complementary errors. The first is that physical sexual activities are often simplistically characterized as passive (to be read feminine) or active (to be read masculine) and that preferences for a participation in these physical activities are read as direct homologues of the complex matters of masculinity and femininity. The second source of the confusion lies in the two situations in which homosexuality can be most easily observed. One is the prison, where the characteristics of homosexuality do tend to model themselves more closely on the patterns of heterosexuality in the outside community, but where the sources and the character of behavior are in the service of different ends. The second situation is that of public homosexuality characterized by the flaunted female gesture

6. Beiber et al., *Homosexuality*.

which has become stereotypic of homosexuality. This is not to say that such beliefs about the nature of homosexuality on the part of the heterosexual majority do not influence the homosexual's behavior; however, just because stereotypes are held does not mean that they play a role in the etiology of the behavior that they purport to explain.

Another major problem that exists for etiological theories of homosexuality based on family structure is the difficulty one finds in all theories that depend on the individual's retrospective memories of his childhood and that call upon him for hearsay evidence not only about himself, but about his parents. We live in a post-Freudian world, and the vocabulary of motives of the most psychologically illiterate is replete with the concepts of repression, inhibition, the Oedipus complex, and castration fears. The rhetoric of psychoanalysis permeates the culture, thanks to a process that might best be called the democratization of mental health. One of the lessons of existentialism is that our biographies are not fixed quantities but are subject to revision, excision, and other forms of subtle editing based on our place in the life cycle, our audience, and the mask that we are currently wearing. Indeed, for many persons the rehearsed past and the real past become so intermixed that there is only the present. Recent research in childrearing practices suggests that two years after the major events of child-rearing, weaning, and toilet training mothers fail to recall accurately their previous conduct and hence sound a good deal like Dr. Spock. An important footnote here is that persons do not always edit the past to improve their image in the conventional sense. Often the patient in psychotherapy works very hard to bring out more and more self-denigrating materials to assure the therapist that he, the patient, is really working hard and searching for his true motives.

As a consequence of our preliminary work and the work of others, such as Evelyn Hooker, Albert J. Reiss, Maurice Leznoff and William A. Westley, Nancy Achilles, Michael Schofield, Laud Humphreys, and Martin Hoffman, we would like to propose some alternative considerations in terms of the complexity of the life cycle of the homosexual, the roles that mark various stages of this cycle, and the kinds of forces, both sexual and nonsexual, that impinge on this individual "actor."[7] It is our current feeling that the problem of finding out how some people become homosexual requires an adequate theory of how others become heterosexual; that is, one cannot explain homosexuality in one way and leave heterosexuality as a large residual category labeled "all other." Indeed, the explanation of homosexuality in this sense may await the explanation of the larger and more modal category of adjustment.[8]

Furthermore, from a sociological point of view, what the original causes were may not even be very important for the patterns of homosexuality observed in a society. Much as the medical student who comes to medicine for many reasons, and for whom the homogeneous character of professional behavior arises from the experiences of medical school rather than from the root causes of the occupational choice, the patterns of adult homosexuality are consequent upon the social structures and values that surround the homosexual after he becomes or conceives himself as homosexual rather than upon original and ultimate causes.[9]

7. Evelyn Hooker, "The Homosexual Community," in *Perspectives in Psychopathology,* eds. James C. Palmer and Michael J. Goldstein (New York: Oxford University Press, 1966), pp. 354–64; Albert J. Reiss, "The Social Integration of Queers and Peers," *Social Problems* 9 (Fall 1961): 102–20; M. Leznoff and W. A. Westley, "The Homosexual Community," *Social Problems* 3 (April 1956): 257–63; N. Achilles, "The Development of the Homosexual Bar as an Institution," in *Sexual Deviance,* eds. J. H. Gagnon and W. Simon (New York: Harper & Row Co., 1967); Michael Schofield, *Sociological Aspects of Homosexuality* (Boston: Little, Brown and Co., 1965); Laud Humphreys, *Tearoom Trade: Impersonal Sex in Public Places* (Chicago: Aldine Pub. Co., 1970); and Martin Hoffman, *The Gay World* (New York: Basic Books, 1969).

8. That this is a crucial issue is only coming to be understood, and it seems impossible to act upon. Merle Miller in his article "What it Means to Be a Homosexual," *The New York Times Magazine,* 17 January 1971, quotes Martin Hoffman: "Until we know about the mechanisms of sexual arousal in the central nervous system and how learning factors can set the triggering devices for these mechanisms, we cannot leave a satisfactory theory of homosexual behavor. We must point out that heterosexual behavior is as much of a scientific puzzle as homosexual behavior. . . .We assume that heterosexual arousal is somehow natural and needs no explanation. I suggest to call it natural is to evade the whole issue; it is as if we said it's natural for the sun to come up in the morning and left it at that."

9. Howard S. Becker, "Change in Adult Life," *Sociometry* 27 (March 1964): 40–53; and Howard S. Becker, Blanche Greer, and Everett C. Hughes, *Boys in White: Student Culture in the Medical School* (Chicago: University of Chicago Press, 1961).

What we are suggesting here is that we have allowed the homosexual's sexual object choice to dominate and control our imagery of him. We have let this single aspect of his total life experience appear to determine all his products, concerns, and activities. This prepossessing concern on the part of nonhomosexuals with the purely sexual aspect of the homosexual's life is something we would not allow to occur if we were interested in the heterosexual. However, the mere presence of unconventional sexuality seems to give the sexual content of life an overwhelming significance. Homosexuals, moreover, vary profoundly in the degree to which their homosexual commitment and its facilitation becomes the organizing principle of their lives. Involved here is a complex outcome that is less likely to be explained by originating circumstances than by the consequences of the establishment of the commitment itself.

Even with the relatively recent shift in the normative framework available for considering homosexuality—that is, from a rhetoric of sin to a rhetoric of mental health—the preponderance of the sexual factor in any discussion of homosexuality remains evident. The change in rhetoric itself may have major significance in the ways in which persons with homosexual interests are dealt with; but at the same time, the mental health rhetoric seems equally wide of the mark in understanding homosexuality. One advance, however, is that in place of a language of optimum man which characterized both the moral and the early mental health writings, there is a growing literature concerned with the psychological characteristics necessary for a person to survive in some manner within specific social systems and social situations.[10] In this post-Freudian world, major psychic wounds are increasingly viewed as par for the human condition and, as one major psychiatric theoretician has observed, few survive the relationship with their parents without such wounding.[11]

---

10. Marie Jahoda, "Toward a Social Psychology of Mental Health," in *Mental Health and Mental Disorder,* ed. Arnold M. Rose (New York: W. W. Norton & Co., 1955), pp. 556–77; and F. C. Redlich, "The Concept of Health in Psychiatry," in *Explorations in Social Psychiatry,* eds. A. H. Leighton, J. A. Clausen, and R. N. Wilson (New York: Basic Books, 1957), pp. 138–64.

11. Lawrence Kubie, "Social Forces and the Neurotic Process," in *Explorations in Social Psychiatry,* pp. 77–104.

Adjustments and Outcomes

The problem of adjustment and mental health becomes a question of whether these wounds are exacerbated by social situations that render them too costly to the individual or to the surrounding community. This trend toward a reconceptualization of mental health is accompanied by a scaling down of the goals set for humanity; instead of exceedingly vague and somewhat utopian goals, we tend to ask more pragmatic questions: Is the individual self-supporting? Does he manage to conduct his affairs without the intervention of the police or the growing number of mental health authorities? Does he have adequate sources of social support? Does he possess a positively balanced and adequately developed repertoire for gratification? Has he learned to accept himself? These are questions we are learning to ask of nearly all men, but among the exceptions is found the homosexual. In practically all cases, the presence of homosexuality is seen as prima facie evidence of major psychopathology. When the heterosexual meets these minimal definitions of mental health, he is exculpated; but the homosexual, no matter how good his adjustment in nonsexual areas of life, remains suspect.

Data drawn from a group of 550 white males with extensive histories of homosexuality, interviewed outside institutions by Kinsey and his associates between 1940 and 1956 (table 5.1), suggest that most homosexuals cope fairly well, and even particularly well, when we consider the historical period involved and the stigmatized, and in fact criminal, nature of their sexual interests.[12] Of this group, between 75 and 80 percent reported having had no trouble with the police, the proportion varying by the exclusivity of their homosexual commitment and their educational attainment.

Following this same pattern, trouble with their families of origin tended to occur in a joint relationship with level of education and degree of homosexual commitment, with the less educated and the more homosexual reporting a greater incidence of difficulties. Only about 10 percent of the group reported trouble at work and less

12. Extensive homosexuality is here defined as a minimum of fifty-one or more times or contact with twenty-one or more males.

TABLE 5.1   *Reported Incidence of Social Difficulties by Education and Exclusivity of Homosexual Commitment*

	Percentage High School		Percentage College	
	Exclusive Homosexual	Mixed Homosexual and Heterosexual	Exclusive Homosexual	Mixed Homosexual and Heterosexual
Trouble with:				
Police	31	22	24	17
Family of origin	25	16	19	11
Occupation	10	8	7	8
(N)	(83)	(83)	(283)	(101)

than 5 percent at school as a result of their homosexuality. Of those who had military experience, only one-fifth reported difficulties in that milieu. In the military, possibly more than in civilian life, homosexuality is a difficulty that obliterates all other evaluations made of the persons.[13]

We do not wish to say that homosexual life does not contain a great potential for demoralization, despair, and self-hatred. To the contrary—as in most unconventional careers—there remains the potential for a significant escalation of individual psychopathology. This potential is suggested by some other aspects of these same data (table 5.2). About one-half of these males reported that 60 percent or more of their sexual partners were persons with whom they had sex only one time. Between 10 and 20 percent report that they often picked up their sexual partners in public terminals, and an even larger proportion reported similar contacts in other public or semipublic locations.[14] Between one-fourth and one-third reported having been robbed by a sexual partner, with a larger proportion among those having exclusively homosexual histories. Even the most cau-

13. Colin Williams and Martin Weinberg, *Homosexuals in the Military* (New York: Harper & Row, 1971).
14. An extended study of the composition of these populations may be found in Humphreys, *Tearoom Trade*.

tious males can fall afoul of this problem, as one interviewee reported:

> *R:* There are a great many people who aren't what they claim to
> be. . . . several years ago, I was in a bar. I was known very well in
> this bar by the bartenders, the owner, the dice girl. I was particularly
> fond of the dice girl and it was a slow night. She was sitting at the
> bar talking to me and there was a fellow on the other side that kept
> moving his leg against mine, looking at me and lighting my cigarette
> and trying to get in the conversation and finally she said to me, "I'm
> gonna leave you alone; looks like you're gonna do all right with this
> fellow next to you." And I said, "I'm not because I says I'm scared
> of him." There was something, I was just so scared of this fellow.
> And she says, "Always let your instincts be your guide." He got to
> talking to me and seemed very nice and by that time I'd had a few
> more drinks, it was later, several hours, and he ended up coming
> home with me and when he left, a collection of some thousand rare
> coins and all the loose cash and whatever could be handily picked up
> was missing.

In addition to risk of robbery, the illegal status of homosexuality results in easy coercion, so that beween 10 and 15 percent of the
cases reported that they were blackmailed because of their homosexuality.

There were further indicators of alienation and interpersonal difficulty in the findings. For two-fifths of the respondents the longest
homosexual affair lasted less than one year, and for about one-
fourth kissing occurred in one-third or less of their sexual contacts.
Even kissing becomes in some cases a test rather than an expression
of erotic intimacy:

> *R:* I don't know how you watch for them [robbers] except that I
> always talk to a person a long time before I go with them for sex.
> I'm always very careful to always be noncommittal; I invite them for
> coffee or a drink or I go to their place for a drink or something. Try
> to kiss them if they kiss; there are a great many people that won't
> kiss if they're not what they claim to be, I get on my guard [if they
> don't kiss].

This sense of fear and anxiety about the consequences of exposure
penetrates very deeply into homosexual life styles, with about 30

TABLE 5.2. *Selected Negative Aspects of a Homosexual Career by Education and Exclusivity of Homosexual Commitment*

	Percentage High School		Percentage College	
	Exclusive Homosexual	Mixed Homosexual and Heterosexual	Exclusive Homosexual	Mixed Homosexual and Heterosexual
Proportion with 60% or more of sexual partners with whom had sex only once	49	43	51	45
Often pick up partners in public terminals	19	18	17	7
Ever been rolled	37	26	34	29
Ever been blackmailed	16	6	12	15
(N)	(83)	(83)	(283)	(101)

percent reporting that they have never had sex in their own homes. One respondent reports that because of his occupation even his own name is off limits:

> *R:* Since my job is connected with federal government, I have a little bit of worry on this account because I have [a security] clearance and all that. I generally will not give my name out except for my first name and I won't tell anyone specifically where I live until I get to know them a bit better. The number of people I have told where I live or my full name has been limited to, I'd say, half a dozen people. In fact, I don't even think it's that many. Probably about five.

Accumulatively, such conditions involve the two-fifths of these men who indicated some serious feelings of regret about being homosexual, and who gave such reasons as fear of social disapproval or rejection, inability to experience a conventional family life, feelings of guilt or shame, or fear of potential trouble with the law. These figures require a more detailed analysis, and there are also uncertainties about case collection bias that must be considered. However, it is our feeling that these proportions would not be substantially changed, given a more complete exploration of these factors. These data, then, suggest a depersonalized character, a driven or compelled quality of the sexual activity of many homosexuals, which cannot be reckoned as anything but extremely costly to them.

Obviously, the satisfaction of a homosexual commitment—like most forms of deviance—makes social adjustment more problematic than it might be for members of a conventional population. What is important to understand is that consequences of these sexual practices are not necessarily direct functions of the nature of such practices. It is necessary to move away from an obsessive concern with the sexuality of the individual, and attempt to see the homosexual in terms of the broader attachments that he must make to live in the world around him. Like the heterosexual, the homosexual must come to terms with the problems that are attendant upon being a member of society: he must find a place to work, learn to live with or without his family, be involved or apathetic in political life, find a group of friends to talk to and be with, fill his leisure time usefully or frivolously, handle all of the common and uncommon problems of impulse control and personal gratification, and in some manner socialize his sexual interests.

There is a seldom noticed diversity to be found in the life cycle of the homosexual, both in terms of solving general human problems and in terms of the particular characteristics of the life cycle itself. Not only are there as many ways of being homosexual as there are of being heterosexual, but the individual homosexual, in the course of his everyday life, encounters as many choices and as many crises as the heterosexual. It is much too easy to allow the label, once applied, to suggest that the complexities of role transition and identity crises are easily attributable to or are a crucial exemplification of some previously existing etiological defect.

An example of this is in the phase of homosexuality called "coming out." This is a complex period, during which there is self-recognition by the individual of his identity as a homosexual, his first major exploration of the homosexual community (or homosexual individuals) and less often his first homosexual experience. However, this entry into homosexuality is not a neat and ordered affair and is probably more complex than the equivalent emergence into heterosexuality. Self-recognition can come very early and first overt behavior very late, as with this respondent:

> *Int:* How long would you say you have been out?
>
> *R:* Well, in a technical sense I suppose for five years.
>
> *Int:* How do you mean "in a technical sense?"
>
> *R:* Well, if you mean how long have I actively been saying, "OK, I know what my desires are, I'm going to do something about them," it would be age twenty-five. But I've known what my desires were since, I'd say, late grammar school. I was consciously convinced of my homosexuality that early.
>
> *Int:* What happened at the age of twenty-five that made you come out?
>
> *R:* Well, I did run into someone that I had known very casually while I was in college and this person was a staff member at the time. We had always had a lot of interests in common but I'd been afraid of him because he's a very hostile sort of person—and I'd always avoided him for that reason.
>
> *Int:* Did you know he was homosexual?
>
> *R:* No, I didn't. It was maybe three weeks after that. He sort of tested me out first. He took me to a sort of in-between bar and then he took me to a bar and it had dancing. That was the first time, for all practical purposes, that I'd ever really had physical contact with a man that led to sex.

A more common pattern involves adolescent experience in homosexuality, but the meaning of such an experience can vary widely.
With some males these first contacts occur in an ambiance of ignorance so that the significance of the behavior is slow to emerge.

> *R:* Well, we lived in the country when I was fourteen. The popula-
> tion of course was very sparse and a lot of things happen that can't
> happen in the city and the boy who lived across the street from my
> house was homosexual and we just happened one day to fall into it.
> We had sex. The realization that you are the same sex didn't occur to
> us at that time. You just did what was natural and you never ques-
> tioned it. I questioned it when I was older although it never came as
> a shock to me. I always knew from that time that I desired men. The
> realization that this was not accepted, that this was not the norm,
> didn't come until I was maybe sixteen-seventeen, but it didn't upset
> me. . . . Maybe it was just a realization.

These same kinds of early experiences can be faciliated by the existence of the homosexual community and its institutions. A
significant factor of late has been increased media attention to homosexuality which at least makes things easier for the homosexual. However, the crucial step (and one which is never formally supported)
is the existence of other people.

> *R:* But I didn't think that that's what I wanted, but the more I
> thought about it and the more I went back to it, it did turn out to be.
> The whole field was green to me. I just didn't know where to go and
> what to do and how to find what I was looking for. There was some
> experience in adolescence. A little bit in high school, a little bit in
> college, but I looked on those as adolescent years, just experimenting,
> having fun, just getting to know what it's all about. I walked into my
> first gay bar I think quite by accident, not knowing what it was at
> first and when I was in there, I didn't know what to do. I stayed for a
> time and then came back to the bar more and more frequently and
> of course talking with people and talking to bartenders you learn of
> other places to go and other things to do.
>   I have to say that I had the feeling and I knew the appetite was
> there, because I would be looking at good looking men more than I
> would at good looking women. There's been more and more pub-
> lished and more and more publicity on the aspects of homosexuality;
> all the ladies' magazines have articles on it, and several of the nation-

wide magazines have come out with extensive articles on it in the last few years. You read the things and you can see yourself there too.

In some cases the intervention and instruction is more direct as in the case of a young man who was "brought out" by a relative of the same age.

> *R:* He [the relative] came in with this friend and he says, "I want you to meet a friend of mine." I ask him if he was gay and he said yes and I asked him how long he has known him, and he says, "We've been going together for about a year now. It was hard to believe, two boys going together and all. They took me down to this neighborhood and they said, "If you are going to be a homosexual you do it right. You don't start running around with these nutty little faggots. You meet nice people and you don't become promiscuous and you don't sell yourself; you don't tell everything you know. Just be yourself." It took a long time but finally, I guess I was seeking hard enough. Right in my little home town I got an address and I went over there and made up this cock and bull story of how I met this friend of his when I was over in Europe and he told me to look you up. While I was there this guy was perfectly straight, in a sense. He had no idiosyncracies or anything. We started talking and then one night he asked me to come in his bedroom and I went in his bedroom and there it happened. That started my life as a homosexual.

This multiplicity of pathways to homosexual self-identification and overt activity is also reported by Barry M. Dank. He describes the process of attributing meanings to physical sexual activity during early adolescence in the following words: "The person who has sexual feelings or desires toward persons of the same sex has no vocabulary to explain to himself what these feelings mean."[15] More generally, this problem also exists for the heterosexual in the process of getting a proper understanding of the content and activities described by the word *sexual* itself—more radically, how does one learn that the feelings and desires *are* sexual in the first place? Dank suggests the valuable concept of those situations of concentrated knowledge which are most productive of coming out.[16]

15. Barry M. Dank, "Coming Out in the Gay World," *Psychiatry* 34 (May 1971): 182.
16. Ibid., p. 83.

Whatever the point in time and order of experiences, the removal of inhibiting doubts frequently releases a great deal of sexual activity. Sexual contacts during this period are often pursued almost indiscriminately and with greater vigor than caution. A young homosexual describes the highly active behavior of a close friend who has just come out and in it sees similarities to his own adjustment.

> *R:* He came out a year ago and he is very promiscuous. He's got this attitude that he's just sought after by everybody and unfortunately he is and it's completely gone to his head. It is very sad because he's screwing up his life. It is just going to bring about bad luck. If he doesn't shape up pretty soon, in the next six months he is going to be out of it. I've talked to —— about him and —— says, "Well, look how long it took you to shape up," which it did. It took me about a year to stop running around. In a homosexual life most people are interested in tricking or having numbers. Not too many people are interested in having affairs, because in affairs too many people are hurt, unfortunately. So I figure well, have a good time.

The intertwined and common aspects of social learning prior to overt heterosexual and homosexual life are such that similar motives are expressed during comparable life periods. The desire for a romantic, passionate, and conclusive amorous relationship exists for both young men and women. Mr. or Ms. "Right" is just around the corner.

> *R:* I do know I was excessively promiscuous—by that, I mean bringing home people like every night or several times a day. In my case, it was strictly a search for someone, maybe like the "romantic ideal type person." It is totally unrewarding as far as I'm concerned except for the immediate instantaneous pleasure; that can be very good or cannot, but it enables you to do better in other areas, like on your job for instance so that you're not always constantly thinking about sex and it gives you some physical release. On the other hand, I think emotionally . . . it doesn't afford an emotional release as far as I'm concerned. It's like the more money you earn, the more money you want to earn, but in this case the more sex you have the more you want to have. But . . . the fond hope that finally you are going to find *the* person or find *the* something that really matters. I think that sometimes you may be so caught up with promiscuity that the person may come along and you don't even recognize it.

This is very close to that period in the life of the heterosexual called the "honeymoon," when coitus is legitimate and is pursued with a substantial amount of energy. This high rate of marital coitus, however, declines as demands are made on the young couple to exercise their roles in the framework of the larger social system. In these same terms, during the homosexual "honeymoon" many individuals begin to learn ways of acting out a homosexual object choice that involves homosexual gratification, but which is not necessarily directly sexual and does not involve the genitalia.

R: The beginning of a homosexual relationship is just the opposite of heterosexual courtship. There you start out with a common social background and have emotional rapport in a mild pleasant recreational sense, then you gradually work up to more intense relationships. You start out with a community of interests. Theoretically you meet these girls in a situation where you have something in common with this girl [*e.g.,* same school, neighborhood club]; if things go well, then you build up to an intimate sexual relationship. Homosexuality, this is the opposite. You start out with sex and it may be the most sensual, hedonistic, animalistic thing you can think of. First you think of your partners as objects, then you get to know them as persons. And if you have a very strong promiscuous background and there is some point about the sexual behavior you don't like, then you go on and get something else which is more interesting. You have to work at building a friendship, it just doesn't happen. Although it's not a necessity, I usually don't consider a person my friend until I've known him a year. You have to see him in a variety of situations, and you have to try to get out of a sexual dead end where you're just seeing him as a bed partner. That's not an easy thing to do. Living in a city, where friendships can easily be replaced, the temptation for anonymity and running around irresponsibly is so great that the urge to build a friendship has to be cultivated.

It is during this period of coming out that many young males (between eighteen and twenty-five) go through a crisis of femininity; that is, they "act out" in relatively public places in a somewhat effeminate manner; and some, in a transitory fashion, wear female clothing, known in the homosexual argot as "going in drag." During this period one of the major confirming aspects of masculinity—that is, nonsexual reinforcement by females of masculine status—

has been abandoned, and it is not surprising that the very core of masculine identity should be seriously questioned. A young male who had largely passed through the crisis reported:

> *R:* The next phase was very emotional but even then I still wasn't the same way I am now. It was more sexually oriented. I wasn't ready to get emotionally involved with anyone. And then I was going out with these younger kids that I had met at parties—I was getting very wild that year. Wearing my hair much longer and I moved in with this ——— and we were using make-up and all sorts of things. And then all of a sudden that fall I just . . . things weren't going right for me, I wasn't meeting anybody. I had very few tricks last fall because they just . . . couldn't seem to find anyone I like that liked me. And now I'm just getting away from the whole business. Now I've been trying to get more masculine myself; trying to get away from this acting effeminate because I don't want that.
>
> *Int:* Why was it you started acting this way in the first place?
>
> *R:* Because most of my friends were doing this. It seemed to me to be the right thing to do, the fun thing to do. That's what happens to these younger kids; they feel the same way but they're not as old as I am so they don't have the maturity to realize that they're doing wrong.
>
> *Int:* In what ways are you making yourself more masculine?
>
> *R:* Oh, I'm just not carrying on. I don't use make-up or hair spray or things like that. I try to walk as normal as a person can walk; I don't try to see how swishy I could get. And I try to wear conservative clothes.

This crisis is partially structured by the existing homosexual culture in which persons already in the crisis stage become models for those who are newer to their homosexual commitment. A few males retain this pseudofeminine commitment, a few others masquerade as female prostitutes to males, and still others pursue careers as female impersonators. This adjustment might be more widely adapted if feminine behavior by men—except in sharply delineated occupational roles—was not negatively sanctioned. Thus the tendency is for this kind of behavior to be a transitional experiment for most homosexuals, an experiment that leaves vestiges of "camp" behavior, but more often leaves traces more expressive of the character of the cultural life of the homosexual community than of some overriding need of individual homosexuals.[17] Since this period of personal disorganization and identity problems is at the same time highly visible to the broader community, this femininity is enlisted as evidence for theories of homosexuality that see, as a central component in its etiology, the failure of sexual identification. Because of the absence of conventional structures of social support, the homosexual at this point of his life cycle is more likely to be in psychotherapy. This search for help is often construed as evidence for those theories which argue for the pathology of the homosexual, which is already based on a missampling of the alternative ways of being homosexual or expressing a homosexual preference.

Another life cycle crisis that the homosexual shares with the heterosexual in this youth-oriented society is the crisis of aging. While American society places an inordinate positive emphasis on youth, the homosexual community, by and large, places a still greater emphasis on this fleeting characteristic. Closely associated with age is appearance and, as one of the respondents commented:

> *Int:* What is the first basis of a homosexual's choice?
>
> *R:* First of all, general appearance. If a person is very ugly, short, obese, or crippled those people are often immediately out. Race can be important, but there's another characteristic that's even more important: that's age. If a person is say past forty or for some people even past thirty, his chances are pretty well reduced. Some people past thirty or forty are in pretty good condition and others are not. Baldness, grey hair, wrinkles and that sort of thing, poor dentition, these may be things that repel people.

In general, the homosexual has fewer resources with which to meet this crisis. The heterosexual has his children, whose careers assure a sense of the future, and he has a wife whose sexual availability cushions the shock of declining sexual attractiveness. In addition, the crisis of aging comes later to the heterosexual, at an age when his sexual powers have declined and expectations concerning the significance of his sexuality are considerably lower. The earliness of the impact of aging in the life cycle of the homosexual is often out

17. David Sonenschein, "The Homosexual's Language," (mimeographed, 1968).

of phase with other aspects of aging (occupational, familial, etc.) and is in part shaped by other aspects of the homosexual life history or life style as well.

> *R:* The point I was trying to make is that if you finally came out when you are older and you had this big struggle beforehand, that is, you were not in the pattern of coming out in your early twenties where sex and youthfulness was the big thing. If you come out early, you get into a pattern of lots of sex and as you get older and older you still have all this sex. Even when you settle down, it's still sex, youthfulness, and all these things—and then comes the early thirties and people are just devastated, they really are. I don't know a single person in the early thirties—some that are incredibly good looking and look a lot younger than they are—they are just zonked out by being so because I think they've just been in this youth pattern. Even if they are not being promiscuous at the time they still know about the promiscuity and importance of youth. It's not as bad as that for people who come out after twenty-five or come out fairly late because they haven't been settled into this pattern.

The management of aging by the homosexual is not well understood, but at this point in his life there are a series of behavioral manifestations (symptoms) attendant to this dramatic transition that are misread as universal aspects of homosexuality. At times this sense of dispair can lead to suicide or prolonged depression, but it is clearly not a function of gender preference. Hence, serious feelings of depression or loneliness are often attendant on the age transition in the middle to late thirties. Such symptoms are not uncommon in male and female heterosexuals (especially single or divorced women) at this same age as well.

> *R:* As far as the future is concerned I don't know. I always have the feeling that if the going really did get extremely rough, I could terminate the whole thing rather easily and painlessly and make it appear to be an accidental death. Sometimes I get to thinking about this—I don't know, sometimes it just seems so hard. Now in about five years or possibly ten I'll consider myself more or less—well I shouldn't say it—unattractive. It'll be harder to make contacts. This is another reason why I prefer maybe just one partner to depend on. I mean it's not like a man and woman getting married and they have their differences and split up—they can always find a new partner.

But if a male does this and splits up with someone and he's around, say, forty-five or so, then I think he would have a very much harder time finding someone. And I feel that I'm the type of person that needs somebody and I don't think I could tolerate the situation.

Here, as with "coming out," it is important to note that most homosexuals, even with fewer resources than their heterosexual counterparts, manage to weather the period with relative success. In part this successful transition from one stage to another in the life cycle depends on the affection and support of the others. As with heterosexuals the waning sexual interest is managed while emotional ties remain the significant basis of individual morale. As a fifty-year-old male reported:

> *R:* We go on vacations together now and of course since we are apart . . . not "apart." I mean we live together, and we sleep together, and we kiss each other good morning and good night. And we sorta neck around a little once in awhile—even at our age; because it is enjoyable, we both want it. As with most married people, when you get older, it's a sense of having somebody around; it's not sex, because there's no attraction, but we love being around each other. We enjoy an evening at home. He'll get busy doing something and I'll get busy doing something. And we feel we have a very happy home life. We've got a nice circle of friends that aren't a bunch of screaming meemies, and they've been together ten, twelve, fifteen years and they're couples too. Once in a while, we'll get a couple of singles in. It's nice to have some young blood around us once in a while; sometimes we like them, sometimes we don't.

A central concern underlying these options and the management of a homosexual career is the presence and complexity of a homosexual community, which for some persons serves simply as a sexual marketplace, but for others provides the locus of friendships, opportunities, recreation, and expansion of the base of social life. Such a community is filled with both formal and informal institutions for meeting others and for following, to the degree the individual wants, a homosexual life style. Minimally, the community provides a source of social support, for it is one of the few places where the homosexual may get positive validation of his own self-image. Though the community often provides more feminine or "camp" behavior than many participants might desire, in a major sense "camp" behavior is often an expression of aggregate community characteristics without an equal commitment to this behavior on the part of its members. They participate in the homosexual bar culture because "gay bars" are a required sexual meeting place. Older or more conventional homosexuals often have ambivalent feelings about such establishments.

> *R:* The bars are not good places certainly, but I don't know any better places. I would wish that in the future that the public in general would accept homosexuality for what it is so that homosexuals could have a means of meeting. You could meet someone who had common interest. I think a lot of times that many homosexuals feel that the only way they are going to meet someone is if they act obviously Nellie. And this is the very type that I feel the most aversion for.

Further "low camp" behavior involving exaggerated feminine mannerisms may also be seen as a form of interpersonal communication characteristic of intracommunity behavior and significantly altered for most during interaction with the larger society. Hence a young male just through the coming out period, but still attached to the bar and the gay scene, describes "camping" as:

> *R:* The only term I can think of is just goofing around. You're out with the boys and you begin talking girl talk. In homosexual life you can make a boy's first name into a girl's name. Like mine is Tabatha, Mark is Mary Ann, and my brother George they call Penny. It's a big joke. At a party it's fine, but on the outside, forget it. Most of them are self-conscious about the fact that they are homosexual and they don't want to start flicking the street and being fruity. If I see someone acting fruity on the street down in the city, well, I've got too much at stake at work and at school, and my folks have a pretty big business. I wouldn't want to wreck them so I keep my mouth shut. If I see somebody like that I avoid them.

A parallel expression to "low camp" in the homosexual community as a form of communication is the playful, intellectual practice of "high camp." In part a style or class-linked practice, "high camp" also penetrates the larger society's interests.

R: I'm camping more than I used to. It means letting yourself go, but it doesn't involve so much the femininity as it involves the spinning out ideas and words—that kind of thing. If you read Susan Sontag's book you can tell more about it. It's something like "playing the dozens" in the ghetto, but it really has a lot of intellectual content with the right people.

The community serves as a way of mediating sexuality by providing a situation in which one can know and evaluate peers and, in a significant sense, convert sexual behavior into sexual conduct.[18] Insofar as the community provides these relationships for the individual homosexual, it allows for the dilution, complication, and enhancement of overt sexual activity by providing sociosexual gratification in ways that are not directly sexual. Consequently, the homosexual with access to the community is more protected from impulsive sexual "acting out" than the homosexual who has only his own fear and knowledge of the society's prohibitions to mediate his sexual impulses.

It should be pointed out that—in contrast to some ethnic and occupational subcultures—the homosexual community, like many other deviant subcommunities, has very limited content.[19] This derives from the fact that the community members often have only their sexual commitment in common. Thus, while the community may reduce the problems of access to sexual partners and reduce guilt by providing a structure of shared values, often the shared value structure is far too narrow to transcend other areas of value disagreement. The college-trained professional and the bus boy, the

18. Ernest W. Burgess makes this useful distinction in his article, "The Sociologic Theory of Psychosexual Behavior," in *Psychosexual Development in Health and Disease,* eds. Paul H. Hoch and Joseph Zubin (New York: Grune & Stratton, 1949), pp. 227–43. Burgess says; "Accurately speaking, the various forms of sexual outlet for man are not behavior, they are conduct. Conduct is behavior as prescribed or evaluated by the group. It is not simply external observable behavior, but behavior that expresses a norm or evaluation."

19. For descriptions of the content of other deviant subcultures see, Harold Finestone, "Cats, Kicks, and Color," *Social Problems* 5 (July 1957): 3–13. Howard S. Becker, *The Outsiders* (New York: The Free Press, 1963); James H. Bryan, "Apprenticeships in Prostitution," *Social Problems* 12 (Winter 1965): 278–97.

white Anglo-Saxon Protestant and the Negro slum dweller may meet in sexual congress, but the similarity of their sexual interests does not eliminate larger social and cultural barriers.[20] The important fact is that the homosexual community, as it exists at the present time, is in itself an impoverished cultural unit. This impoverishment, however, may be only partially limiting, since it constrains most members to participate in it on a limited basis, reducing their anxiety and conflicts in the sexual sphere and increasing the quality of their performance in other aspects of social life.

Managing life cycle crises in the midst of the homosexual community presents problems of one sort to the homosexual, problems that are often shared by heterosexuals; there are other general norm life cycle changes that they share: earning a living, maintaining a residence, relations with family, and so on. At this point we might consider some of these in greater detail.

First there is the most basic problem of all: earning a living. Initially, the variables that apply to all labor force participants generally apply to homosexuals also. In addition, there are the special conditions imposed by the deviant and criminal definition of the homosexual commitment. What is important is that the occupational activity of homosexuals represents a fairly broad range. The differences in occupational activity can be conceptualized along a number of dimensions, some of which would be conventional concerns of occupational sociology, while others would reflect the special situation of the homosexual. For example, one element is the degree of occupational involvement—that is, the degree to which occupational activity, or activity ancillary to it, is defined as intrinsically gratifying. This would obviously vary from professional man to ribbon clerk to factory laborer. Evidence of these occupational constraints on sexual expression, which can be set by even the trivi-

---

20. The homosexual community does provide for an easing of strain by training working- and lower-class males in middle-class lifestyles and even middle-class occupational roles to a greater extent than most people realize. In contrast, for those whom homosexuality becomes the salient organizing experience of their lives there may be a concomitant downward mobility as their ties with commitments to systems of roles that are larger than the homosexual community decrease.

al problem of the hours of work, is reported by a young medical student:

> *R:* Well, it took awhile for me to stop running around so much, but I went right into a program in the medical field. Fortunately my hours were that I had to be in bed at a reasonable hour, like about 9:30, 9:00 if I could make it, because I had to be up at 5:30. I have to be in surgery at 7:00 and I'm on my feet from 7:00 until 3:30 and I am tired. I'm the kind of person that needs eight hours sleep or I'm not any good for the next day. So this affected me a lot.

A corollary to this is the degree to which the world of work penetrates other aspects of life. In terms of influence upon a homosexual career, occupational involvement very likely plays a constraining role during the acting-out phase associated with "coming out," as well as serving as an alternative source of investment during the "crisis of aging." The impact of a strong career commitment can directly shape the homosexual interest, dominating as it does with heterosexuals all aspects of life.

> *R:* I usually don't think about long-term relationships because I think I have very little control over it and it involves somebody else. I mean I can never tell who I am going to meet or what's going to happen, but as long as whatever happens doesn't affect my career or anything connected with that in my profession, I would probably let it happen if I thought it was beneficial for my personal life. But I'm not planning everything out—"I'm having a future lover who is going to live with me for ever and ever" and things like that. I would just let happen what happens. If a permanent love doesn't come along it really won't upset me. It is not my primary interest. My primary interest is my professional life.
>
> The more I learn about myself of course, the more discriminating I become about my associations with people. I only want to associate with people who are professionally very much like I am. The older I get the more I want this common factor between my friends and myself. And I find to a great extent, that most homosexuals do not fit into the same things I fit into. This is true I suppose with heterosexuals, but I don't think it is any more true with homosexuals than heterosexuals. The older I have gotten, I have limited my associations, and the only time I would come into contact with homosexuals

would be in the field of —— where I know quite a few of them. They would not necessarily be friends of mine but I would work with them. That's probably the only way I would associate with them.

Another aspect bears directly upon the issue of the consequence of having one's deviant commitment exposed.

R: You're careful that you don't go around with a sign on your back or anything—the scarlet letter is still scarlet as far as most people are concerned. You wear the red H on your forehead, people are going to avoid you. I think most people today are a little more broadminded than they were, say, ten years ago, but when it comes to the economics of daily living—I have had an experience where I lost a job because I was gay. They found out I was gay and the boss wasn't going to have any queers working for him; it's as simple as that. It was never given as the excuse, but I know that that was why I lost my job. And after that I vowed that I wasn't going to work any place that did not know it, and I had several interviews where I made it a point they knew it. There was one job that I was very qualified for and he asked me why I lost my last position, and I said "I got fired because I was queer, and I'm telling you this because I would not want that to happen again." And he says, "Oh, that doesn't have any effect on us. We have several people of that type of personality up here," which was true, I happen to know that—including him—but nevertheless I did not get hired. Finally I gave up on it and the job I have now I didn't mention it. I couldn't go along without making a living forever. You can't find a job if you're gay and want to admit it.

For some occupational roles disclosure would clearly be a disaster —the schoolteacher, the minister, and the politician, to mention just three. There are other occupations where the disclosure or assumption of homosexual interests is either of little consequence or —though relatively rare—has a positive consequence. It should be evident that the crucial question of anxiety and depersonalization in the conduct of sexual activity can be linked to this variable in a rather direct way.

A second series of questions could deal with the effects of a deviant sexual commitment upon occupational activity itself. In some cases the effect may be extremely negative, since the pursuit of homosexual interests may generate irresponsibility and irregularity.

Some part of this might flow from what we associate with bachelor-hood generally: detachment from conventional families and, in terms of sex, constant striving for what is essentially regularized in marriage. Illustrations of this kind of behavior include too many late nights out, too much drinking in too many taverns, and unevenness in emotional condition. On the other hand, several positive effects can be observed. Detachment from the demands of domestic life not only frees one for greater dedication to the pursuit of sexual goals, but also for greater dedication to work. Also, a compensatory occupational conservatism can occur so that job effort is increased to reduce anxiety and fear of exposure. Such a compensatory strategy can even be ideologized in some cases into a traditional Horatio Alger posture.

> *R:* You try harder because you think you have to. Try to make yourself indispensable. I think that's probably the basic secret of it: do more than is expected of you and do your job well and continue education and study, improving your abilities and positions, and after you reach a certain point and if anyone makes any snide comments to anyone in the organization, well the boss would say "Well, I wish you'd do your job as well." What people do in their own time, as long as they're not getting involved or anything like that, that's their own business. I think that any homosexual that faces the issue and is satisfied with the fact that he is as good as anyone else, and probably better if he applies himself, is going to be real happy in the homosexual world.

The ability of some jobs to facilitate homosexual activity—certain marginal, low-paying, white-collar jobs, for example—serves as compensation for low pay or limited opportunity for advancement. There may be few simple or consistent patterns emerging from this type of consideration, yet the tendency to overemphasize the sexual element in the study of the homosexual is due to our prior reluctance to consider nonsexual questions which are both complex and pedestrian.

Similarly, just as most homosexuals have to earn a living, so must they come to terms with their immediate families. There is no substantial evidence to suggest that the proportion of homosexuals having significant relationships with relatives differs from that of

heterosexuals. The important differences rest in the way the relationships are managed and, again, the consequences they have for other
aspects of life. Here also one could expect considerable variations
containing patterns of rejection, continuing involvement without
knowledge, ritualistically suppressed knowledge, and knowledge
and acceptance. This becomes more complex because several patterns may be operative at the same time with different members of
one's family constellation. In some cases we can observe a continuing and positive structure of relations beginning in early life. An
older man reports:

> *R:* I came from a beautiful family. My father has been dead now
> for about eighteen years, but mother is still living—she's seventy and
> still working. I have a sister who is five years younger than I am; she
> is married, and she has had three children, a boy and two girls. The
> boy's in college; the girls are married and they have children, so that
> makes my mother a greatgrandmother, which is very happy for her.
> In fact, my sister, mother, and I went west for two weeks, just the
> three of us, and I said, after the trip was over, "Now, isn't it unusual
> that a family after all these years can still go and have a tremendous
> time, just the three of us." We enjoyed it, and there haven't been any
> squabbles, but the main point is that I had this tremendous home life.

Here again, it is not unreasonable to assume a considerable degree
of variation in the course of managing a homosexual commitment,
because this kind of factor varies. Yet the literature is almost totally
without reference to these family relationships. Curiously, in the
psychiatric literature—where mother and father play crucial roles
in the formation of a homosexual commitment—they tend to be
significant by their absence in considerations of how homosexual
careers are managed. The dynamic and changing character of family relations is obscured in the analytic literature with its historical
emphasis. Hence the process of parents and children coming to
terms with each other is as apparent in homosexual as heterosexual
life:

> *R:* My parents were always very understanding if I wanted to go
> away for the weekend. All they asked was where I was going and
> who I was going with. While I didn't like to be questioned so much,
> if anything happened it was only right for them to know anyway; I

was still just a kid. As long as they were helping to foot the bills, I owed it to them. They were really good parents. They're quite understanding.

Int: Did you always feel very close to them?

R: I didn't used to. I always liked my mother, but my father was very businesslike in our house and I never got very close to my father. I was always more or less afraid of him because I got so tired of listening to his lectures. But now that I am getting older, I see he's a very wise man and I love him very much. Every day he tells me something else just a little smarter and makes me listen. I used to sit there and let it go right through one ear and out the next. I had no interest whatsoever. But I got hit in the face a couple of times, not physically, but mentally, and I know it's either shape up or be a flop. I can't work it all out myself and so I listen to him and he's a very wise man.

This order of discussion could be extended into a large number of areas. Let us consider just one more—religion. As a variable, religion (as both an identification and a quality of religiosity) manifests no indication that it plays an important role in the generation of homosexual commitments. However, it clearly does, or can, play a significant role in the management of that commitment. Here, as in other spheres of life, we must be prepared to deal with complex, interactive relations rather than fixed, static ones. Crucial to the homosexual's ability to "accept himself" is his ability to bring his own homosexuality within a sense of the moral order as it is projected by the institutions surrounding him as well as by his own vision of this order. The process of coming to terms with a religious commitment is deeply involved and can often involve a stronger as well as a weaker attachment to religious values:

Int: May I ask your religious preference?

R: I am a Christian. I read the Bible as much as I can, though I don't go to church as much as I should. I'm of no set denomination, but I believe in the Lord. I take the Bible for what it's worth and I try to live this day in and day out in anything I do, even in homosexual life. This contradicts what it says in the Bible about homosexuality, but unfortunately I'm not strong enough to help myself just yet. Someday, I hope, maybe I can look back and say I was going through a homosexual stage, but obviously this is playing cat and

mouse with myself. I know there's somebody up there helping me because I could never do it alone.

This strong but troubled attachment is frequently countered by a
drift away from religion:

> *R:* As far as religion is concerned my eyes have been opened to a
> lot of the fallacies of religion. It's not the idea that I'm trying to poke
> at religion, and I feel I'm not. Sure don't intend to be a hypocrite,
> and I feel that by being associated with a religion that says "you
> can't do this and you can't do that and you must do this"—but you
> still have the option of going in to confess it, and you can still go
> back and do it again—this is being hypocritical. I'm not doing any-
> thing that I'm ashamed of; I'm doing what nature has provided for,
> whether it might be warped in some people's minds. And so I grad-
> ually eased myself out of the Catholic Church and Mother knows it.

It may be that the issue of including homosexuality within a religious definition is the way the question should be framed only part
of the time, and for only part of a homosexual population. At other
times, and for other homosexuals, to frame the question in terms of
bringing religiosity within the homosexual definition might be more
appropriate. In the two following instances, strong religious commitments were retained but reshaped to meet the exigencies of
homosexuality. The conventional religious values are expanded to
include homosexuality, in one case by an appeal to tolerance, in the
other by examples of good behavior outside of homosexuality.

> *R:* I feel that I'm drawing a bigger circle than they are. I'm ac-
> cepting them. I think their attitude is wrong and they are losing out.
> I'm bigger than they are, so to speak. This doesn't drive me away
> even though I hear it in the sermon once in a while—something re-
> lated to homosexuality. I feel I have understanding they don't have,
> and I cannot do without God and the Church.
> *R:* Well, I mean, the way I feel about it, you believe in God, and I
> think you lead your life the way you see fit to lead it, and I'm sure
> that God will accept it, I mean, it isn't that you're committing a sin
> and I always feel that believing in God and doing his wishes as far as
> your Christian life is concerned, I think that he'll accept it. I mean,
> that he won't condemn you, as far as the Lord is concerned. I mean,
> I don't think that he would condemn you, because it's your life and

you actually are not committing a sin, so I feel that he'll accept you and won't turn you down.

By personalizing the deity, an approach shared by many noninstitutionally committed persons, homosexuality itself is revalued.

The need for damnation (that rare sense of being genuinely evil) and the need for redemption (a sense of potentially being returned to the community in good standing) can be expected to vary, given different stages of the life cycle, different styles of being homosexual, and varying environments for enactment of the homosexual commitment. And our sense of the relation suggests that, more than asking about the homosexual's religious orientation and how it expresses his homosexuality, we must also learn to ask how his homosexuality expresses his commitment to the religious.

Criminality and Decriminalization

Central to relationships between the conventional and the unconventional aspects of the homosexual's life is the disadvantaged position that he is placed in by the existence of legal sanctions against homosexual behavior. The law is at the center of a good many of the male homosexual's dilemmas, because it converts an unchosen condition into a legal disability. There has been a recent press for change in these statutes by both homosexual and nonhomosexual members of the society in an attempt to move homosexual behavior, insofar as it does not involve force, seduction of minors, public outrage, or the misuse of authority, outside the realm of criminal law. It is important to consider at least some of the consequences of this attempt at legal reform and its effect on the homosexual and the society at large. Such a change, by and large, is in agreement with the recommendations of the American Law Institute, the Wolfenden Report in England, and the current Criminal Code of Canada and four states of the Union. It involves, however, a larger segment of the society than merely the homosexual. If one is to say that homosexual contacts between consenting adults should not be against the law, then why should one have heterosexual offenses against the law unless they fall under the same prohibitory headings: those that involve force, great disparities in age, abuse of authority, and public outrage? In this sense offenses such as prostitution, pornography, adultry, fornication, and mouth-genital contact in or out of marriage would cease to be violations of the criminal statutes[21] and would fall into that zone of behavior which is covered by religious codes but is not subject to the police power of the state.[22]

The request of the homosexual that his sexual behavior be considered part of the private rather than public zone of action and the concern of morality rather than the statutory law involves a series of questions:

1. In what manner does the imposition of criminal sanctions on adult homosexual behavior affect the genesis of homosexual development?

2. Does the imposition of criminal sanctions reduce the total number of homosexual actors or acts through the principle of deterrence?

3. Does the existence of the law have any secondary impacts on the mental health of the homosexual?

4. Does the law aid persons in being able to leave a homosexual career; that is, does the existence of the criminal code aid in a reentry into a heterosexual way of life?

If some of the roots of homosexual (as well as heterosexual) potential are to be found in early family life, and if most of the early, overt reinforcements of this potential occur between adolescents, then the imposition of sanctions on homosexual adults seems beside the point. Few of us would propose a situation wherein the psychological patterns of mothering or fathering came under the scrutiny of the criminal law. It would appear that the genesis of homosex-

21. As they still are in most states of the Union.

22. The crucial thrust of these ideas is that sexuality is part of the private life of the individual. The role of the homosexuals in this struggle for change is quite interesting, for they represent a group of persons who are organized to promote change and who will cause change in other areas as a result. Thus, the intense stigma attached to the homosexual in contrast to the fornicator or the adulterer is what gives him some social power and cohesiveness. This is parallel to the argument that the American Civil Rights movement is a vanguard for the rights of the poor of whatever race. The black laboring under a special disability can call attention to the problems of class, poverty, and opportunity.

uality is probably outside the control of any such set of legal mechanisms.

It is in reducing the numbers of homosexual actors and acts that legal sanctions against homosexuality are likely to be most effective; that is, they can make the conditions of homosexual behavior sufficiently risky and unpalatable to the individual so that he will either remain inactive or reduce the frequency of his activity. In the case of the inactive male, the option is to remain homosexual in his wishes but celibate in his behavior. In the case of the man who operates with great caution, his sexual life is pursued under conditions of considerable anxiety. Such deterrence of homosexual acts does occur; however, the dimensions of it are obscure and the psychological consequences for the individual who accepts these options of coping with his homosexual impulses may be very unhealthy.

The criminal law and the stigma given to homosexual behavior result in some considerable mental health risks for the individual homosexual. There are those males who have major homosexual preferences but who, through processes of inhibition and repression, deny these impulses and take up heterosexual marriage. In a recent study these males were found to have the strongest propensities for sexual contact with children and youth.[23] Their homosexual behavior is often connected with conditions of unbearable stress in other areas of life, and they suddenly fall into homosexual contacts that almost invariably lead to arrest and legal involvement. Such males rarely appear in the homosexual community and are rarely identifiable prior to the criminal act.

The conditions imposed by the law affect those homosexuals who have entered upon a homosexual career as well as those who have dealt with their impulses in other ways. The law and the stigma attached to being homosexual make the life of the homosexual open to other disabilities; he is vulnerable to blackmail, to being assaulted or mugged by his sexual partners, to being entrapped by the police, and is often driven to seek sexuality under extremely unpleasant and ugly circumstances. In an attempt to show a basically

23. Paul H. Gebhard, J. H. Gagnon, W. B. Pomeroy, and C. V. Christenson, *Sex Offenders: An Analysis of Types* (New York: Harper & Row, 1965).

conventional façade to the world, many homosexuals become over-conformists in all other aspects of life. But at the same time, their sexual activities are performed in bus stations, public toilets, and public parks. In this sense, the sexual life remains unsocialized and invulnerable to the emotional attachments and affections which serve as stabilizing forces for the personality of the individual. Self-hatred on the part of many homosexuals is commonly observed, and is not unlike the self-hatred of other despised minority groups who receive harsh treatment from society. This self-hatred is self-defeating and self-damaging, and it arises more out of the legal and social status of the homosexual than from deeper psychic roots.

The existence of the law, and its tendency to segregate the homosexual, also has negative consequences for those who wish to change their sexual patterns. The existence of a homosexual community and culture that is outside the law is double-edged, for it not only makes life more bearable for the homosexual in the society but makes it difficult for him to leave this adjustment. Just as the significant element in the phrase "the culture of poverty" is not poverty, but culture, the significant problem for the homosexual is that he is embedded in a series of satisfying and meaningful social relationships that serve to make his world orderly, intelligible, and integrated. The existence of this culture, while serving the individual well in some ways, makes him less reachable by conventional therapies and social agencies when he suffers from problems, whether or not these problems are associated with a homosexual preference. While the utility of individual therapy is often in doubt, until structural conditions are changed the individual homosexual remains at considerable risk and may require this intervention.

The tendency to define the person in terms of his homosexuality rather than in some larger way also creates therapeutic problems, since it reduces his relationship with the conventional world through which he might return to society. Thus, for the delinquent boy, one route back into conventional society is an honorable discharge from the army that wipes out the past or a marriage to a respectable girl who takes him out of the gang by giving him a new and meaningful set of relationships to the rest of society. The tendency to make sex excessively important in the life of the homosexual decreases his capacities to use other routes of communication with the larger world in order to deal with any problem.

It is certainly possible to suggest that there would be far more circulation of persons out of the homosexual world into the heterosexual one than vice versa if the sanctions and stigma were not so heavy and so overwhelming. Indeed, our very sense of a boundary between one preference and the other derives from these legal sanctions. Without the boundaries between the behaviors the very idea of a restricted life style existing for what we now call heterosexuals or homosexuals may disappear. What often amazes an observer of the homosexual world is the small amount of serious pathology that really exists, given the conditions under which the homosexual life is lived.

Once one has raised the issue of changing the homosexual, the quite important but often overlooked question is: Into what, sexually at least, should he be changed? Most people would prefer that the homosexual be changed into a heterosexual. However, what is not dealt with is the problem of where the homosexual will get heterosexual practice—that is, with whom will he have essentially therapeutic sexual experiences? There is rarely a confrontation with the fact that many of the heterosexual activities that the homosexual is to perform are also against the criminal law if performed outside marriage. It is very difficult to prescribe a treatment for homosexuality that does not include creative and positive emotional attachments to new persons—women for the male homosexual and men for the female homosexual.

The law is one of the major forces that shapes the context in which the homosexual lives out his life. However, it is not the sole institution which effects his behavior. Often, though forming a backdrop against which he performs, it is not the most salient factor. The problem is to locate the homosexual life within a context of both the pedestrian and the seemingly exotic. It is only at the intersection of these individual and situational forces that we can examine the contingencies of the homosexual career.

Homosexual Prostitution

Like all forms of collective sexual deviance, male homosexuality tends to create at its periphery a substantial number of persons who are involved in the staging or performance of various parts of the homosexual life. The owner of the homosexual meeting place, the bartenders, the owners and clerks in boutiques for men, the models, the makers and purveyors of erotic photographs and films of males are all service personnel generated by the existence of a homosexual subculture. The majority of personnel in these service occupations are themselves homosexual, and are more likely to be publicly homosexual than homosexuals in other, more conventional occupations. These are occupations which can tolerate and even promote the exaggerated feminine or camp elements of the homosexual life style. In a very important sense, these occupations are the ones that promote a great deal of continuity in the homosexual subculture and, by virtue of their visible nature, produce a public image of homosexuality that is at variance with the behavior of the largest number of the subculture's members. Even though these occupational locations are the most deviant from the point of view of the larger culture, as a result of their public nature they do not require so much concealment of homosexual interests. Therefore, they may not be so psychologically costly in terms of keeping major components of the self secret from the larger society.

In addition to these roles which promote homosexual presentations that are public in nature, there is one other central figure in the homosexual world who often depends in large measure for his success on being, or at least presenting himself as, exclusively heterosexual. This is the male prostitute.[24] The male prostitute plays for the male homosexual many of the same roles that the female prostitute does for heterosexual men, but the role takes on additional complexity since the male prostitute faces a client population that has a subcultural aspect quite unlike that of the female prostitute's heterosexual client. Furthermore, there are certain aspects of male prostitution that arise specifically from the way in which male homosexual preferences are organized in this culture.

One of these central differences is that the female prostitute is paid so that her client can have an orgasm, while in nearly all of the cases the male prostitute is paid for his orgasm. Therefore, unlike the female prostitute, the male prostitute must have sufficient sexual arousal from the contact to become erect and have orgasm. Thus,

24. Estimates of the frequency of contact with prostitutes by homosexuals are presently unknown.

unlike the female prostitute, the male prostitute is limited in the number of contacts he may have over a short period of time by the refractory period to sexual stimulation that follows orgasm in the male. While there are males who can have more than one orgasm over a single twenty-four hour period (and there is evidence from non-Western cultures that this is a more common physical capacity than Western men exhibit), the capacity for two or three orgasms per day is usually limited to the young and the healthy. The requirement of arousal to the point of orgasm in these sexual encounters on the part of men who are either predominently interested in females or make such a presentation has consequences for both patterns of recruitment to the occupation and to levels of economic reward. Since the female prostitute needs to have neither arousal nor sexual pleasure, she may engage in prostitution without sexual interest in her partner and have contact with substantial numbers of males over relatively short periods of time.

The Homosexual as Client

Much of the content and character of contacts with homosexual prostitutes arises from the character of the homosexual lifestyle itself. Even though a substantial number of homosexuals do go to prostitutes, paying for sex is evidence that one is unable to compete for it on the free market—that is, that one is unattractive or inept at making a sexual approach. It is clear from our discussion of female prostitution (chap. 7) that a certain proportion of a prostitute's clients are those physically unable (the ugly, the handicapped) or socially unable to operate in normal sociosexual encounters. While these persons represent some of the customers of prostitutes—those who find the usual channels of sexual access too difficult to manage —they are clearly not the majority.

Once again, like prostitution in the heterosexual world, there are elements of erotic degradation in paying for a sexual encounter. However, unlike the heterosexual world where the paying of money degrades the woman—making her into a more erotic object, an object to which anything can be done without consequence—in the homosexual world the payment of money often has the effect of degrading the customer.[25] In the heterosexual world, power in some limited sense in the interaction falls to the customer following the exchange of money; in most acts of homosexual prostitution the customer remains the supplicant of the prostitute. The range of sexual techniques permitted will be highly stereotyped and limited, especially when the partners are playing out a situation in which the heterosexuality of the prostitute is what is being paid for.

This commitment to the heterosexual character of the male prostitute is often central to the relationship. Much of the sexual content of some homosexuals' lives is stereotyped around the heterosexual pattern. The contact between heterosexuals is well differentiated in terms of sets of defined modes of approach and withdrawal, linked to the playing out of nonsexual gender roles. Such self-other differentiation is often sought by homosexuals in seeking persons with whom to have sexual contact. Commonly, this search for differentiation occurs along some symbolic axis that relates to masculine or feminine role presentations that the homosexual (as much as the heterosexual) mistakes as a commitment to heterosexuality or homosexuality. It is this drive for differentiation from the self that often leads homosexuals to contacts with men in uniform, truck drivers, stevedores, or men in other masculine-typed occupations, to men of other races, and to prostitutes who are commonly referred to as "rough trade." Two motives may be untangled in these kinds of contacts. The first is one of self-degradation. Contact with men who are symbolically more powerful gives the sexual act a greater sense of tension through increased risk. At the same time, a desire for power over the heterosexual is also evoked. By the act of arousing the prostitute and "making" him ejaculate, the homosexual male acts out a drama in which he is in power over the heterosexual male. He also reduces his own deviance by confirming his belief that there is an element of homosexuality in all men.

A less complex set of motivations exists among those male homosexuals who, like heterosexuals, are in positions where their sexual needs must remain anonymous and protected.[26] The homosexual

25. Thomas Painter, "Male Homosexuals and their Prostitutes in Contemporary America," 2 vols. (unpublished, 1941).

26. For the distinction between overt and covert homosexuals see Maurice Leznoff and William A. Westley, "The Homosexual Community," *Social Problems* 3 (April 1956): 257–67.

businessman or executive is even more vulnerable than the hetero-sexual who engages in deviant sexual activity. Contact with prostitutes provides an outlet that does not have the risks that creating a series of close sexual friendships might, nor does it necessarily contain the risk comparable to that of going to locales where known homosexuals congregate. (Not untypically, such homosexuals fear disclosure to other homosexuals almost as much as they fear disclosure to nonhomosexuals.) This is especially true when contact with prostitutes occurs outside of the city or neighborhood where the individual lives or works. There are risks in contacts with prostitutes, as we shall see, but often these risks are run by men who find that conventional access to homosexual contacts is denied them. Another group of men in this class, who go to prostitutes out of convenience or because of restrictions of sexual opportunity, are those males who are themselves homosexual but have heterosexual families. These men, often bisexual, go to prostitutes because they are unable to create other liaisons due to the great social risks involved.

A final major component in going to male prostitutes is a desire among many homosexuals for young men. Here, many of the components of heterosexual contacts are to be found in homosexual relationships. The society of the United States is youth-oriented in both its heterosexual and homosexual worlds. The physical attractiveness of the young is a major element in sexual desirability. To gain access to the young and the attractive, it is often necessary to pay some kind of price whether one is heterosexual or homosexual —in today's world the young desire the young. In order for an older male to enter this world, he must pay either in money or in allowing access to rewards that would not normally be available to the young. While real affection can and does exist in both worlds between people of disparate ages, this is not a common phenomenon, and such encounters are often contaminated by other considerations.

The Transient Majority

Unlike the female prostitute, whose first paid encounter often comes after a fairly substantial career of unpaid heterosexual contact, for many men (perhaps the majority) payment for a homosexual experience is either part of a single homosexual experience or one of just a few experiences.

A substantial number of young men in relatively isolated social situations (out of money, without friends, traveling, and the like) are approached by homosexuals who offer them money for a simple act of fellatio. The encounter goes no further in terms of physical intimacy. It begins and it is over within a few moments. Sometimes the encounter will involve returning to the homosexual's quarters and staying the night, but more commonly the encounter will have little social dimension. Such an experience may occur while young men are hitchhiking, living transiently in a youth hostel or hotel, or wandering in a marginal bright lights section of a community.[27] For the heterosexual young man this social isolation, the fleeting nature of the contact and the money serve to reduce any sense of personal homosexuality. He must, however, have the minimal capacity to symbolically transform the homosexual act by neutralizing it into a merely physical response or to imagine a heterosexual stimulus. Without these circumstances of isolation and the minimum ability to transform the situation, he will be unable to sustain his sexual response. Outside of this circumstance, it is unlikely that he will pursue homosexual relationships.

Another relatively common situation for transient homosexual prostitution occurs when a collection of young men, often in the military service in a strange community, are seeking heterosexual adventure. Often their search is in vain. In a state of mild sexual excitement and commonly somewhat intoxicated, they may be approached either singly or as a group by a male homosexual. If the young man is approached singly, his reaction will be similar to the young man who is approached in social isolation. If the group is approached, what occurs is dependent on the prior experience of the members and the power structure of the peer group itself. If the consensus is for cooperating, the group values themselves serve to neutralize the homosexual character of the event in addition to the mechanisms cited above.

Another common collective situation that can lead to paid homosexual encounters comes out of the street group culture of many U.S.

27. Reiss, "The Social Integration of Queers and Peers."

cities. Many lower-class young men spend a great deal of time in gang behavior engaging in delinquent and quasi-delinquent activities.[28] Depending on many characteristics of the local community and the gang, some or many members of the gang will engage in transitory contacts with homosexuals for pay. The act is perceived by the heterosexual participants as ways to make money when they are out of funds. Depending on the local gang culture, such encounters may be relatively aggressively pursued, or they will be waited for almost passively. Gangs can develop a fairly long-term contact with a series of males who buy liquor for underage members, supply them with money, drive them around in their cars, and do over favors. The contacts are viewed in much the same light as contact with female prostitutes or contacts with promiscuous girls in the neighborhood.

All of these relationships with males who are predominantly heterosexual have serious elements of risk. The etiquette of the contact requires that the client very carefully refrain from raising the homosexual nature of the contact, that the physical contact be only with the genitals, and that there is no expectation of reciprocity.[29] The image of the self as heterosexual on the part of the prostitute is very delicately balanced, and if there is an imputation that the prostitute is enjoying the act out of homosexual motivations serious violence can result. Some of these reactions may well be what has been clinically described as homosexual panic. The prostitute, formerly secure in his heterosexual self-image, suddenly suspects that he is being aroused by the homosexual content of the transaction. The reaction is often a retreat to physical violence, since assaulting the homosexual now reasserts his dominance and his masculinity. This potential is especially true in group encounters with young men where, after the sexual contact occurs, the group of men assault the homosexual in order to continue to see themselves and each other as heterosexual. This same process also occurs in delinquent gangs where the homosexual contact is followed by assault and robbery of the homosexual. Among some delinquent gangs, members deliberately play the role of prostitute in order to rob the

28. Ibid., p. 199.
29. Ibid., p. 214–26.

customer. Since the homosexual was engaged in what is illegal behavior, he has no recourse to the police. As we will see, the robbery
and blackmail of the homosexual occurs among more professional
prostitutes as well.

These transients make up the majority of men who in their lives
have had a homosexual contact for pay. The vast majority remain
heterosexual and continue to see their homosexual contacts as
merely "playing the queers."

Apprentices, Hustlers, and Call Boys

The apprentices in the life of homosexual prostitution are drawn
from the subgroup of originally heterosexual males and some homosexual males. For many young men living at the edge of conventional social life, living lives of bare economic subsistence and
lacking skills or training, the first accidental homosexual encounter
may lead to still others. The relatively easy money, the personal
attention, the comparatively exciting life can be attractive to the
young, unattached male. If he is physically attractive he will find
that by going to certain street locations in large cities or to specifically homosexual gathering places he will be approached by a
substantial number of men who will pay him for sexual contact.[30]
He may be advised to these locations by his first customer. If he
wishes to continue in the trade, he will learn that there are modes of
receiving money and maintaining the normative character of the relationship. The life on the street leads to further detachment from
conventional life. He will come into contact with other prostitutes
and they will describe and discuss customers, homosexual techniques, and the ways of the life. His newness on the street will at
first assure him of customers simply because he is new. Like any
prostitute his physical attributes, including penis size, will be talked
about in the client world, creating his market price and desirability.
To the degree that he maintains a physical attitude of nonreciproci-
ty in homosexual acts, he will retain a certain set of customers; but
he will find that the longer he is around the life the greater the sus-

30. H. Lawrence Ross, "The 'Hustler' in Chicago," *The Journal of Student Research* 50 (September 1959): 15.

picion is that he is, in fact, homosexual himself. As a protection against homosexual ideation and reaction, many of these young men have extensive contacts with the pre-prostitute females who are to be found in the same half-world of the street.

In some cases, young men who are themselves homosexual also go through this process as their way into a homosexual lifestyle. An earlier homosexual commitment takes on its beginning form through prostitution, just as if the individual were totally heterosexual. This role-playing is often a transitory phenomenon, and a young male with strong prior homosexual proclivities begins to reciprocate in the paid encounters. If such young men are attractive, they will continue to be paid for sexual relationships that either do or do not involve reciprocity, but their own homosexuality will drive away those customers who are paying for the illusion or the reality of heterosexual conquest or degradation.

Time and self-conception combine to move the young man from apprenticeship to hustler status. When the young man moves from sporadic, unsought encounters to spending time on the street or other locations where he is available to clients on a full-time or weekend basis, his status changes both for himself and for others. Once a young man has appeared on the street often enough and has had sex with enough men, he may maintain his self-image as heterosexual but becomes identified as a hustler. This status, however, is not nearly as irreversible a situation as the movement into female prostitution.

The bulk of even these young men will, as apprentices or hustlers, drift out of the world of prostitution if they remain heterosexual, since the search for newness and variety is endemic in this sector of the homosexual comminity. New faces and new bodies will replace these young men in the street and bar culture, and they will disappear back into the mainstream of the society or take up other delinquent occupations. Some of these originally heterosexual males will drift into a homosexual self-image and fall into conventional roles in the homosexual world. Those who were previously disposed to homosexuality will do much the same. It is this small proportion, of all those who came in as transient members of the world of homosexual prostitution, who verify the homosexual folklore that "this year's trade is next year's competition," meaning that this year's prostitutes will be paying prostitutes next year. This occurs often enough to keep the folklore going, but it is an insignificant source in terms of recruitment to adult homosexuality. From this street population a few will go on to other roles as courtesans and call boys.

For those young men marked by substantial physical attractiveness and quick wits, it is possible to move into more specialized prostitute roles. The street or bar hustler can, if he has good manners and social graces, move upward socially through his physical attributes. He may attach himself to an older male who is affluent and become his lover, attendant, or servant; or he can become a relatively highly paid call boy. This later occupation can be performed singly or through a male madame. Like the call girl, this is the pinnacle of the profession, and it is organized in much the same manner as the highest echelon of female prostitution. The profession at this level is marked by discretion, since the clients are men of considerable substance and reputation. The prostitute must by this time be prepared to participate in nearly any kind of sexual activity, either actively or passively, either heterosexually or homosexually. The most complex and extended group of this sort known to the authors includes both males and females who can be supplied in almost any numbers or combinations.

Movement into this world is much the same as movement into the world of female prostitution. Individuals become almost totally detached from conventional lifestyles, and customers are regulars who return relatively frequently. Unlike the erratic and disordered street world, this can be a world of considerable stability and continuity. The homosexual call boy's goal is very similar to that of the call girl—to move into a permanent relationship with someone who is extremely affluent. The job, however, has the same disadvantages as well. It is dependent, for most of its members, on continuing good looks and amenability. At the same time, detachment from conventional lifestyles and work habits encourages (except for the best organized call boys) general dissipation and laziness that decreases attractiveness. The male prostitute begins to live in a world dominated by other prostitutes and by the accoutrements of prostitution, its attitudes, and exploitative lifestyles. One real advantage, however, is that this world seems more protected from the police and less vulnerable to arrest than is the world of the female prostitute.

Conclusion

Like all worlds of secondary deviance organized to facilitate the lives of other deviants, the world of homosexual prostitution is a shifting and diffuse community.[31] Its values and norms overlap and differ from the values and the norms of the world of female prostitution, but at the center of each is the confluence of sex and money. In the one, the money serves to create the image of eroticism on the part of the client; in the other, the money serves to protect the self-image of the prostitute. For the males, the taking of money is often the first step toward the world of prostitution; for the female, the taking of money is the last step in the process. Both prostitute types are continuous with the character and values of the world that they serve, the female with the world of the heterosexual as a deviant alternative, the homosexual prostitute as a form of deviance for the deviant.

31. The cost of sexual encounters with male prostitutes, unlike contacts with females, has not increased with general affluence. This may be a function of the large number of transients and apprentices who drive down the price. See T. C. Esselstyn, "Prostitution in the United States," *The Annals of the American Academy of Political and Social Science* 375 (March 1968): 133.

6

A Conformity Greater than Deviance: The Lesbian

The lesbian differs from other women in the gender of the object that engages her sexuality. This is a significant gesture and one that engenders a potential for the emergence of deviant adaptations in other aspects of her social life. It is unfortunate that in the very limited body of research on the lesbian the significance of this difference in object choice tends to consume nearly all of the researcher's attention.[1] This disproportionate concern results from the vulnera-

---

1. The scientific literature on the lesbian is exceedingly sparse. Some of the more useful materials are: Anonymous, "Some Comparisions Between Male and Female Homosexuals," *The Ladder* 4 (1966): 4–25; Virginia Armon, "Some Personality Variables in Overt Female Homosexuality," (Ph. D. diss., University of Southern California, 1961); Donald Webster Cory, *The Lesbian in America* (New York: Citadel Press, 1964); Helene Deutsch, "Homosexuality in Women," *International Journal of Psychoanalysis* 14 (1933): 34–56; Sylvan Keiser and Dora Schaffer, "Environmental Factors in Homosexuality in Adolescent Girls," *Psychoanalytic Review* 36 (1949): 283–95; Brian Magee, *One in Twenty: A Study of Homosexual Men and Women* (London: Secker and Warburg, 1966); Marijane Meaker (pseud. Ann Aldrich), *We Walk Alone* (New York: Fawcett, 1955); J. D. Mercer, *They Walk in Shadow* (New York: Comet Press, 1959); Lionel Ovesay, "Masculine Aspirations in Women: An Adaptational Analysis," *Psychiatry* 19 (1956): 341–51: Joseph C. Rheingold, *The Fear of Being A Woman* (New York: Grune and Stratton, 1964), pp. 372–80; C. B. Wilber, "Clinical Aspects of Homosexuality," in *Sexual Inversion: The Multiple Roots of Homosexuality,* ed. Judd Marmor (New York: Basic Books, 1965), pp. 268–81. *The Ladder,* published by the female homophile organization, The Daughters of Bilitis, is useful and often insightful reading, as is the publication of the Minorities Research Group in England, *Arena 3.*

176

bility of the researcher to the same impulses that motivate the lay audience in their erotic enrichment and complication of the homosexual role. This enhanced eroticism derives from beliefs about the degree to which the interests and capacities of homosexuals are organized around the sexual impulse with an attendant increase in the amount, variety, and pleasure in their sexual performances. In contrast to the male homosexual, however, the female homosexual has perhaps a more labile stereotype, one which is capable of greater integration into the fantasy life of the society. Because the society seems less interested in the repression of homosexuality among females than that among males, there is perhaps less pressure to conceive of the behavior as narrowly, nor is there as much need to protect the self against the fantasies generated by thinking about the behavior.[2] Indeed, since males are the producers of most sexual fantasies, it is perfectly possible for them to conceive of the lesbian as simply being unawakened heterosexually, merely waiting for the right man to appear. Since thinking about the aroused female is a significant source of sexual arousal for the male, the source of her arousal is a matter of indifference.

As a consequence of the difficulty of separating sexual talk which is sexually arousing from that which is informational, we generally neglect the degree to which the lesbian shares all of the problems of a woman in the society prior to usual age of marriage, some of the problems of the single heterosexual female later in life, and some problems of the single person in a married society whether that person be male or female, heterosexual or homosexual. Thus the problems of dealing with family and friends, of earning a living, of finding emotional and social support, and—possibly of greatest importance

---

2. Even though the society does not seek to repress female homosexuality in quite the same manner that it does male homosexuality, the numbers of females involved in overt female homosexual contact are somewhat lower than for males. Using data on female college students comparable to that referred to in chapter 5 for college-attending males, there is a remarkable difference in the rates of single homosexual experiences. The incidence figure for males is 30%, while the comparable incidence for females is 6%. Of this small proportion, two-thirds (or 4% of the total) have had homosexual experience limited to early adolescence with a few scattered experiences later in the teens. This leaves only 2% of the college-attending women who were interviewed with any significant homosexual experience and less than 1% who were exclusively homosexual in behavior and object choice.

—struggling, as all persons do, to create and live with a constantly changing self are common to persons with all forms of sexual commitments. Even at the level of sexual activity we generally neglect the degree to which the lesbian's commitment to sexuality largely reflects general female patterns of sexuality, the difference in the gender of the object choice notwithstanding. Central to the contention of this book and reflecting a concern that is the thread of this work is that the female homosexual follows conventional feminine patterns in developing her commitment to sexuality and in conducting not only her sexual career but her nonsexual career as well. This should not be particularly surprising considering that despite the specific experiences that influenced her sexual object choice, which are still obscure, the lesbian is exposed to the numerous and diffuse, subtle and unsubtle, experiences and relationships that generally serve to promote conventional gender-role identification in the society. Moreover, many of these experiences and relations occur prior to the emergence of adult-like sexuality during adolescence. There is little reason to assume that these sources of sex-role learning are not assimilated in much the same way as occurs with females who are exclusively heterosexual.

One of the major characteristics of female socialization in the United States is the degree to which the general outlines of its processes are relatively simple and devoted to a single outcome—what Talcott Parsons has called, after Ernest W. Burgess, the domestic pattern.[3] Whatever the desires of females for glamour, career, or companionship patterns, the most pervasive commitment of the society is the production of wives and mothers among all females. Much like the United States military's inability to conceive of a soldier who is not modeled on the rifle-carrying infantryman, the society does not conceive of, nor does it train except by inadvertence, females who have more complex roles than wife and mother. In the process of socialization, patterns of both assertion and aggression are specifically restricted through comparative statements about the appropriateness of such behavior for females. Such control over the early development of a capacity for dominance in interpersonal re-

3. Talcott Parsons, "Age and Sex in the Social Structure of the United States," *American Sociological Review* 7 (October 1942): 604–16.

lationships results in greater personality lability and conformity to the needs of the male.[4] Much of the bargaining behavior observed between mothers and their children points to this lack of moral assurance that their orders will be carried out.

This single model system of producing women has other consequences that are discernible in the language of the psychoanalytic theory. It is in this literature that the enigma of female sexuality as well as the problem of femininity and womanhood has been most frequently, if not most profoundly, confronted.[5] In keeping with the biological biases of the analytic tradition—i.e., in contrast to an author like Simone de Beauvoir—the psychoanalyst Joseph C. Rheingold discusses what appears to be the role that biological differences play in the development of femininity and the sexual commitments of women.Given his belief in the preeminence of the body, he says, "The denial of the body is delusion. No woman transcends her body."[6] Such an orientation turns historical conditions into biological necessity. That the role of women has been so limited, controlled, and simply packaged has allowed the psychoanalyst and most other observers to grant to the biological organization the character of an absolute sign. As a consequence of this simplistic training system, regardless of its historical source, the biological fact of childbearing has been allowed to become central to the social meaning of womanhood. Thus the female is subjected to social training processes which focus their energies on molding the woman

4. This may account for the Kinsey finding that there were no differences in the sexual patterns of females when socioeconomic status was held constant, except for age at marraige and therefore age at first coitus, a fundamentally dependent variable in this case. Female sexuality is designed to conform to a relatively wide range of male sexual performance without major upset or anxiety.

5. Some analytic and nonanalytic discussions of this problem are: Simone de Beauvior, *The Second Sex* (New York: Alfred A. Knopf, 1953); Therese Benedek, *Psychosexual Functions in Women* (New York: Ronald, Press, 1953); Marie Bonaparte, *Female Sexuality* (New York: International Universities Press, 1953): Sigmund Freud, "Female Sexuality," in *Collected Papers* vol. 5 (London: Hogarth Press, 1950), pp. 252–72; Stephen R. Graubard, ed., "The Woman in America," *Daedalus* 93 (Spring 1964): 579–808; Jerome Kagan, "Acquisition and Significance of Sex Typing and Sex Role," in *Review of Child Development Research* vol. 1, eds. M. L. Hoffman and L. W. Hoffman (New York: Russell Sage Foundation, 1964), pp. 137–67.

6. Rheingold, *The Fear of Being a Woman*, p. 215.

to become the "mother of the family" rather than into other roles.[7] Indeed, the alternative roles available for women, especially those of "career," whether professional or glamorous, are almost as deviant for the society and nearly as impregnated with sexual stereotypes as is the role of the "lesbian."[8]

Previous research in the sexual behavior of the lesbian (there has been little interest in any other aspect of their behavior) clearly supports the contention that the patterns of overt sexual behavior on the part of homosexual females tend to resemble closely those of heterosexual females and to differ radically from the sexual activity patterns of both heterosexual and homosexual males.[9] The exceptions to this generalization result either from research in prison environments or from certain other limited situations where the constraints operating on sexual performances and role assignments are basically different from those observable in the rest of the society.[10] This homogeneity of behavior among women in the sexual realm (regardless of the gender of the sexual object choice) and

7. Alice Rossi, "Equality Between the Sexes: An Immodest Proposal," *Daedalus* 93 (Spring 1964): 607–52. The author points out that for the first time in history there is a situation in which child-rearing is the full-time business of the woman rather than being simply one of her many duties, as in the past.

8. Changes in the technology and social organization of work have considerably lessened the strain of choosing between family roles and work for middle-class females. However, the problems of managing a strong career commitment, including aspiration levels appropriate for a given career, appear to remain problematic. As Mervin Freedman observed in describing his study of Vassar students: "The interviews also reveal some reluctance on the part of women to assume leadership in various professions or fields except for those which possess considerable female connotation—for example, social work. They are likely to retreat from any exceptional accomplishment which may threaten the security of men. . . . All in all, as I see it, most women today are striving to maintain the integrity of the family and, at least to some extent, the continuity of traditional sex roles." Mervin Freedman, *The College Experience* (San Francisco: Jossey-Bass, 1967), pp. 119–20.

9. Alfred C. Kinsey, Wardell B. Pomeroy, and Clyde E. Martin, *Sexual Behavior in the Human Male* (Philadelphia: W. B. Saunders Co., 1948): Alfred C. Kinsey, Wardell B. Pomeroy, and Clyde E. Martin, *Sexual Behavior in the Human Female* (Philadelphia: W. B. Saunders Co., 1953).

10. Rose Gialombardo, *Society of Women* (New York: John Wiley & Sons, 19611); D. A. Ward and Gene G. Kassebaum, *Women's Prisons: Sex and Social Structure* (Chicago: Aldine Pub. Co., 1965).

the profound differences between men and women begin, overtly at
least, in the different introductions of the two sexes into sexual experience.

Early adolescence is for most females a profoundly nonsexual
period, both in the sense of sexual fantasy as well as overt sexual
activity. During this period when the genital fixations of males are
being determined either in masturbation or in heterosexual experimentation which is linked to peer group ties, the female is learning
patterns of behavior that are only indirectly invested with sexual elements. It is not that female sexuality is inhibited while male sexuality is not, nor that the sexual drive is stronger in the male than in
the female, but that the opportunities for learning and performing
sexual activity are not provided. The appropriate language of female sexuality in adolescence is not the language of repression, but
the language of the absence of learning. There are those females
who during adolescence do become detached from conventional
female patterns and develop an interest in sexuality for its own sake
or for the sake of pleasure. This detachment and the opportunity to
learn sexual as opposed to cosmetic patterns is more likely to occur
much later (if at all) for most females, often in their late twenties
and early thirties. About half of all women who masturbate to orgasm do so after experiencing orgasm in heterosexual relations.
This indicates that the capacity for the females to experience the
self as a sexual object develops differently than is the case with
males. Even the experience of orgasm comes much later than for
males.[11] It is a common experience for the latter during adolescence (about 90% experience it by age sixteen). It becomes common for the female only later in life (90% by ages twenty-nine to
thirty).

These differences do not indicate anything about the biological
elements of sexuality, but they do suggest the profound differences
that result from the period in social life when the sexual is directly
engaged. For the male sexuality is learned in adolescence prior to
profound linkages with the rest of life, and such earlier experience
allows greater experimentation and greater detachment from other

11. Kinsey et al., *Sexual Behavior in the Human Female,* figures 148–50,
p. 717.

societal elements. For females the acting out of sexuality occurs much later and in response to the demands of males and within the framework of societal expectations. For the female sexual activity does not occur for its own sake, but for the sake of children, family, and love. Thus sexuality for the female has less autonomy than it has for the male, and the body (either of the self or of others) is not seen by women as an instrument of self-pleasure. This vision of sexuality as a form of service to others is continuous with the rest of female socialization. Even though the lesbian occupies what is conventionally seen as a sexually deviant role, this same pattern of socialization remains in control. For most women, including most lesbians, the pursuit of sexual gratification as something separate from emotional or romantic involvement is not particularly attractive; indeed, for many it is an idea so strange as to be impossible. This is in part reflected in the number of sexual partners that women report. In the original work of Kinsey and his associates it was observed that, of the lesbians interviewed, only 29% had sexual relations with three or more partners and only 4% had contact with ten or more partners. These figures are extremely close approximations of the proportions for females *per se* whether homosexual or heterosexual.[12] They contrast dramatically with the same figures for heterosexual males which in turn are far less than for homosexual males.

The adolescent and pre-adolescent learning environments seem to be as denuded of sexual elements for the lesbian as for the heterosexual female. That this absence is not the result of repression of drive is demonstrated by the fact that during adolescence, or even after involvement in heterosexual activity, women rarely report profound feelings of sexual deprivation. Similarly, sexual arousal by fantasy or the presentation of visual sexual materials is far less common for females than for males. The very content of dreams is less sexual, as in the content of daydreams and other fantasies. The greater diffusion of sexual arousal is paralleled on the physical level where females are less genital and less visually oriented toward sexual materials. Sexual arousal for females is both more tactile and tends to result from exposure to materials (nonerotic read-

12. Ibid., p. 475 and table 78, p. 336.

ing materials or Hollywood-style movies) where the sexual elements are presented in the context of legitimizing emotional circumstances.[13] What is significant here is that females do respond to sexual stimulation, but not at an emotional distance.

The reported rates of sexual stimulation in absence of emotional contexts is somewhat higher for homosexual than for heterosexual females, but it is far lower than for homosexual or heterosexual males; and it is also far lower for the lesbian than one might suspect, given the obviously greater salience of sexuality. Sexuality for the lesbian should be more self-conscious, if only because it becomes the basis for her commitment to deviant patterns; however, the more general character-molding processes of the society are the dominant factors. Despite the currently oversimplified image of the lesbian as a counterfeit man, the gender of the object of her sexual desires is one of the relatively few attributes that she shares with males.

The remainder of this chapter is focused on the various aspects of the lesbian's life, hopefully beginning to detail those aspects that she shares with the conventional world and on the way in which conventional imperatives interact with a deviant adaptation. The interview materials were drawn from a series of open-ended interviews with about twenty lesbians. Much of the rest of the material is drawn from research with heterosexuals and association with persons in the homosexual community, both male and female. The findings from these experiences should begin to express the diversity of lesbian experience and to suggest some of the sources of the variation in that experience.

On Becoming a Lesbian

The detachment from conventional life that lesbians experience may ultimately focus on sexuality, but rarely will specifically sexual events organize this detachment. The sense of alienation that leads to a vulnerability in the direction of sexual deviance may find its roots in many sources, but what seems to be conspicuous is the feeling of estrangement. Even with the existence of such a feeling, the

13. Ibid., pp. 642–89.

staging of a lesbian's overt sexual involvement is as delayed as it is for her heterosexual counterpart. For the lesbians we interviewed, this appears as a rather consistent pattern. The discovery of their homosexuality usually occurred very late in adolescence, often even in the years of young adulthood, and the actual commencement of overt sexual behavior frequently came as a late stage of an intense emotional involvement. Indeed, in many instances their first emotional attachments, which began to generate in them a recognition of their special sexual inclination, involved only the most preliminary forms of sexual activity, unmarked by anything as unambiguously sexual as genital contact.

This romantic drift into sexual behavior was typified by one lesbian who described the beginning of her first homosexual affair in he following way:

> The fall after graduation from high school I started at [a residential school]. I met a girl there who was extremely attractive. She had a good sense of humor and I was drawn to her because I like to laugh. Many of the girls used to sit around in the evenings and talk. As our friendship grew, our circle narrowed and narrowed until it got to be three or four of us who would get together at night and talk. Then there was only three. Then two—us. And maybe after a couple of months of this our relationship developed into something more. Starting out by simply kissing. Later petting. That type of thing. It didn't actually involve overt sexuality [genital contact] until February [A period of about nine months].

Clearly, for the woman in question there was only a vague sense of what was associated with such behavior. There was little awareness of what a lesbian is and what she does.

> *Int:* When was the first time you began to talk about yourself using terms like *lesbian* or *homosexual?*
> *R:* Even when I was involved with her for five or six months, we didn't talk about it. We didn't give ourselves names. We spoke about how much we cared for one another. But we didn't discuss it. I may have thought it, but I don't know.

A second lesbian described a situation that was very similar. In this case there actually was some mild homosexual play during mid-adolescence, though with no apparent recognition of a homosexual inclination.

It was at home with my cousin. It was like a game we played in bed at night. It really wasn't, to the fullest extent, sex. It was caressing, fondling. It was, as I said, something we did at night . . . we never talked about it.

However, her strongest emotional attachment was to come several years later. Between the first relation with the cousin and this second attachment, there was no sexual involvement, and the second "affair" was itself overtly sexual only to a limited degree.

R: We met at the [a residnetial hotel for women]. We started out just being friends and then it became something special. She taught me a lot of things. I love music and she taught me how to listen to it and appreciate it. She liked things I liked, like walking. We read a lot together. We read the Bible, we read verses to each other. We shared things together. We caressed each other and kissed. I think it was a need to have someone there. And I was there and she was there and we just held on to each other.

Int: Did you ever become sexually involved on a more physical level?

R: Not to the fullest, and when I say not to the fullest extent I mean we didn't take off our clothes and lie in the nude with each other. I enjoyed being with her. I got something from her without going through the actions of sex.

Yet, although the young woman in question went on to become involved in several overt homosexual affairs, the above-described relationship and the woman involved became and remained for her a model of what an ideal relationship and love object should be like.

What is common to all of the above statements is the low order of significance given to performance of sexual acts. The delay of entry into sexuality parallels that of the heterosexual woman, and indeed, given the absence of a male who conventionally begins or initiates physical sexual expression in the course of interaction, there should be (and is) a greater delay in the beginning of physical sexual involvement for the lesbian than for the heterosexual female. The "nondiscussion" of the sexual aspects of behavior also derives from a lack of acceptable or even available names for the activities that are to be engaged in. Without such names the sexual act stands alone without an available set of verbal cues that reinforce a desire for the act in the absence of either the other person or other physical cues for the evocation of desire. A major element in the sustaining of sexual experience is the act of thinking about the experience, for without such internalized language, fantasies, and symbols, the experience is rarely self-generating. Indeed, the lesbian who moves most easily into the physical aspects of homosexual experience is the one who has had a prior body of heterosexual experiences that organize her sexual life.

It is not uncommon for lesbians to report that the realization of their own homosexuality appeared early in adolescence or even during childhood. Typically, one lesbian reported acute "shock of recognition" upon encountering a dictionary definition of homosexuality during very early adolescence. Another reported a sense of tentative recognition in childhood.

> I always had this fantasy about being a cowboy or Robin Hood. And then I realized they always had a girl friend, a Maid Marion. So in my fantasies I began to have my girl friends.

There is a sense in which such a report is difficult to evaluate. After the child or adolescent experiences a "sense of difference" in her relations to others, her problem is to resolve this difference by explaining it or finding social roles either in fact or in fantasy that organize the sense of difference and make it meaningful. The amount of existential distortion in such recall remains an unknown quantity. One must remember that this retrospection occurs after an identity has been refashioned to contain an active homosexual component, and it is not uncolored by an understandable desire to establish a sense of continuity with the past.

What is interesting in these two cases of early recognition of a label for their "sense of difference" (as was true for others like them) is that active involvement in sexual behavior did not occur until the subjects were in their early twenties. For them, apparently, labeling themselves as having, however tentatively, a socially deviant choice of sexual objects was not a necessary or immediate stimulus to alienation from other socially ordered aspects of sexual career management. Most lesbians are not exempt from the constraints and norms that regulate the development of female sexuality in general. This appears to be particularly true of the timing or phasing of entry into active sexual roles, as well as of the quality of relationships required to facilitate that entry.

While the pattern described above has the suggestion of modality, in this, as in most things, human behavior is complex and tends to present itself as a range. One does encounter modes of entry that were immediately sexual and that occurred earlier in adolescence. In one case (though there are surely others), the onset of early homosexual activity was associated with sexually segregated, institutional arrangements. Such environments have historically been charged with generating large proportions of homosexual behavior, though the degree to which this experience has consequences outside of the institutional context is equivocal. When these institutions are penal in nature there is a selection factor operating since many girls who are sentenced to such institutions have had prior sexual experience. Thus the homosexual activity occurs among a more sexually experienced population and, indeed, may well link to other than sexual needs (see chap. 8). In the case of other, nonpenal, sexually segregated institutions, there may be a greater likelihood of passionate schoolgirl attractions, but the acting out of these attractions is more likely a figment of male imagination than female eroticism.

Our limited number of interviews yielded only one example of a young woman who actively sought a test of her lesbian tendencies. One must note the degree to which her extensive heterosexual experience did *not* predispose her to aggressive sexual pursuit of females, even though she had the model of males to follow in her own case. It would appear that the expression of dominance in sexual interaction is probably independent of the dimension of preferred sexual object choice.

R: I've had these tendencies ever since I can remember. In high school I'd look at this or that girl and I'd have the desire to talk to her, get to know her better. I was never aroused by just any girl, I always had to have a special attraction to her. I just didn't want her, I'd want her to want me. I didn't want to be the aggressive one. . . . I started dating boys when I was twelve and a half and just stopped a month ago. I had light petting when I was thirteen or fourteen, I had intercourse when I was sixteen or seventeen. I'm not a tramp or anything. I don't like having sex with a guy, I just did it to cooperate when they got too pushy. I've never enjoyed it, I never had an orgasm with a guy.

Int: How did your homosexuality become sexual?

   R: Through this guy I was going with. He wasn't satisfying me and so I told him how I felt. That I had this attraction for girls. I heard that there were lesbian bars and I told him I wanted him to take me to one so I could find out if this was what I wanted. And he went along with it, thinking that after I found out I might go back to guys. So he asked a friend who knew about these things and got an address. Te took me there and left me. I met a girl there and went home with her.

The number of homosexual careers characterized by an experience comparable to this is hard to determine. We suspect that the proportion is very small, much smaller than the proportion of females who have such an extensive history of sexual activity during adolescence. What might be necessary, in order to be able to articulate a sexual need as this young woman did, is an unsatisfying learning of heterosexual experience which produces a sense of personal alienation.

Curiously, the experiences that followed for this respondent fell into an essentially feminine pattern despite the seemingly "masculine" and detached character of her pursuit of the lesbian experience. In short succession she had brief contact with three females, all of whom left her as unsatisfied as did her previous encounters with men. It was only the fourth contact, which had a more extended and intense emotional content, that provided the respondent with her first positive sociosexual experience with either gender as well as her first orgasm. Apparently, the process of development that constrains the female in our society to become trained in the rhetoric of love prior to the rhetoric of sex can be discarded only with a more total rejection of feminine identification than most lesbians are capable of.

Missing in the interviews was one of the most popular representations of the introduction into homosexuality provided us by modern fiction: seduction by an older woman. While there were some instances in which the initial partner was an older woman, in most cases there was advance evidence of movement away from conventional heterosexual patterns. In several of these cases the older woman was the object of seduction rather than the seductress. This is not to say that seduction by an older woman cannot occur. There is the likely possibility that we failed to talk to lesbians for whom seduction by an older woman was the mode of entry into homosexuality and, more importantly, the cause of detachment from more conventional patterns. Even so, the size of such a group is probably not very large. The real social importance of the image of the older seductress, an imagery providing the basis for many popular "explanations" of the "causes" of homosexual behavior, lies in its function of reducing a sense of parental guilt and shame. Suddenly, as the image of the corrupt and corrupting seducer appears on the scene, the need to examine relationships and processes closer to home is considerably reduced.

The Roots of Female Homosexuality

As has already been suggested, the great concern to identify and label the sources that supposedly induce homosexuality is reinforced by the guilt- and anxiety-reducing functions of such labeling. The availability of certain explanations allows the homosexual to counter societal rejection and the inevitable and terrible cruel sense of self-rejection with an "it's not my fault" posture. Explanations which postulate biological accidents or seductions as the cause of homosexuality allow parents to avoid the unanswerable question: What did I do wrong? In a society in which the repression of the homosexual is commonly punitive and nonrational, there is a requirement to view homosexual behavior as pathological. Out of this requirement a number of pseudo-rational etiologies, cures, and preventatives have arisen.

Clearly, understanding the sources of homosexual behavior is possible on some ultimate level. This is very important, if only for what might be learned about general human behavior in the process. However, it is our feeling that a better understanding of the sources of this behavior will reveal a complex process in which there is great variation in the combination of attributes that produce similar outcomes. What is most important is to avoid the frequently made assumption that the possession of extensive knowledge about the processes initiating a homosexual commitment would provide substantial knowledge about the processes that initiate a homosexual career. Implicit in such an assumption is the belief that subsequent homosexual behavior will represent, to a significant degree, a reenactment of the originating circumstances. Such assumptions seem to be unwarranted. The factors that initiate a homosexual career—indeed, any career—remain only a part of a series of elements in a dynamic and variable process.

Much of the literature on the lesbian, particularly the psychiatric literature, emphasizes the quality of life in childhood when crucial sex-role distinctions are learned and places a special emphasis upon the significance of parent-child or parent-parent relations which appear to impinge upon this development. In our small group of lesbian interviews, two factors emerged with noteworthy consistency: first, about half of the women reported that their parental homes were broken by death, divorce, or separation; second, although our discussion of group attributes should not be interpreted as hard statistics based upon an unbiased sample, it was particularly impressive that in almost every case there was a strongly expressed preference toward one of the parents, with attitudes toward the other parent or substitute parent ranging from condescending neutrality to open hostility. However, the preference for the male or female parent was almost equally divided.

Thus, some described their parents in the following way:

> If I never had to see him [father] again, I wouldn't mind one bit. . . . I remember when I was a kid I caught my parents fooling around. It made me sick. I hated my father for touching my mother.

Another described her stepfather as follows:

> I was five when my mother asked me if I cared if she married him. He wasn't a threat to me. I ruled the roost when I was five and I have since. It wasn't because I was spoiled. If I did something wrong, I was spanked for it by my mother. And when I was young, by my uncles. But I never thought much of him as a man and neither did my mother. My mother couldn't look to him to do the things other men did. She'd either do it or have me do it. There was nothing wrong with my stepfather, but she wouldn't think of asking him because he always whined or cried if she asked him. *(Discussing her stepfather's reaction to the disclosure of her homosexuality.)* My father, I don't know, you could call him dense, but homosexuality—or almost anything—they don't seem to register.

On the other hand, descriptions by other lesbians of relations with parental figures took a totally different cast:

I lived with my grandmother till I was ten and then I went to live with my father. My mother was a surgical nurse and was constantly on call and couldn't take care of the kids. I feel pretty close to my father. We liked to go fishing together, build things like bookcases. We get along, but we both have tempers.

Or:

Mother was sick a lot of the time. She was just there. Someone to be taken care of.

While it is evident that extreme relations with parental figures in any direction appear to predispose individuals to deviant patterns, the same predisposing factors are equally evident in many families that do not produce homosexuals. Clearly, the term to be underscored is *predisposing*. The question simply stated then becomes: such predisposing factors, plus what, lead to lesbian commitments? And this is a question that is not likely to be answered in any comprehensive way in the near future.

A second approach to the roots of homosexuality is found in a listing of physical, genetic, or homonal "faults." Within the limits of currently available research findings, there is little to suggest that homosexual populations can be differentiated from heterosexual ones on these characteristics. The only marked biological difference for the lesbian group interviewed was that a large number began menstruation earlier or later than most girls with whom they were growing up. None reported difficulty with menstruation. Among those who felt they were late in arriving at menarche, most reported a sense of relief when they began sharing the experience of their peers. Like unconventional family situations or attachments, the out-of-phase onset of menstruation appears not to tie in specifically with a homosexual adaptation but rather to a tendency to experience alienation from modal development and socialization processes.

Linked to this interest in physical explanation is another argument about the sources of female homosexuality, one that is difficult to take seriously. This argument states that female homosexuals are really heterosexual rejects; more simply stated, the lesbian becomes such because she is not sufficiently attractive to "make out" as a woman. Our own findings run contrary to this. Few of the women interviewed were in any sense obviously homosexual (what-

ever that might mean), overly masculine, or physically ugly. Though
there is a great deal of subjectivity involved, the interviewers' opinion was that, as a group, the women were conventionally feminine
in appearance.

Another line of explanation involves social rejection and holds
that the crucial factor involved is an inability to manage conventional social relationships successfully, a kind of social ineptitude
that leads individuals to seek a more supportive social milieu. Experiences exemplifying this possibility were noticeable in several of
the interviews. One lesbian, for example, described herself in adolescence in the following way:

> I was unhappy, unsure of myself socially, though not intellectually. I
> wore braces and had acne. My sister, who was ten years older, was
> quite beautiful. I was always the other daughter. Following behind
> her in school, I got used to the expression of disbelief that followed
> when teacher realized that I was her sister.

Or in another case:

> I was the original clumsy dolt. If there was anything to break, I
> would break it. I was too large to manage. I couldn't say the right
> things. After a while, I was just scared all the time. And that just
> made it worse.

On the other hand, another lesbian reported:

> My high school years were very happy simply because I was active in
> so many things. President of this and a member of that. I went to
> many parties. I was in charge of many functions. Being active, hav-
> ing lots of friends, being smiled upon by the gods because I was also
> an honor student, which wasn't difficult for me, and I was happy.

However, this latter kind of report was relatively rare. Most described some moderate amount of social activity during school; very
few could be described as isolates. The essential factor that appeared to be emerging was an estrangement from conventional heterosocial involvement which was beginning to flower among their
peers.

It is possible to speculate that this sense of alienation, regardless
of source, may well be one of the central elements in the genesis of
much of deviant behavior. The sense of difference, regardless of its

source, whether some internally felt discontinuity, or an affirmation of difference provided by legal agencies, opens the way to detachment. At the same time, there are major forces seeking to decrease this sense of difference, rarely directly, but merely through participation in routine social arrangements. It is often difficult to predict what direction or particular form of deviance will arise from the sense of difference. Judging what the alternative potentials were at the beginning of a deviant career is nearly impossible from examining an actor at the point of completion of a deviant adaptation.

Almost all the women reported some heterosexual dating and mild sex play during their high school years. Only two carried it to the extent of intercourse, although a larger number indicated that they had experimented with heterosexual coitus after homosexual experiences. The sense of difference seemed in most cases to precede their withdrawal from conventional social life rather than the reverse. The young woman who reported such a happy period during her high school years described dating activity during that same period in a way that begins to foreshadow an eventual departure from that happy world.

> It was when I was fifteen or so, the sophomore or junior year. That's when everyone really started dating. I had a very close girl friend. It was very traumatic for me at the time. We had gone to junior high and through the freshman year together very intimately. We shared everything, did everything together. And then, in our sophomore year, she began going steady with this boy. And then it hit me. You know, all of a sudden she wasn't around anymore. This boy friend was a good friend of mine and he said to me this buddy of his wanted me to go out, the four of us to go out. I didn't particularly want to go, but I'd just go so I could be with my friend. After a while I did go out. I dated as much, if not more, than the other girls, I enjoyed going out to an athletic thing or to dances because I like to dance. But as far as the boys were concerned, I wasn't interested like the other girls were interested. You know, looking for someone to care for or marry. At that time, they were thinking about things like that.

Lastly, we might consider the casual explanation that attributes a corrupting influence to literary representations of deviant behavior. Generally, there is scant evidence that literature serves as a crucial triggering mechanism for deviant sexual tendencies. In only two cases did respondents report reading about lesbian behavior prior to becoming homosexual. For one young woman, such reading apparently had little consequence, since her homosexual experiences were not to begin for some five or more years; she remembered it as merely "a trashy sex novel where the beautiful girl is rescued from an evil lesbian by being made love to by a "real man." In the second case, *The Well of Loneliness* was read by one lesbian while she was in her late teens.

> As I look back now, it really is a silly book. But then . . . it was like an explosion. I had had these strange feelings for a long time, and then to discover that I wasn't the only one in the world like that. . . .

Even though extensive reading is absent from the early histories of the lesbians interviewed, almost all had later read extensively in the available "lesbian literature." But once again, the pattern of general adult reading resembles that reported by Kinsey for females as a group—that is, relatively limited sexual arousal from literature.

On Being in the "Community"

For both male and female homosexuals one can talk about the existence of a community, at least in most relatively large cities. As for many ethnic or occupational groups, which also can be said to have a community, this subcommunity does not require a formal character or even a specific geographical location. It is, rather, a continuing collectivity of individuals who share some significant activity and who, out of a history of continuing interaction based on that activity, begin to generate a sense of a bounded group possessing special norms and a particular argot. Through extensive use such a homosexual aggregate may identify a particular location as theirs. In almost all large cities this location includes one or more taverns that cater exclusively to a particular homosexual group. In these bars the homosexual may more freely act out her self-definition as compared with less segregated situations. Recently, several homophile social and service organizations have appeared, and they offer a more public image of the homosexual. These various kinds of social activity reinforce a feeling of identity and provide for the homosexual a way of institutionalizing the experience, wisdom, and mythology of collectivity. The cultural content of this community has been described in the past with irony, but more recently with a sense of affirmation, as the "gay life."

For the individual homosexual, the community provides many functions. A major function is the facilitation of sexual union; the lesbian who finds her way to the community can now select from a population that, while differing in other attributes, has the minimum qualification of sharing a lesbian commitment. This greatly reduces what is for the isolated lesbian the common risk of "falling for a straight girl," i.e., a heterosexual. The community provides a source of social support; it is a place where the lesbian can express her feelings or describe her experiences because there are others available who have had feelings and experiences very much like them. It is an environment in which one can socialize one's sexuality and find ways of deriving sexual gratification by being admired, envied, or desired, while not necessarily engaging in sexual behavior. Lastly, the community includes a language and an ideology which provide each individual lesbian with already developed attitudes that help her resist the societal claim that she is diseased, depraved, or shameful.

While all the lesbians interviewed were part of a community to one degree or other, a larger proportion of lesbians avoid such communities than is the case for male homosexuals. This possibly occurs because the lesbian has less need for the community, since her homosexuality is not so immediately alienating from the conventional society. The lesbian may mask her sexual deviance behind a socially prepared asexuality. Not all categories of women in our society are necessarily defined as sexually active, as, for example, the spinster. In line with this, the image of two spinsters living together does not immediately suggest sexual activity between them, even when considerable affection is displayed. The same is not true for men. The bachelor is presumed to be even more sexually active than the married man, and the idea of two males past young adulthood rooming together strikes one as strange indeed. It is possible that the differences in the staging of entry into sexuality and the concomitant variation in learning situations between males and females also allow the female to handle later sexual deprivations more easily. More female homosexuals than male homosexuals, then, should be able to resist quasi-public homosexual behavior that increases the risk of disclosure; they are also more able to resist relations that involve only sexual exchange without any emotional investment.

One lesbian, who had previously avoided the community (during a long period of heterosexual marriage followed by a period of no sexual activity) and now was only involved with the community on a fairly marginal basis, expressed resistance to "the gay life" and its tendency to reinforce lesbian commitments at the expense of greater alienation from conventional society.

> No, I didn't consider myself part of the gay world and I consider myself fortunate. From what I've seen of the gay world, not the elite, but kids who hang around the bars get too . . . involved. Particularly the young girls. It drains all of her energy, all of her time, and her money. I see an awful lot of girls who have a lot of potential and ability which has never been used and will probably never be used because they waste all those good years. They hang around the bars and just because they're homosexual the gay life becomes everything.

Another lesbian, who had spent eight years defining herself as a homosexual and had experienced three fairly long homosexual affairs before she encountered the homosexual community, represented one of the positive aspects of the community. She came initially from a working-class background and had previously worked at a fairly low status, semiskilled occupation. Her affairs, initiated largely on the basis of adventitious meetings, were conducted with the most limited awareness of other lesbians and with lovers who were drawn essentially from similar social backgrounds. Entry into the gay world for this young woman provided her with her first sustained experiences and relations across social class lines which were not organized to maintain her lower-class status. The very salience of sexuality in this community provided a basis for her transcending many conventional social barriers existing in the larger society. In rather short order, her aspirations in many other areas of life began to rise. She became dissatisfied with her occupation and started training for one that paid more, possessed higher prestige, and required greater skill. Her commitments to art, music, and eating, and thus the very style of her life, began a rapid transformation. Clearly, for some persons the homosexual community represents a new kind of opportunity structure, while for others it is a resource that is paid for by withdrawal from the larger community.

Women Without Men

The most common image of the lesbian is probably that of a pseudo-male, a female who, in her biological inability to be a male, is a caricature of maleness. This is the denotation that stands behind that hackneyed word *dyke*. There are a few lesbians for whom a masculine identification is terribly important, and for some it manifests itself as transvestism (wearing of male clothing). This need for adopting a masculine self-image or playing a masculine role emerges from very shadowy origins, and, if little is known about the etiology of homosexuality in general, still less is known about this phenomenon. Where transvestism appears, it is associated with a feeling of alienation that leaves few viable connections with conventional social life, although the language of cause and effect somehow seems out of place. Some of this apparent masculine behavior is surely linked to the dilemma of the female having to engage in initiatory behavior in zones of life where she had been trained to be reactive. This takeover of male imagery may well be most likely to occur among those females whose family patterns have given them an imagery of initiatory behavior as being exclusively a male behavior. Those who have the most rigid distinctions between male and female gender-role behaviors may be the ones who find that their deviant object choice must be integrated into pseudo-male public performances. The great intensity of feeling and a quality of over-determination are other distinguishing characteristics of this commitment, both of which may justify labeling the behavior "compulsive" in a way that is not justified in describing most lesbians.

The polarity of sexual roles, which is part of the content of sexual learning for the lesbian as well as everyone else in our society, has fundamental consequences for such a woman who is now involved in homosexuality. It is this tendency of the lesbian to model her experiences on heterosexuality that produces such role categories as "butch" (the supposed male-husband surrogate in the lesbian relationship; the partner is the more aggressive, controlling, managerial, money-making, etc.) and the "fem" (the female-wife surrogate with an attendant attention to feminine attributes and activities). The very existence of these role categories in the homosexual community's argot results in an uncritical acceptance of their validity both by the homosexual world and by heterosexual outsiders. Indeed, the importance of the continuing value of the terms may lie more in their clarification of the structure of interaction in the community than in guiding any of the members of the community itself as they interact with persons they already know.

While, as suggested, few lesbians become committed to this totally masculine role as a near-permanent lifestyle, many more lesbians may experiment with this kind of strategy for a short period, particularly during the identity crisis that occurs at the time of the first self-admission of a deviant sexual commitment, or at entry into the culture of the homosexual community. During this early phase of career development, it is not unlikely that many lesbians overreact because they are still imbued with the essentially heterosexual language of their earlier socialization and think of themselves as an accident of nature: a man trapped in a woman's body. Such a self-conception surely helps in reducing uncertainty and in creating the necessary distance from previous and less viable identities. At this extremely crucial moment of transition, overidentification with masculinity helps the deviant to reduce dissonance.

It is the experience of one researcher who has dealt with lower-class lesbians that homosexual patterns among these females are nearly identical with male-female relationships in the slum community. These women take over the most immediate surrogate role behaviors that are available in the local community, with some females acting out clear-cut "stud" roles compared to the other females who continue to operate within the usual definitions of femaleness in the ghetto.

Another reason that this rolestyle may be attractive for short periods is the obviousness of that style. This obviousness becomes helpful to the newly "turned out" lesbian, who may not yet have become adept at other styles of handling sociosexual relations. One young lesbian commented:

   R: For instance, when I first got into the gay world with the first girl, there was no butch or fem. We didn't know, though I was slightly more aggressive.

Int: In making love?

R: No, I mean in taking care of things, managing, planning. When we made love, there was a kind of flow, a sharing. So I eventually came out in the gay world as kind of butch. Mostly because I felt you had to be somewhere. Later, if someone asked, I said I was butch, but mostly because I didn't want any of these bull dykes coming to me.

Almost all of the women we interviewed saw themselves as women who wanted to become emotionally and sexually attached to another woman who would, in turn, respond to them as a woman. This was expressed rather clearly by a lesbian who thought of herself as being classified as a "fem."

Int: Do you have a preference as to active or passive role?

R: For me it would be reciprocal. But among the gay people I know, I guess I am classified as fem. Probably because I'm not the aggressive type. I don't go around asking girls to dance—I can't lead for one thing.

Int: Do you prefer girls who are butch or fem?

R: That's hard to say. I think that most of the girls that I have been attracted to were also attractive to men, some of them very much so. Also, there has to be some community of interests so that there is something to talk about. A way of seeing things the same way.

Another young woman, whose first two lesbian contacts were both "butch" types, commented:

They didn't like me to touch them, or anything. They had to do everything. Just like most men. If that's what you want, you might as well go "straight."

Despite what we feel to be an essentially feminine quality that pervades the sexual commitments of most lesbians, there is often a distinct masculine aspect to lesbian life. What is deceptive is that many of these masculine elements arise from nonsexual sources and have nonsexual roots that are missed because one is dealing with a specifically homosexual population. One such partial, nonsexual explanation is offered by Simone de Beauvoir in her discussion of the lesbian in *The Second Sex*.[14] There she observes that the descrip-

14. de Beauvior, *The Second Sex*, pp. 421–22.

tive phrase "women without men" has a literal meaning beyond just describing sexual behavior. When they abandon the social route that for the majority of women culminates in heterosexual marriage, most lesbians must take responsibility for a whole range of activities and skills that ordinarily fall to the male in the family. For these women such skills as repairing a lamp, learning how to handle tools, and managing an independent personal economy leads to a different set of expectations with reference to many other functions in the rest of the world. Without a male figure to manage relationships between her and the demands of the external world, the lesbian must learn a whole set of instrumental tasks which are only learned to a very limited extent by other women.

A quasi-masculine appearance also insulates the lesbian from the relations that create demands she either cannot or does not desire to accept. One young lesbian, who is both feminine and attractive in appearance, described the dysfunctions of her femininity at work in the following way:

> At work all the people are "straight" [heterosexual], and I have to put on this big scene of being heterosexual. And I don't like putting on fronts. But the men who come in like to flirt and expect me to flirt back. If I could just tell everyone that I'm homosexual, I wouldn't have to put on this big front, but everyone won't accept it.

In considering this insulation function of a nonfeminine presentation of self, it is important to remember that it need not be considered by all persons as indicative of homosexuality; it can also be defined merely as asexuality.

Another aspect of this question of the style of self-presentation involves the lesbian community. For lesbians who are involved in the community, there may exist a constraint to appear less feminine than many of them might individually be in a free choice situation. In the community context, uniform or recognizable styles of dress or presentation quickly establish group membership and heighten the sense of group solidarity.

Family Relationships

One thing of which we may be fairly certain is that parents do not deliberately raise their children to be homosexuals, for in all •

known societies exclusive adult heterosexuality is an intended outcome of the child-rearing process. Nonetheless, homosexuals do emerge from families, and no matter how unusual or strained the family may have been, the lesbian is confronted with the same problem that everyone faces upon becoming an adult—she must work out some relationship with her parental family so that her new self-definition may be expressed (either in concealment or in public identification). The mere fact that a commitment has been made to a deviant sexual pattern that limits the possibilities of realizing some of the conventional parental expectations, such as getting married and having children, makes this transition more difficult for the lesbian. However, there is no indication that the distribution of solutions to this dilemma for the lesbian population differs substantially from those adopted by heterosexuals. At the same time, it must be acknowledged that substantial strains on more specific levels do occur.

For a small proportion of the lesbians we talked to, family connections were minimal. This severing of family ties varied between rejection of the lesbian by the family, rejection of the family by the lesbian, or a mutual rejection. But this was the case for few, and in most instances some partial family ties were maintained, if only through one sympathetic member. This was typified by one lesbian who described her family relations in the following way:

> The only one I see is my brother and his wife. At least once a month I will go and have dinner with them. Their children are always glad to see me, and I am very fond of them. They know, but we don't talk about it. Once I brought a girl friend along, but it seemed to create too much embarrassment. I am sure, though, if I were ever in trouble, they would come through for me. We don't talk about them [parents and another brother] often. Even though it's been a long time, it still hurts.

So, while cases like this one appear and while it is evident that homosexuality played an important role in the rupturing of family ties, there are numerous instances in a general population where family ties are ruptured over factors having nothing to do with sexual deviance.

Some larger proportion of lesbians manage this problem by masking their homosexual activity from all or almost all family members and seem to cope with family relations fairly well. One commented:

> Once mother accepted the fact that I didn't want to live at home and that I wasn't going to get married, it worked out very well. I talk to them about once a week and go out every few weeks. My girl friend comes along, and she gets along very well with the family. Mother, particularly, is pleased that I have such a well-educated and refined roommate. I am sure that she doesn't know. I don't think mother or father can conceive of something like homosexuality.

Frequently parents suspect, or even know, but decide to ignore the possibility or the fact of lesbianism. In one case it was quite clear that the mother was fully cognizant of her daughter's sexual preference, since it was the reason for the daughter's expulsion from a school. However, following that event no further reference was made to lesbian activity. Indeed, in most families where there is knowledge or partial knowledge there is avoidance of the issue. In relatively few cases, perhaps as few as those involving complete rejection, there is full knowledge and an open, casual acceptance.

What should be clear is that there is no one pattern of family adjustment for the lesbian, particularly not one predicated exclusively around the fact of lesbianism. There are satisfying family relations and unsatisfying ones, relations that are disruptive for the individual lesbian and those which are highly supportive, relations of intimacy and of distance, and relations where the family simply is not a very significant factor. The tendency for strain is evident. For example, in a large number of cases the disclosure to parents of her homosexual commitment was made by the lesbian as a manifestly aggressive and hostile act directed toward one or both parents. The pattern of alienation that we commented upon in our earlier discussion suggests that in many instances disordered family patterns can be observed; however, these family problems might be best understood in terms of general approaches to the study of the family rather than in terms of a special theory organized around the concept of homosexuality.

Earning a Living

Most lesbians are confronted with the problem of earning a living. When a woman foregoes the conventional path where a husband would perform this role, labor force participation becomes much more important. In some cases this more serious involvement with work adds to the public misconception of the masculine character of lesbians, for, in our society, "serious" work still remains predominantly in the masculine sphere. This is, of course, a problem that all women who take work seriously, homosexual and heterosexual alike, must face. As we have noted before, it is often assumed that the occupationally committed female is somehow imperfect. Serious commitment to work remains in most cases for females an unexpected outcome of the childrearing process; more than the suggestion of deviancy is implicit.

The heterosexual female with strong work commitments, particularly where work becomes career, is still treated as exceptional, with abundant ambiguities and indications of role strain. This is marked by the fact that the "career woman" is frequently defined in many of the stereotypical characteristics that are found in the stereotype of the lesbian (e.g., aggressive, castrating, man-hating, driven, and frustrated). Clearly, what appears as preferences or capacities for authority roles in the public sphere of work are too often too automatically translated into comparable preferences in the privacy of the bedroom. (Ironically, the lesbian with limited commitments to work tends to have that attributed to the same "character disorder" that gave rise to her homosexuality, rather than an expression of conventional female socialization.)

One lesbian who worked at a fairly skilled job wrote an article in a British lesbian publication that described her sense of frustration at constantly being passed over for promotion by men whom she felt were no more (and often less) competent than she. This woman understood that the judgment was being made that most women are only temporarily involved in the world of work and that there is little point in training them for higher positions, since they ultimately marry and withdraw from full labor force participation. She commented that she wants to tell her superiors that she is a lesbian and unlikely to marry, but her desire to do so is curbed by her anticipation of the firm's reaction to her sexual object preference.

Most lesbians, then, appear to be more seriously committed to work than most women. Reflecting this, they tend to have relatively stable work histories. Most movement between jobs is associated with an upgrading of jobs. Some lesbians, to be sure, display extremely erratic work histories, and this is frequently associated with difficulties in managing personal and sexual relations. One commented:

> When I broke up with ——, things just went to hell. I must have had six different jobs in less than a year. Just when things were settling down, I met ——. Off on the merry-go-round I went. Nothing seemed to matter, just being with her. Then I realized that she was supporting me and that was a drain on the relationship.

Other lesbians are persons with a very limited commitment to the world of work, who might be termed highly dependent. Such lesbians, however, may not differ in many respects from their heterosexual counterparts who find in marriage many of the supports for their dependency needs. Parenthetically, this relatively small proportion of highly dependent lesbians may be "overrepresented" in both lay and professional views because these women are among the ones most likely to seek therapy and the ones most likely to participate in the visible part of the homosexual community. As a consequence, they help sustain the "fem" motif in the "butch-fem" polarization of the female homosexuality; such a view is, of course, a caricature of heterosexual relations. It would appear that, for whatever reasons, lesbians with disordered work patterns constitute a minority of all female homosexuals. Knowing what we do about the problems associated with adopting a deviant social role, we should not be surprised to observe that some part of a lesbian population has this kind of difficulty; rather, we might better be surprised at the number who appear to function well in the world of work.

A significant factor in the work adjustment of the lesbian is obviously the character of the occupation or profession that she selects. For some occupations, aspects of a lesbian commitment may actually prove helpful. The lesbian's sexual commitment frees her from many of the normal demands of family life and particularly from the demands of childbearing and rearing. In other occupations this same sexual commitment may prove difficult to manage or at least may constrain the lesbian, either by restricting her occupational activity or by limiting her sexual activity. Also important is the degree to which work can be separated from other spheres of life.

Many jobs place demands on aspects of the individual's conduct that would be considered private activity in other occupations. For example, the job requirements of the public school teacher or federal government employee set severe limits on the conduct of one's personal life. And, while lesbians are employed as teachers and government workers, they must either learn to conduct their sexual relations with greater discretion than many other lesbians (and conduct these relations in an atmosphere of greater fear and anxiety) or be prepared to have their careers suffer. One lesbian occupying a high-paying position with private industry commented on this:

> My company advertizes me as one of the features of our service. My name is on the letterhead. It has been hard work and it has taken years to arrive at this position, this reputation. The hardest thing is knowing that all of this can be wiped out at any moment because of some publicity. I don't think the people with the company would object, but the customers? Who knows? —— [her girl friend and roommate] likes to go to the gay bars. I do too, but not so much. So we go, but I keep waiting for someone who knows me at work to come walking in. It's like living under a sword or with a time bomb.

Another factor which is important in understanding the homosexual's work problems is the degree of involvement with other people that the occupation requires. Many people have very strong feelings about homosexuality, and many more feel uneasy in its presence. One lesbian who worked at a routine office job for several years said:

> I work very hard at not letting people at the office know. I don't think I would get fired or anything. It's just the nervousness I know it would start. The other girls look at you curiously. Any touching, even accidental, is taken for a pass. I've had it happen before, when I got careless and let someone know who talked. I got so that I'd wait for the john to be empty before I'd go in. I don't want to go through that again.

Another woman observed:

> You can't get too close to people at work. It gets too complicated. You start going out and they want to know too much about you. One girl tried to fix me up with her brother. It is really better to be a little stand-offish.

Still another factor is the amount of interest the lesbian takes in her job—that is, the degree to which work itself is rewarding or engaging. For many people work is merely a way of earning a living; for others it is an important and gratifying activity. In the latter case, work not only becomes a constraint on, but also an important substitute for, many of the relations and gratifications that the lesbian, almost by definition, is denied. The potentialities that work offers the lesbian obviously differ widely, and the fate of the professional woman is different from that of the shop clerk or waitress.

Friends

None of us has an opportunity to select our parental family, although as adults, even with the pressure of social expectations, we can modify the degree and extent of our involvement. But part of growing up means that it is frequently very difficult to share new experiences or tastes with parents who are, by definition, a generation away in experience, or even to share such things with siblings with whom one has had a prolonged, diffuse, and complex relationship. This fact makes friendship so very important; friendships tend not only to be supportive and reinforcing but also to be more specific and controlled than familial attachments. So the lesbian must count available friendships as an important resource in the process of coping with the contingencies of her existence. Perhaps more than in the other areas of social life we have considered, the homosexuality of the lesbian becomes a highly conspicuous factor in her friendship selection.

None of the lesbians we interviewed could be considered isolates, although it is probable there are some who had been, particularly during various transitional states. For most, the inclination to speak aloud their feelings and desires becomes something of a constraint in forming friendships with other lesbians. Although it is interesting to note that almost all the lesbians we interviewed included some male homosexuals among their friends, for some of the lesbians male homosexuals constituted their only close male friends. This need for the socialization of deviance is one of the major foundations of a homosexual community. One relatively isolated lesbian, who was very critical of certain aspects of the homosexual community, described the importance of her few lesbian friends in the following way:

> There are two or three girls here I think I could talk to, get some sympathy. I don't think it would be a matter of seeking advice so much as letting off steam. As a matter of fact, that did happen last spring. One of the girls, we both cried on each others' shoulders for awhile.

While a homosexual commitment endows friendship with a special significance, it may also be the factor that makes friendship less stable. This instability arises partially from the fact that the population from which the individual lesbian is likely to select her friends is the same population from which she also is likely to select her lovers and sexual partners. As a result, most discussions of friendship were filled with a sense of anticipated impermanence. The fact that friends are often ex-lovers or are current or recent rivals appears to foster an ultimate reserve or, in some extreme cases, a constant mistrust. Almost paradoxically, the instability of many lesbian alliances, a fact that contributes to making friendships among female homosexuals so important, also tends to limit the quality of friendships that develop. However, despite this reservation, most of the lesbians interviewed reported managing their friendships fairly well, at least in the sense of having friends with whom they could spend their leisure time and to whom they could turn in moments of stress.

Many of the women also reported having close friends who were not homosexual and who had knowledge of their homosexuality. The existence of such friends obviously facilitated adjustment. This seemed particularly true for those lesbians who had made the best occupational adjustments—i.e., those who had jobs they enjoyed or those who had relatively stable work histories. Both of these —nonhomosexual friendship ties and work adjustment—may well be linked, however, to the somewhat elusive elements that are associated with meeting the conventional world on its own terms. Friendship with knowing nonhomosexuals often appeared to have a limited quality, indicating something like a "separate worlds" phenomenon. Indicative was the fact that very few lesbians can handle an attempt to bring their two worlds together, but of course, this would be characteristic of virtually all deviant subcultures.

Another large proportion of the lesbians reported having non-homosexual friends who did not know they were homosexual. Such friends play a role in filling the lesbian's social life with people, but to the extent that these friends do become an important resource in a lesbian's life, they also become a source of considerable anxiety. One lesbian described her situation in the following way:

> Some [friends] may suspect. I don't know. Normally I just don't tell people unless there is a reason for it. You know, where the question comes up, where I might have to explain some peculiar behavior. Once or twice it came out when I had too much to drink. I try to watch it, but you can't be on your guard all the time. Normally, my practice is not to tell people unless I'm pretty sure what the reaction will be.

The lesbian population observed represents, then, differing basic styles of handling the question of friendship. For some, it meant living in almost exclusively homosexual social circles, while others lived in homosexual and nonhomosexual social worlds simultaneously. There were also different styles of living in the nonhomosexual world. Little is systematically known about what determines these alternative patterns, although the ways they relate to work and family certainly are involved. And perhaps here, more clearly than elsewhere, it is evident that the content of social life for lesbians can be more adequately grasped by understanding the social response to homosexuality than by understanding the psychodynamics involved.

Finding Love

Romantic love as a mass experience is an invention of the modern world. As such, it plays a peculiarly important role in stabilizing social life. This is particularly true for that form of love that embodies, and is partially expressed through, sexuality. Few people grow up in our society without an understanding of the desirability of love. Even fewer doubt that its absence represents a crucial personal impoverishment, and extremely few fail to respond to the rhetoric that emerges from it. The lesbian is no exception to this. The difference here, as in many other spheres of life, is that for her the establishment of an enduring love relationship is more problematic.

Almost without exception, the lesbians we interviewed expressed a significant commitment to finding such an enduring love relationship. Perhaps because their alienation from the larger society is centered in the sexual area, and as a result, they are more conscious of its role, their sense of its importance appears to be even greater than it would be for other populations. What apparently is involved is an almost nineteenth century commitment to romantic ideals. Their aspirations were fundamentally those embodied in "the American dream": a comfortable home, an interesting job, access to enjoyable leisure activities, and, above all, a sustaining and loving partner. This may rest in the fact that love, as a social value, becomes a way of overriding the inevitable uneasiness accompanying a deviant commitment.

Unfortunately, as frequently occurs with goals that are extremely important, the very enormity of the importance of love often frustrates success. This frustration may take several forms. One is the endowment of casual relations with a greater intensity of feeling than the relationship can sustain. One older lesbian observed:

> This falling in and out of love is something that the younger girls do. They turn on to each other and it fulfills a certain psychological need of the moment. They think they're in love. And, of course, it breaks up after a while. What would you expect? Sometimes they've only known each other two weeks.

Another form of frustration stems from the tendency to develop impossible expectations regarding the performances of their partners. This was expressed with considerable clarity by one young woman.

> Maybe it will pass, but right now love is very important to me. Being very near someone all the time. Wanting to love them and having them love you back. It's like being on a high and not wanting to come down. Maybe it's my fault. Maybe I've just had bad luck in the lovers I've known. They seem to come down too quickly and then it becomes ugly and sordid.

Still another tendency is a balancing and frequently self-defeating reserve that derives from an understandable anticipation of instability in relationships; it is a means of self-protection against a very likely unhappy ending. One lesbian, whose commitment to a substantial emotional investment was strong, described her reluctance to share living quarters with her current lover in the following way:

> *R:* I guess I feel a sense of security with her. It's not just sexual attraction. I don't know how to explain it. I can talk to her; she understands me. If it broke up, I'd be crushed. There's something there that I've never had before. It's just like I can't let her go. The only happiness I find in life right now is her.
>
> *Int:* Would you like to live with her?
>
> *R:* I don't want to live with anyone. I've been stuck with too many lemons. I find living by myself very enjoyable. She can come over whenever she likes. But if she's living with me . . . I just feel crowded. I want to know that whatever happens, this place will be me . . . mine.

So, as with friendship, the lesbian appears to have both a greater need for love and, out of that greater need, a greater probability for frustration.

It also should be remembered that some lesbians do manage long, enduring relationships, but others have difficulty managing even temporary affairs. In this, as in other areas of life, there is considerable variation in the capacities between lesbians at any given point in time and for given lesbians during different phases of the life cycle. The differences emerge as the need for and meaning of love change. Moreover, while the quest for love is problematic for the lesbian, it is not totally lacking in its problematic aspects for heterosexuals, who, after all, have at their disposal a larger number of substitute rewards and formal constraints that function to bolster a love relationship.

Self-Acceptance

Perhaps the single most important variable in understanding the adjustment of the lesbian is the process or the degree to which she comes to accept herself—that is, to manage her feelings about her emotions and preferences and to bring into some balance what she is and what she wants to be. Put into its simplest terms, this is her ability to like herself. Much,, of course, depends upon the outcome of many of the things we have discussed: relations to family, extent and quality of friendships, utilization of and role in a homosexual community, work adjustment, and success in the quest for love. These, of course, function in a complex and interactive system about which we know relatively little, primarily because of the scarcity of inquiry into these areas of life. How significantly success or failure in any of these specific areas of life leads to more general effects remains an important, but unanswered, question. However, it is clear that the most crucial expression occurs in the area of existential self-consciousness, for it is here that these more abstract judgments of success or failure are translated into the alternatives of contentment, happiness, confidence or despair, demoralization, and self-hatred.

Once again, what is problematic for most heterosexuals becomes more problematic for the lesbian. The problems have their sources in some elements that are particular to the lesbian adjustment, other elements that are shared with those who occupy nonmarried or childless roles in the society, and still others that are shared with persons whose sexual choices are regarded as odd or peculiar. Like most individuals, the lesbian can expect positive confirmation from the world on most of the roles that she strives to maintain. To the degree that these role performances elicit negative responses, the lesbian will be further detached from those living more conventional lives. From what we have suggested before, however, the majority of lesbians do maintain a major commitment to a number of conventional relationships. At the same time, the lesbian does experience a continuing sense of doubt when in interaction with conventional persons whether they know or do not know about her homosexuality. If the guilty secret is discovered by those who do not know, the lesbian fears that she will be rejected; if she is among those who already know, there is the danger of their interpreting her behavior solely through the screen of the deviant element in her life. This problem is clearly not omnipresent, nor does it necessarily infect every encounter. But nonetheless it is a background element, a sense of uneasiness that may serve to distort interaction with persons who appear conventional. Indeed, the existence of a pervasive deviant adaptation can lead to interpreting the behavior of others toward the self when such behavior seems ambiguous in nature.

When someone's reaction to a lesbian is purely in terms of her nonmarried status, she can still interpret it in terms of her homosexual interests, thus making her world more dangerous than it is.

The homosexual adaptation, for the individual actor if not for the audience of interaction, has a potential both for organizing life and for the consequences of failure. What little public language there is for the lesbian is predominantly negative, and her sexuality is certainly more striking than her other social roles. Perhaps it is not surprising, then, that many lesbians appear to have difficulty at this level and that most talk about it at one time or another. Nor is it surprising that the search for an effective basis for self-acceptance is fairly costly and most typically involves learning to deny the importance of certain activities, relationships, and forms of status that the society defines as eminently desirable and part of the "natural" course of life.

Several of our respondents indicated just how costly this process can be. One lesbian fled her homosexual commitment by entering an unsuccessful marriage that continued for six or seven years. This was followed by a period of sexual inactivity and later by involvement in homosexual activity. She commented:

> *R:* Sex is not very important to me now, in spite of the fact that there is greater sex activity. It is not as important as it was when I was in my twenties by any means. I've had too many years of conditioning; having lived without it, I made a conscious effort at psychologically conditioning myself not to think about sex. And I was fairly successful.
> *Int:* Are you happier now?
> *R:* Yes I have . . . well, I don't know about happier. I was happiest when I decided not live a straight life. In other words, I wasn't going to try to look for another man or to get married again. I'm not sure I am happier now that I made a second decision to live as if I were a lesbian. But there was a great deal of . . . peace is not the word. I felt I was reconciled with myself.

Decisions for this lesbian were problematic, but she is not entirely exceptional. A majority of the lesbians we talked to had experimented with the possibility of heterosexual relations, and a good proportion of these had seriously considered marriage. One described her situation as follows:

> *R:* The first fellow was the dashing type, involved in everything. He was part owner of ———. I was serious because I enjoyed being with

him; I found him interesting, even fascinating. But he didn't excite me physically; as a person he excited me. I enjoyed doing things with him. But physically, for instance, when he touched me I said I felt nothing, absolutely nothing. So if he made any attempt or made any suggestions, I put him down and said I didn't want it. And if he argued, I'd get sick to my stomach and think: my God, is he going to force me? But he never did. He wasn't pushy about it. I guess he thought it would be all right after we got married, so he proposed. I cared for him, but I didn't love him. It got to a point where every time he took me out, he proposed, so I broke it off.

Int: Did you ever feel the temptation to try to fake it?

R: Of course I thought about it at the time. He really was a nice boy and I thought . . . well, maybe it won't be such a bad idea. I might even be surprised. But then I realized I couldn't; it would be too much a lie.

The temptation is clearly to sacrifice the sexual gratification for significant gains in the availability of conventional rewards and statuses: the approval of friends and family, a recognized position in the general community, a family of one's own, and so on. Another young lesbian, reporting an almost identical occurrence, added:

For a while we all thought I would get married; my parents were happier than I can recall. One of my mother's big disappointments was the fact that there would be no grandchildren. I love both of my parents a great deal, and I would do almost anything for their happiness, but I couldn't do that. I think I was saddened, too, when I broke it off. Then I knew that I wasn't ever going to have children. And I would like to have some . . . for myself.

For the lesbian who learns to accept herself, this surrender of access to major cultural goals may be among her most difficult tasks. Moreover, we suspect that this surrender is never final, but that the desire for such goals tends to re-emerge at different degrees of intensity, at different points in the life cycle, either as nostalgia about the past or as anxiety about the present.

The need to see oneself as conforming to the moral order of the society also creates problems. The entry into a deviant career does not automatically bring release from moral constraints; to the contrary, the need to deal with conventional morality may loom more sharply for deviants than for persons following sexually conforming patterns who can readily assume universality of their moral commitments. More specifically, religiosity plays an important role, and nearly all of our society's organized religions take hostile positions with respect to homosexuality, defining it as wicked and sinful. This frequently creates a great problem for the lesbian who—like the male homosexual—must somehow attempt to reconcile her religious commitment with her sexual identity. For one lesbian, this was the greatest obstacle to her self-admission of homosexual preferences. She observed:

> I just felt that it had to be unnatural. I knew how men and women made love. It was present in their very biology. I didn't have the slightest idea of how women might; I didn't know what I could do to provide pleasure for another woman. I somehow decided that if God had intended women to love one another, He would have made it more obvious, like He did for men and women in love.

For most lesbians there is a movement away from religious involvement, particularly from the conventional communions. For some, this involves a kind of agnosticism or merely an avoidance of religious subjects and thoughts. For others, however, the roots of religious training and conviction run too deeply. Some of these women manage by rearranging their religious beliefs, thereby developing a personal style of religion and a personal image of God. One very religious woman described her feelings by saying:

> I stopped going to church when my minister told me that if I couldn't control the feelings, I could control acting on them, that it was a challenge. I just knew that God would not have given me these feelings if they were so bad. Somehow I know He understands.

Other lesbians, unfortunately, can't make this kind of transformation in their beliefs, and for them the resultant sense of self-rejection and self-hatred becomes severe. A number of such lesbians attempt to anticipate divine punishment by self-punishment, thus risking the disruption of their lives generally. One such lesbian accounted for her refusal to follow up many encouraging prospects in her field of work by saying: "I didn't because I felt I didn't have the right; I was too unworthy." However, the role of the church may change as an increasing number of the major religious bodies are now in the process of rethinking their original position on the question of homosexuality, particularly the question of whether it is, by definition, sinful and is a sufficient basis for exclusion from the religious community.

Psychiatry and the growing use of the language of mental health increasingly play a role in this process of self-acceptance. A large number of the women interviewed had been in one kind of psychological therapy or other, and a large number of them displayed considerable familiarity with the literature of psychology and psychiatry. The effects of such experiences appear to be mixed. On the one hand, it should create problems for full self-acceptance, since the prevailing clinical view of homosexuality is that it is an expression of pathology. On the other hand, use of the language of psychotherapy lessens the risks of self-hatred, because it permits the lesbian to see herself as the outcome of a process over which she had little control.

Conclusions

The major shortcoming of many previous discussions of the lesbian has been one of omission rather than commission; the lesbian has been described almost exclusively from the perspective of what has appeared to be her distinguishing characteristic—her sexual conduct. What has always been missing in these discussions is the rest of the activity that fills the lesbian's daily life. Even when such aspects of life have been considered, they have been used to show the way her sexuality expresses itself in this nonsexual activity. Rarely, for example, has her sexual activity been viewed as something that can be, and is, an expression of other forms of social activity. In our present, tentative, unsystematic, and incomplete investigation, we are attempting to alter this perspective somewhat—to impose a sense of this complexity upon the study of female homosexuality.

A second goal of this study has been to present a sense of the diversity of forms that female homosexuality may take, and to relate this diversity to a number of different dynamic factors and contingencies. While we may be inaccurate in selecting or recognizing these factors and contingencies, we feel confident in asserting the need for this kind of complex view. More than anything else, our success rests upon our ability to help move consideration of this problem away from dangerously simplified notions of *the* lesbian or *the* cause of female homosexuality.

We are *not* trying to argue that female homosexuality is natural. To the contrary, we are arguing that it is unnatural, but unnatural in the way that all human behavior is unnatural: it is without an absolutely predetermined and fixed shape and content. It is a complex condition that derives from the human ability to think, act, and remember, and the need to live with other humans.

7
The Prostitution of Females

Prostitution is conventionally defined, in order to distinguish it from other sociosexual activity, as the granting of sexual access on a relatively indiscriminate basis for payment, either in money or barter, depending on the complexity of the local economic system, with the payment acknowledged to be for a specific sexual performance. This service may be performed by either males or females for either males or females, though in practice in nearly all societies acts of prostitution are commonly performed by females for males or by males for males. While the prostitutes may be selective about the kinds of sexual activities that they will perform for money, it is clear that some kind of sexual act is available from them. Likewise, prostitutes may be relatively selective about their clientele, choosing not to take those who are dirty or deformed, those who request sexual activities that they think aberrant, or those who violate certain of the norms of conduct between prostitute and customer. However, within these idiosyncrasies the entrée to the prostitute is the capacity to pay for the relationship. Payment for the specific act is what distinguishes the prostitute from other sexual partners who accept a variety of gifts while having sexual contact.[1]

1. From the point of view of the radical feminist, this generalized description of the prostitute-customer relationship is universally applicable to the relations between women and men, including the relation between husband
(continued on p. 218)

This definition provides only a limited meaning of the prostitution of females to males, which is the exclusive focus of this chapter. Female prostitution is as much if not more vulnerable to the processes of social and scientific simplification than are other kinds of sexual relationships. While it is easy for us to recognize that there are profound social and psychological differences between similar physical acts that are called homosexual when they were performed in classical Greek society, in the Plains Indian cultures, and in public toilets of large cities in the United States, the prostitution of females remains too easily characterized as the world's oldest profession. While it has been recognized by some sociologists that the rate of males going to prostitutes or the prostitutes' significance in the sexual milieu is somehow connected to other outlets for sexual activity, such easy functionalism is limited to a relatively narrow band of history and to a limited set of cultural contexts. Indeed, the implied assumption of such a functionalist position is a fixed level of biological sexual appetite (commonly that of men) which requires a fixed amount of satisfaction and which will be necessarily found in some cultural arrangements.

The idea of the "world's oldest profession" largely conceals from us the central relation of female prostitution to conventional relations of men and women, both in their familial and economic positions in the specific historical societies in which they live. The label conceals the process of recruitment to prostitution, the social norms about gender and sexual behavior among the groups from which the women were recruited, the possibilities of exiting from the prostitute role, and the differing relation between prostitution and conventional sexual relations between the sexes. The term *prostitu-*

---

and wife in all sexist societies. From a political point of view, and for certain scientific purposes, this focus on the commonalities in the political, economic, and social statuses of women vis-à-vis men is both useful and powerful. Both the raising of consciousness and political mobilization depend upon women seeing that their current social condition, whether it is at present normatively legitimate or illegitimate, depends on their inferiority. This strategy of seeing similarities is also useful from a scientific point of view, because it seeks explanation for behavior not in a limited and given situation, but looks to larger relationships for the source of explanations of behavior.

tion tends to mask the significant differences between prostitution as it has occurred in such diverse locations as seventeenth-century England, the city of Kyoto in eighteenth-century Japan, the nine-teenth-century frontier communities of the United States, the cities and villages of Southeast Asia (before and after Western colonial-ism), or the Tenderloin of San Francisco in 1970. To see each in-stance as equivalent in some cross-cultural scheme is to rip it from its historical context in some dubious search for cultural universals.

To decry the search for cultural universals is not to impugn a concern for cultural continuity and the existence of historical proc-esses that allow older forms and values to interact with and, at times, shape current social life. Our attitudes toward prostitutes are based on the same origins as our current conventional vision of the natural order that should exist between women and men—i.e., nine-teenth-century English models. Though the contours of most of our society have changed in the intervening century, the available legal, moral, and social scripts that exist for the act of prostitution are remarkably stable.

In the middle and latter half of the nineteenth century large num-bers of women in the English urban working class (including mi-grants from both Ireland and the rural counties) were vulnerable to prostitution. Economic and social dislocation, the frequent deaths of husbands or parents, and the brutality of the factory system ex-posed large numbers of women to sexual as well as economic ex-ploitation. The conditions of vocational and familial life for lower class women were sufficiently appalling that a medical observer of prostitution in England stated that the working conditions of the prostitute seemed to be less physically damaging than either work in the factories or the exhaustion of repeated childbearing.[2] While adult women were at considerable risk, there existed a parallel trade in young girls and female children who were kidnapped or purchased for the bordellos of continental countries.

When large numbers of women and female children were forced into, were seduced into, or volunteered for lives of prostitution, it

2. William Acton, *Prostitution Considered in its Moral, Social and Sani-tary Aspects in London and Other Large Cities* (London: John Churchill, 1857), p. 59.

was close to impossible for the society to attend to what was a visible social condition. The state of relation (or perhaps irrelation) that existed between men and women was such that while novelist George Eliot allowed that her husband in his kindness used her but once a month, the anonymous author of *My Secret Life* could wander the streets of London seducing or buying large numbers of young women and children. The deep moral crises of English life were expressed in the sexual relations of men and women as they occurred both within and across classes.

The prostitute in this social situation came to occupy a very particular and symbolically enriched role in the Victorian mind. While it is evident that the actual experience of prostitution was highly varied—child and adult prostitutes in expensive bordellos, streetwalkers in the port cities, kept mistresses in St. John's Wood—the combined reforming and condemning impulse of the Victorian middle classes stylized the image of the prostitute, giving her motives and a life history and, indeed, inventing an entire social apparatus through which she could be experienced directly or in fantasy and put to social use. The Pre-Raphaelite paintings of the lost woman, given up to degradation amidst the finery of her suburban flat yet more inviting than the good women around her, are visual exemplifications of the profound moral ambivalences attached to prostitution by the cultural elite. A number of themes formed the relations between the sexes in this bourgeois world and had direct impact on the image of the prostitute: first, all (or nearly all) life chances for women had to be obtained through men; second, the opposition between the maternal and the erotic, the innocent and the impure was both an economic and a moral issue; and third, there was a deep confusion between women's social mobility and sexual adventurism, a confusion that can be traced in terms of declining female eroticism and increasing degradation from *Moll Flanders* to *Vanity Fair* to *Jane Eyre*.

The joining of money and sex was crucial to prostitution and the social connection which set the prostitute and men's sexual relations with her in a particular light. The sexual contact with the prostitute is that moment when the most private and most public in a bourgeois society meet. Even the metaphors for sexual expenditure that emerged at the beginning of capitalism involve an imagery of sexual excess as the spending of vital body fluids.[3] Sexuality itself was experienced by cultural elites through the language of Calvinist econometrics.

Sexual gratification in the nineteenth century among the middle classes in England (and for large populations today) was legitimately expected only within the marital bond. Even those presently quasi-legitimate forms of sexuality that are proscribed but not punished today because they are tacitly thought to promote either marriage (premarital coitus between those in love) or because they apparently reduce sexual "drives" or "tensions" during the absence of a marital partner (masturbation, either in adolescence or during marriage) were not normatively available to the nineteenth century bourgeoisie in England or the white Anglo-Saxon Protestant sector of the United States.[4] In contrast to these restrictions prostitution was thought to have quasi-legitimate functions during the last century and the first quarter of this century in the United States and England; for, within the strictures against premarital coitus and masturbation that grew out of the eighteenth century, the function of the bad woman was to protect the virtue of those who were good —i.e., the "bad woman" aided a covert and often overt maintenance of a "good" female's property value. Given the large number of migrant males, many of whom would not marry, it was not unexpected that police officials would conclude that the existence of prostitution was either a necessary evil or that it was a positive good

3. The significance of this idea of a limited amount of sexual capital that needed to be saved and expended in legitimate sexual works (i.e., reproduction) seems to have been codified in the first half of the eighteenth century. It has parallels in Tantric Bhuddism where vital fluids in the male are to be retained during coitus and in the film *Dr. Strangelove,* where the character General Jack D. Ripper will not share his vital body essences with women. The most significant use of the limited sexual economy model is, of course, in Freud where limited libido (a psychic energy equivalent to a humor or fluid) must be rechanneled to do cultural work.

4. Premarital coital practices in Northern Europe (which in prior centuries allowed premarital coitus among those potentially marriageable to test the females' fertility) find their continuity in a high incidence of premarital coitus in Scandinavia, but a premarital coitus which is now restricted to a fiancée. The early steady dating and multiple petting partners that characterizes the United States is only beginning to appear there. In the United States and England these patterns of fertility testing either never existed, or for England did not survive the rise of capitalism.

in that it reduced the number of rapes of good women in the community.

Most of the current values as expressed by individuals or collectively in welfare institutions and the processes of criminal justice are inherited from expressions of a nineteenth century cultural elite. The symbolic structure through which we experience the prostitute (the whore with a heart of gold, the bad woman who loves and dies for the good man, the lost and unadjusted girl, the lustful wench, the hardened whore, the victim of vice) is largely a cultural inheritance or cultural survival. While the character of recruitment, the locus of the activity, and the social sectors from which women are drawn have changed substantially, the prostitute is experienced by the customer in many of the same ways, and the legal structure that imposes sanctions uses the same explanatory rhetoric for legitimating arrest and imprisonment. This interaction of an inherited symbolic structure being imposed on novel sexual materials is not uncommon compared to other forms of sexual behavior. The development of the sexual sector is largely unplanned, and members of Western societies are, to a great extent, indirectly socialized into sexual roles.

A basic shift from the nineteenth-century pattern of the use of prostitutes in the United States correlates with a major campaign against prostitution after World War I. This involved an increase in penalties, lowered tolerance of houses of prostitution, and a national campaign against venereal diseases. This change seems to be tied to shifts in the structure of premarital coitus and the rise of romantic love as a collective ideology and individual option in mate selection. Romantic love and passionate sexuality, which now appear as such necessary and ubiquitous elements in woman-man relationships, are relatively new ideas. Indeed, the majority belief in romantic love probably does not antedate the 1920s in American society and is a post-World War II phenomenon in some working-class populations. The Kinsey figures published in 1948 chronicle this shift in overt behavior. While the proportion among males born in 1910 and after who have ever gone to a prostitute is the same as for males born before 1909, the frequencies at which the post-1910 group went to prostitutes were two-thirds to one-half of the frequencies of the earlier.[5,6] reductions were observed even in the already low frequencies of the college educated; however, the most substantial changes were among those of lesser education. The differences between the college and noncollege rates in all groups show the impact of social class factors in this area of sexual behavior.[7] Nowadays it is clear that contact with prostitutes accounts for only a small proportion of the sexual experience of males in early life. Furthermore, most of this experience is centered around peer-group activity and initiation into heterosexual coitus.[8] Significantly, it is among males who do not marry or who are divorced or separated in their thirties that the proportion going to prostitutes increases to about 15 to 20 percent of all sexual contacts.[9]

At first glance, it is possible to argue that these effects might be due to the decreasing visibility and accessibility of prostitution resulting from increased enforcement and increased sanctions. However, given the difficulty of controlling most victimless crimes, it is more likely that this change was the result of other forces which affected the proportion of never-married males in the society as well as a shift in the courtship patterns and an increasing importance of sexual contact in sealing the love-marriage bond between premarital couples. During the same time as this reduction in the frequency of going to prostitutes occurred, there was a concomitant rise in the proportion of respectable females who were having premarital coitus. This was a shift from about one-quarter of all females in the statistical groups born in 1900 and before in contrast to about one-half in all groups born between 1900 and 1929.[10] This shift oc-

5. A. C. Kinsey, W. B. Pomeroy, and C. E. Martin, *Sexual Behavior in the Human Male* (Philadelphia: W. B. Saunders Co., 1948), pp. 595–609.

6. All of the published Kinsey data for males and females is based on white samples. Data on blacks exist, but have not yet been published as of December, 1971.

7. Kinsey et al., *Sexual Behavior in the Human Male,* pp. 351–55.

8. Lester Kirkendall, *Premarital Coitus and Interpersonal Relationships* (New York: Julian Press, 1961), pp. 22–25.

9. Kinsey et al., *Sexual Behavior in the Human Male,* pp. 249–59.

10. Mervin Freedman, "The Sexual Behavior of American College Women: An Empirical Study and an Historical Survey," *Merrill Palmer Quarterly* 11: 1, 33–43; and A. C. Kinsey, W. B. Pomeroy, C. E. Martin, and P. H. Gebhard, *Sexual Behavior in the Human Female* (Philadelphia: W. B. Saunders Co., 1953), pp. 298–302.

curred at all social levels and is equally true of females with grade school educations and those with college backgrounds. These changes in rates represent a fundamental shift in the role of coitus in the mate selection process of our society, indicating a major break from nineteenth century values and a change in the status of women.

Premarital Coitus and Recruitment for Prostitution

While the data from Kinsey and others indicate that there are substantial differences in the measured sexual behavior of males when social class indexes are examined, there is no such finding in terms of the sexual behavior of females. To wit: the incidence and frequency of premarital coitus among males tend to be a great deal higher than those for females, except among the college educated where the differences are more moderate.[11] It appears that at the educational levels below college, especially among lower lower-class males, that the rates of premarital coitus were much greater than for females.

The explanation of these differentia in rates resides in two sources. First, the data on males in the 1948 Kinsey volume is heavily contaminated among the educational levels prior to high school and especially grammar school populations with males who had delinquent, criminal, and prison records. The comparable data in the Kinsey female volume did not include females with delinquent or criminal records or those who spent time in prison. The processes that exposed these men to criminal experiences and imprisonment also served to inflate their rates of casual premarital coitus. The problems in interpreting these data are extremely well analyzed by J. Richard Udry.[12] However, even with these corrections, male premarital coital rates are still higher than those of females, and this difference seems to have the following significance. Intercourse involving the majority of females at all social levels, but most significantly among the better educated, takes place primarily with one to three males, often limited to only the fiancé; in the Kin-

---

11. Kinsey et al., *Sexual Behavior in the Human Female,* pp. 78–80.
12. J. Richard Udry and N. M. Morris, "Method for Validation of Reported Sexual Data," *Journal of Marriage and the Family,* Vol. 29 (1967), pp. 442-46.

sey data nearly half of females with premarital coitus had it only with the fiancé.[13] Overall, about 55 percent of females reported premarital coitus in that research and did so with only one male, and 35 percent with between two and five males. For women who marry before twenty, as is often characteristic of lower-class girls, the proportion with contact with five or fewer males was 90 percent.[14] What these figures suggest is that the patterns of premarital coitus are relatively similar for females across the social class spectrum, but that there exists a minority of females, both black and white and primarily from working- and lower-class origins, who serve as sexual targets for fairly large numbers of males and at fairly high rates of contact without pay. The conditions of middle and later adolescence for many of these females is disordered and demoralizing. In large measure this early sexual activity is homosocially defined by the males—that is, it is most important in enhancing their social status among other males. Early involvement (ages twelve to fifteen) in heterosexual activity on the part of a female means, in nearly all instances, that the specific relationship will fail, that she will in large measure be "tarnished goods" to both male and female peers. For young women who have few interpersonal or familial resources during adolescence, repeated sexual contacts with males becomes a device for gaining acceptance and social status. Unfortunately, few males are capable at this age of dealing with overt sexual activity without reference to male peer group norms and standards. It is this group that makes up the largest proportion of young women who are adjudged incorrigible or sexually delinquent by courts that deal with adolescents and children. It is also this group who make up the largest number of women who become prostitutes.

Entry Into Prostitution

The conventional imagery of the first experience of prostitution has commonly been one of innocence betrayed or, if one follows the biographies of literary prostitutes, a severely traumatic experience. It is our belief that most biographical documents (not only those of prostitutes) require as subtle a reading as do most works of fiction.

13. Ibid., pp. 291–93.
14. Ibid., p. 335, table 78.

Prostitutes, like their customers, live their lives and their individual sexual contacts through received categories that have an historical dimension both individually and collectively. The act of writing a biography for publication is as scripted a performance as entertaining a client. For most young women who enter the world of prostitution, the transition is untraumatic, at least in the conventional middle-class meaning of trauma. There is often a good deal of vacillation and drift, sometimes when males accidentally or intentionally leave money as an act of goodwill or as a way of expressing their detachment from the relationship. In certain black subcultures a gift or what used to be called "show-fare" is part of the transient sexuality that characterizes the group which Eddington called the aristocrats of the ghetto.[15] For most girls who go into the life of prostitution following personal histories of adolescent disorder and premarital promiscuity, the transition is problematic (primarily in terms of accepting money, not the sex itself). However, for some it may be an entry into what appears to be a far more leisurely and unpressured life.[16] The effects of entering a life of prostitution are far more subtle than the simple shock of discovering that one is a "bad girl." The consequences of being "in the life" are attendant upon an increasing involvement in the world of prostitution, with a correlative decrease in social relationships outside that world. A sense of detachment from family or community often precedes the entry into prostitution. The detachment is expressed through geographic mobility, lack of contact with family, and disordered heterosexual relationships or marriages. To the degree that the entry into prostitution involves a time-specific trauma, it appears more often among females who have not had earlier sexual conditioning by multiple sexual contacts with a variety of males, who still maintain relations with conventional alters or who conceive of themselves within the narrow range of "good girl gone wrong."

With the decline in the numbers of brothels or houses of prostitu-

15. Neil Eddington, personal communication.
16. Anonymous, *Streetwalker* (London: The Bodley Head, 1959); C. H. Rolph, *Women of the Streets* (London: Secker and Warburg, 1955); Wayland Young, *Eros Denied* (New York, Grove Press, 1964), chap. 14, "Prostitution;" and Virginia McManus, *Not for Love* (New York: G. P. Putnam's Sons, 1960), pp. 81–86.

tion—institutions that remain only in some portions of the American South and in other rather anomalous locations—the apprenticeship experience in prostitution is now dependent upon dyadic relationships between the apprentice and either a more experienced prostitute or a male who operates as a pimp.[17] The apprenticeship involves learning on two levels. One level is restricted to activities which are specific to the narrow scene or stage which begins with the presentation of self as sexually available for money and continues to the exit line when the client departs. This learning experience involves more tasks than simply getting over the experience of exchanging money for coitus, though this is the informing and central dilemma of the prostitute. It involves learning ways of approaching males, ways of setting the price, ways of collecting the fee, ways of managing the sexual contact, and then ways of letting the customer go.

The narrow situation of learning how to do the work varies, depending on the site where the sexual presentation is made. In boredellos men come to the women and the act is restricted to a single place. Bar and street girls, like call girls, need to learn a wider set of skills in social management (many men are approached, turndowns are obvious, a private place is required). The individual entrepreneur is in a far more vulnerable position legally and psychologically than one who works in a business enterprise. Each of these events taken as a total experience involves making explicit what may have only been implicit in all prior heterosexual contacts because, no matter how many of these prior experiences there might have been, they could always be regarded as part of a conventional structure of female sexual expectations. When the commitment to taking money has been made, it means that the female gives up pretending that her sexual contacts with most males take place on an individual, affectionate, or romantic basis comparable to that of male selection. The situation is no longer one of courting or dating, but the specific exchange of sexual access for money. This means that, even if she has refused no one previously, her present lack of discrimination is now a public event.

17. James H. Bryan, "Occupational Ideologies of Call Girls," *Social Problems* 13:4 (1966): 441–50.

During this apprenticeship period she must also manage the non-sexual context of prostitution and the methods for bridging the gap between the nonsexual and the sexual. She must learn to name, recognize, and attribute motives to other significant persons in the environment: customers, steerers, the police, and other prostitutes. Part of this learning involves an argot that is itself highly value-laden, and which in and of itself constrains the neophyte into patterns of action and belief.[18] One of the most complex of these tasks is learning the capacity to speak openly (this is not always achieved; prostitution is not a form or a precursor of sexual freedom) about sexual acts and sexual preferences, which in the past have arisen and been performed in the context of gestural and nonverbal contexts, and then to tie the new talk to the pricing of the specific activity that is requested. The problem for the customer is that, while the relationship between money and sexuality is what makes the act possible, the economic portion of the act must not be allowed to intervene in the nature of the sexual performance. The structure of prostitute-client talk, once learned, becomes highly ritualized and predictable, though it varies from one social level of customer to another and from one situation of prostitution to another. Thus, the centrality of the cash exchange is high for the lower-class customer, the sexual activities preferred are limited, and the content of the sexual talk is small. On the other hand, in contacts with middle class males the price is set and not referred to again (though there may be psychic gain for the male as a result of payment), the sexual interests may be wide, and there is a certain expectation of talk that transcends the immediate sexual character to the relationship. The capacity to meet all of these epxectations is a relatively limited skill and may account for the mobility problems of girls who enter at various levels in the profession.

In this sense, entering "the life" is a process of managing a new conception of the self, a new relationship to males, a new way of talking about the self, and learning to meet a new world populated by special kinds of others. At the same time, there is concomitant decrease in the frequency of interactions with conventional others

18. D. W. Maurer, "Prostitutes and Criminal Argots," *American Journal of Sociology* 44: 546–50.

(except men in the new role of client) and in this process a further alternation of a previously decreased capacity to return to the conventional world. The life of prostitution, like many other forms of deviance, commits a person at the most deeply held portions of the self and, in the process, produces far greater similarities between prostitutes than would have been expected from any set of etiological characteristics.

World of the Prostitute

The culture of prostitution is, like all cultures, composed of significant individuals who lay claim on each other in terms of time, energy, and affection. The culture requires a large number of new definitions of others. However, these new definitions often inescapably cut off many of the older, more conventional definitions. The older definitions may still latently lay claim on the prostitute and in some ways entangle her even when she is most enmeshed in her new activities.

The world of the prostitute is primarily composed of other prostitutes, clients, steerers, and procurers, and in some cases pimps; it may include lesbian lovers or madams; and—finally—the police and other agents of law enforcement.[19] Relationships among prostitutes are enormously complex, but they seem in all circumstances to carry with them a substantial amount of mutual dislike and mutual exploitation. The content of conversations is often limited to the occupational life, for exposure of the self on other levels invites exploitation due to increasing personal vulnerability. However, the sharing of a special alienation and distance from the conventional society forces the prostitute back to other prostitutes for her social life. There is no one else with whom she can share a significant daily experience. Relationships with clients are equally difficult, but are most easily handled when they do not impinge on or have prop-

19. James H. Bryan, "Apprenticeships in Prostitution," *Social Problems* 12:3 (1965): 287–97; Sheila Cousins, *To Beg I Am Ashamed,* (New York: The Vanguard Press, 1938); Norman H. Jackman, Richard O'Toole, and Gilbert Geis, "The Self-Image of the Prostitute," *Sociological Quarterly* 4:2 (1963): 150–61; and Wardell Pomeroy, "Some Aspects of Prostitution," *The Journal of Sex Research* 1:3 (1965): 177–87.

erties of relationships that might have been sought in nondeviant contexts. Thus, the house girl who lives in a world of other prostitutes and who services a lower-class clientele is less likely to develop attachments to clients and more easily sees them as a series of replaceable objects. The call girl, on the other hand, to the degree that she must pose in public with her client in the roles that are defined as either conventional or at worst indiscreet, runs the risk of becoming emotionally involved with clients. This emotional involvement is expressed in demands that clients pay lawyers' fees, pay for bail bonds, or help out when she is in trouble, and it results in intense anger when they do not. In this case there is a residue of older expectations still involved, and the girl has not fully made a separation between her work life and her personal life. It is for this reason that the call girl may report more intense feelings of antipathy for the customer than the street or bar prostitute. This is complicated by the fact that the call girl may well have had middle-class origins and be more committed to the romantic love ethic and hence more susceptible to prior self-definition.

Prostitutes are used by clients for a variety of reasons.[20] For lower-class men, such reasons are often defined simply as sexual relief or the opportunity to experience a novel sexual contact, either in terms of a new female or a tabooed technique (usually mouth-genital contact). For the middle-class male resorting to the prostitute is often more complex and is invested with greater ambivalence than for nonmiddle-class males. Novelty in terms of the female and the sexual technique are certainly involved, as is the lack of future responsiblity for the consequences of sexual contact. Since many of the organzing constraints on sexual activity are related to maintenance of the family and its future, the contact with the prostitute is significant, because it allows sexual expression without such controls on behavior. The guilt consequent on the violation of the norms commonly deepens and intensifies the erotic character of the relationship, as does the degraded status of the prostitute who pro-

---

20. T. C. N. Gibbens and M. Silberman, "The Clients of Prostitutes," *British Journal of Venereal Diseases* 36:2 (1960): 113–17; Charles Winick, "Prostitutes: Clients' Perception of the Prostitutes and of Themselves," *International Journal of Social Psychiatry* 8: 289–97; and Kinsey et al., *Sexual Behavior in the Human Male*, pp. 605–99.

vides sexual access separated from the entanglements of nurturance and affection. In addition, there is available a sexual contact that does not involve the male in the time-consuming, conventional buildup to coitus and frees him for other pursuits. The frequency of contacts with prostitutes by males at conventions and in other situations that are separated from the home suggests the loosening of social controls that are necessary for such contacts to take place.

There are also those males whose sexual interests are sufficiently bizarre that there is no population of conventional women who could understand these desires or provide for them. Indeed, the expression of desires such as sadism or masochism commonly, but not always, undermines the rest of a nondeviant relationship. The proportion of such men is small, yet there exists a small number of prostitutes who will provide such services. The prostitute has to learn to cope with the various demands of these clients and to sort out those who request things that she will not do—even for a price. Prostitutes tell each other about clients, and it is in this interaction that patterns of client management are learned.

The relationship of the prostitute to the pimp is poorly understood, and the anxiety that this relationship raises in other men is considerable. This reaction against the pimp is related to the impropriety of a man living off the earnings of women in a society where men must provide for women; in addition, males who are not pimps envy the man who gets free that for which all others pay. The strength of the tie of the prostitute to the pimp is best understood in terms of her deprived emotional relationships with other males. In a world of changing faces, in terms of both prostitutes and clients, the pimp remains a stable figure who will speak in the terms of love and affection. Given that this is often a very minimal relationship, it still provides a stable anchor for the prostitute in a world where her private sexual experiences have been depersonalized; and the replaceability of not only the client, but also the self, has been made most apparent. Inadequate as it might seem to others, the tie to the pimp remains for many prostitutes the single human relationship where she may combine both sexuality and love, even if it is contaminated by money. Indeed, the very act of giving the money away to the pimp is like divesting herself of filthy lucre. Lesbian relationships have much the same character, but are probably less demoralizing. They arise from the need for affection and the alienation from men that is implied in the exchange of sex for money. It is not that lesbians become prostitutes, but that prostitutes, out of their reaction to the emotional proverty of their world, seek loving human relationships.

The world of the prostitute's secondary support-figures—the bell boy, the bartender, the hotel clerk, and the cab driver who direct the customer and the prostitute to each other—is a shadowy one. The prostitute learns the cost of these individuals and their services, their relative unreliability, and the exploitative nature of their relationship to her. These support figures live in a quasi-delinquent underworld that verges on the straightforwardly criminal. Because the act of prostitution is illegal, the prostitute is thrust into a world of police, courts, and correctional institutions. By this act of exclusion from the larger society, she is included in a set of relationships with the criminal world that complicate her life through contacts with narcotics, petty and major crime, and the corruption of the agencies of criminal justice. Since the law is enforced only against the "delinquent" participants in the act of prostitution, she is forever confronted with the facts of unequal treatment. Since enforcement of prostitution laws is uneven and often tied to changes in political climate, she is vulnerable to financial blackmail by the police; and, since her position at the margin of the underworld makes her a listening post, she is often pressured to give information to the police. In all of this she is further alienated from the society and forced into a criminal conception of herself within that society. All of the enforcement procedures fail in their intent to reduce prostitution, since they more often confirm persons in the activity rather than remove persons from it.

Given that all forms of deviance may be seen as at least potential situations for the development of major psychopathology, one of the major functions of the culture of the prostitute is to reduce this potential by providing a system of supporting social figures who operate as a community. While there is a good deal of evidence for pathology among prostitutes, it is probably reduced by the existence of the culture of prostitution. At the same time, the existence of this culture means that the prostitute's capacity to return to the conventional society is reduced. The potential for pathology is located first of all in the amalgam of sexuality and money at its most obvious level. It is complicated by the nature of the legal control procedures that are invoked.

Departure from Prostitution

Most prostitutes do not spend their entire lives in the career. Looks and physical health are eroded—if not by the life itself, then by the very process of aging. Some prostitutes marry out of the life into relatively stable family systems, while others drop out into service and related occupations, some of which are at the margins of delinquent and criminal communities. There is probably some degree of upward mobility for women who enter the life at the call girl level from lower social-level backgrounds; however, this is probably relatively rare. Others remain in the system as a result of police involvement and prison sentences, and still others through the use of drugs. The problem of how the ex-prostitute copes with her past and learns to separate money from sexuality is not known. Part of this capacity may be due to the very alienated relationship that she had with clients, so that they really do not count as part of the sexual past that she has had. It is definite that conditions in the United States make escaping from the life of prostitution more difficult than, say, in Denmark, where there is no statute against the act of taking pay for a sexual act as long as the female has another occupation. Danish authorities hope that through such a mechanism sufficient ties will be maintained to the conventional community so that the woman may have a past other than one of prostitution when she chooses to leave this career.

Conclusion

As far as the immediate future is concerned, the social organization and culture of prostitution will continue to have some strongly national characteristics. However, its illegal status will account for a great many of the nearly universal elements of secrecy, intense occupational involvement, and difficulties in leaving the profession. Its ties with the criminal underworld will leave the prostitute open to harrassment, not only by the police, but also by other prostitutes and other members of the criminal subgroups.

Even without the stigma of illegality, the dilemmas of managing an identification of money with sexuality and the problem of establishing an economic measurement for sexual access will produce certain strains toward the creation of a prostitute subculture. Learning how to manage the new concept of self and the management of the elements of the social world of prostitution will create a situation in which the prostitute must be provided with an occupational world—one in which the normal needs of social relationships will be provided by reducing the effects of attenuating conventional ties. While it has been pointed out that even the marriage tie and the courtship process involve the exchange of economic and emotional security on the part of the female and sexual access on the part of the male, the critical component in prostitution is making explicit the nature of this exchange and determining its value in the public medium of money.[21]

21. Kingsley Davis, "Prostitution," in *Contemporary Social Problems* eds. R. K. Merton and R. A. Nesbit (New York: Harcourt, Brace, and Co., 1961), pp. 262–88.

8

Homosexual Conduct in Prison

The last half-century has seen some extremely uneven progress in some areas of prison management, while at the same time there has been a marked progress in the creation of a new ideology of prison management. However, despite evidence of material and ideological progress, there remains a major area of behavior with which prison systems have been unable to cope—the problem of sexual adjustment that occurs in all institutions where one sex is involuntarily deprived of social or sexual access to the other. In the area of sexuality the prison is perhaps more spastic in its response than it is rigid (its conventional posture to most behavior). Attitudes of prison managements unpredictably vacillate from one extreme to another, both in their intra-institutional activities and in their public pronouncements. For the benefit of the public, prison officials pretend that the inmate population is neuter or they act as if homosexuality is rampant and uncontrolled. In the latter case, the institution's practices range from ignoring the behavior, if it is not troublesome, to periodic witch hunts, punishments, and internal transfers. This erratic course is partially attributable to both the very limited social and sexual resources of a single-sex institution for most of the keepers and the kept, and the extremely ambivalent guidelines for sexual pleasure that exist in the surrounding society.

Aspects of Prison Social Organization

The prison is one of a number of closed, single-sex institutions —what Erving Goffman has called dramatically the "total" institution—that becomes nearly the exclusive environment of its captives during the time they are sequestered.[1] The category of total institutions includes prisons and jails, asylums, and boarding schools, all of which are designed to keep people detained for some purpose. There are, in addition, institutions that are not normally conceived of as belonging to this class which are designed for partial social detention (of either time, work, or a stage in the life cycle), such as schools for the lower classes and the army in peacetime, both of which serve certain kinds of jailing functions for the society. These institutions of partial detention often share to a greater or lesser degree some of the problems of total institutions.

The prison, however, is the major single-sex institution in the society that has (unlike the mental hospital and other closed institutions) within its walls a population that is physically, and, for the most part, psychologically intact and is, at the same time, sexually experienced. The prison in the United States (and perhaps universally) is faced with unresolvable dilemmas in its attempts to manage such a population, either sexually or nonsexually. The prison managers' first duty is to maintain order among the prisoner population and prevent escapes. Failure in these tasks, regardless of successes in such peripheral goals as rehabilitation, will result in the replacement of the prison management. The rehabilitated prisoner disappears into the stream of the society and fails to be credited to the competence of the prison management. Escapes or riots, however, attract public attention and become evidence of the incompetence of the administrator. Rehabilitation and, often, minimal humane treatment become, as a consequence of this imperative of control, secondary and in many cases unrealizeable goals. In addition, the prison manager is also confronted with the fact that under all circumstances his institution will be underbudgeted, under-

1. Erving Goffman, *Asylums* (New York: Anchor Books, Doubleday & Co., 1962).

staffed, and overcrowded. The budgets for penal institutions are most heavily supported by the legislature and other budgetary agencies when the funds are for increased levels of control (especially after a riot or excape) and are commonly slashed when the funds are for increased treatment efforts. These circumstances are the normal circumstances of the majority of American penal institutions. An earlier reference to these institutions as the "cloacal region" of modern society is still appropriate.[2]

In the drive for control, management implements measures that are antipathetic to the rehabilitation of the prisoners and create aspects of the penal situation that shape the acting out of sexual behavior. As part of this attempt to totally control (and hence totally predict) inmate behavior, a series of degradation ceremonies are visited upon the newly imprisoned.[3] Such ceremonial degradation of the prisoner is the mechanism by which his relatively complex identity as a "free citizen" is transmuted into the relatively simple role of "convict." The sudden elimination of heterosexuality is part of this whole deprivation procedure, but it is rarely the most critical. Loss of most bodily pleasures, the capacity to direct one's own movements, the choice of work, the kinds of clothing, the times available for cleanliness, the hours of sleep, the size of income—all of these things besides sexual enjoyment—are denied the prisoner. These losses are important social psychological elements, first in identity stripping and second in identity creation.

It must be remembered that this process of identity change is never complete, and only in institutions of total terror do the majority of inmates become creatures of the institution itself.[4] Thus, while the character of the penal institution as demonstrated through its practices, procedures, and demands may create the context and set some of the limits on the expression of inmate behavior (including the sexual), equally important are collective standards of behavior that govern relations between men outside the prison and the

2. Holley Cantine and Dachine Ranier, eds., *Prison Etiquette* (Bearsville, N. Y.: Retort Press, 1950), p. 95.
3. Harold Garfinkal, "Conditions of Successful Degradation Ceremonies," *American Journal of Sociology* 61 (1956): 420–24.
4. See the extensive literature on the concentration camp for the techniques that were imposed to create this condition.

individual life histories and socialization experiences of the inmate population. Qualitatively similar norms govern superiors and inferiors in power in nonprison situations on the outside; this is the legitimating source of the inmates pleas to be treated "like men" or "with dignity" by their keepers. This version of the forces acting on the character of prison life is counter to some elements in the sociological literature on total institutions, which conceive behavior as nearly wholly situationally determined and fundamentally, even in the life cycle sense, ahistorical in character.

The significance of nonpenal experience for the shaping of behavior in prison not only arises from external norms and prior individual experience, but from the fact that, while many prison managements seek a situation of total control, none of them succeed. Hence the *de facto* procedures and demands of prison life are always an accommodation between the administration and the inmate population.[5] It is this accommodation between the keepers and the kept that shapes and controls the kinds of sexual expressions which the latter will have. Two interlocked but analytically separate inmate social structures emerge in this accommodation between inmates and the prison staff. The existence of such social structures requires that the staff lose or give up power over a certain amount of goods and services of the institution and allow inmates either shared or total control over their allocation. One of these structures emerges around the existence of the favorite prisoner phenomenon; that is, a prisoner who has a position of trust or control over the lives of other prisoners or who is selected for "soft" jobs in the prison. This is the formal, visible inmate elite (the librarian, servants in the warden's dining room, the clerical assistant to various prison officers) who have more mobility, more access to information, more food, better clothing, more access to the power centers in order to make requests.[6] In addition, there is the invisible inmate hierarchy

5. Donald Cressey, *The Prison* (New York: Holt, Rinehart and Winston, 1961); Donald Clemmer, *The Prison Community* (New York: Holt, Rinehart and Winston, 1960); George H. Grossner, ed., *Theoretical Studies in the Social Organization of the Prison* (New York: Social Science Research Council, 1960); Gresham Sykes, *The Society of Captives* (Princeton, N.J.: Princeton University Press, 1958).
6. As a consequence of low salaries, the tendency of prisons to be built in rural or depressed areas as forms of subsidy, the fact that the custodial

of higher- and lower-status persons, depending on the content of local criminal or penal norms. In this structure inmates have power over each other through the methods of force or fraud or through status positions gathered through nonprison exploits. In these two ways an inmate social structure emerges which dilutes the direct controls of the institution, cushioning the arbitrary exercise of power. There is a limit on this accomodation, however, for the custodial staff must not lose total control of the institution. It must at least control the perimeter of the prison (whether walled or not) so that the prisoners do not escape, and the interior insofar as publicly noticeable disturbances are concerned.

The inmate social structure is responsive to the intensity of control and to those in whose hands it is located. There is a balance of power between both the staff of the institution and the inmates *and* between the custodial staff and the rehabilitative staff (if the latter exists). In many American penal institutions the inmates have more power in the institution than does the rehabilitative staff. Power in the institution is represented primarily in the control of work assignments and discipline, and by and large, the final decisions in these matters are predominantly in the hands of the custodial staff. Rehabilitative staffs are often only of negative value to the inmate, since their positive recommendations are rarely mandatory, but the record they create of the prisoner's antisocial behavior and dangerous propensities will continue to dog his steps, not only in the institution in which he currently resides, but in other institutions to which he may go. The riot situation is often a consequence of a power struggle between custody and the rehabilitative staff and the breakdown of previous social relationships between custody and the inmate staff. Favorite inmates lose their positions of strength and the capacity to give out rewards and services to other inmates as the award of such goods and services becomes the right of the treatment staff.

The difficulties between inmates, custody, and treatment may arise even if the treatment staff merely exists, for the promises of re-

---

staff is often undereducated, and an aversion to having women work in prisons, nearly all the clerical work is performed by prisoners. This makes it impossible to keep any information confidential.

form that its very presence intimates will generate discontent in the population. The implication that the institution will reform or aid and abet men to live new lives provokes unrest when it is obvious to the inmate population that the promises will not be fulfilled and that control of the institution remains in the hands of the custodial staff. In this case the promises of rehabilitation are used as levers in the bargaining process against control by custody, especially by inmates who are out of power, and even by those in power, to gain further advantage. When there is a direct confrontation between custody and treatment, the institution may be ripe for a riot or at least major dissension. Custody and the favored inmates covertly join together using the influence of the latter and the residual powers of the former to gain control of the prison. By and large, such struggles are won by the custodial faction in the prison.

The bargain that is finally struck in any penal institution between the inmates, the custodial staff, and the professional-rehabilitative staff will be the major institutional factor creating the sexual adjustments of the inmate population. This bargain represents the degree of control over individual behavior (both staff and inmate) that the institution demands. In some institutions the daily life of the inmate population is almost completely controlled by inmates, and the custodial staff merely guards the walls. In other institutions nearly all of the power is vested in the custodial staff (or, more rarely, the professional staff) and each act of the inmate is determined. These two conditions represent the rare ends of a continuum and most institutions fall between them in the degree of management intensity.

Noninstitutional Factors Affecting Prison Sexual Adjustment

Despite our focus on the character of the prison itself, it is not the sole nor in some cases even the major determinant of inmate patterns of behavior. Institutional behavior rarely arises *sui generis,* and it is only in the complex interaction between the preinstitutional experience of inmates and staff and the institutional structure that an adequate picture of the final mixture may be formed.

There is an unfortunate tendency to view the sexual adjustment of prisoners as arising exclusively from the contexts of prison life. It is frequently assumed that any group of people who were incarcerated for any period of time would react sexually in the same way as those who are presently in prison. This is a major oversimplification brought about primarily because of a lack of information about the prior sexual and nonsexual lives of those who are imprisoned and the way in which this prior experience conditions a person's responses not only to sexual deprivation, but also to a general loss of liberty.

It is important to specify the range of sexual responses that are available to those imprisoned. With the exception of the small number of prisons that allow conjugal visits, there are only three forms of sexual behavior that are generally available to prison populations (except for animal contact for those males on prison farms). These are nocturnal sex dreams, masturbation, and sexual contact with other inmates of the same sex. The meaning, amount, and the character of these adjustments will be strongly dependent on the meaning that these same behaviors had for the inmate before he or she was incarcerated. Thus, the problem for the inmate is not merely the release of sexual tension, but the social and psychological meaning that such release has and the motives and beliefs that it expresses for him. The source of this set of values does not reside in the prison experience, but outside the prison in the community at large. Thus, the prison provides a situation to which prior sexual and social styles and motives must be adapted and shaped.

There are two major dimensions on which most sexual activity is based. One is that of age, with the primary break occurring between adolescence and adulthood. The other, perhaps of greater significance, is the differential meaning of sexuality to the two sexes. Thus, the striking differences between the sexual orientations of men and women noted in the Kinsey volumes offer the best starting point for a discussion of sex in prison.[7] The discussion that follows focuses on the responses of adult male and female inmates to the prison experience, with only passing reference to institutions for adolescents, as they are not unlike the adult institutions.

Male prison populations are not random selections from the larg-

---

7. Alfred C. Kinsey, Wardell B. Pomeroy, and Clyde E. Martin, *Sexual Behavior in the Human Female* (Philadelphia: W. B. Saunders Co., 1953), pp. 642–89.

er society and do not reflect the usual distributions of the population in terms of education, income, ethnicity, occupation, social class, and general life style. The men who make up the bulk of the imprisoned populations tend to be drawn from deprived sections of the society or from families embedded in what we have now come to call the culture of poverty. As a consequence, the sexual experiences of these men and the meaning that sex has for them differs in significant ways from other portions of the population that are less likely to be imprisoned.

A number of dimensions of these differences may be found in the work of Kinsey and his colleagues in which they report the substantial differences among the sexual activity and attitudes of men who have differing amounts of education.[8] These findings are further amplified in the volume *Sex Offenders,* where a comparison of imprisoned men and men of the same social origins without delinquent histories showed that the men with prison histories generally have wider sexual experience of all kinds than do men leading conventional and nondelinquent lives.[9] These variables suggest that at least the model male prison population enters institutions with differing commitments to sexuality than would a middle-class or working-class population. We can therefore suggest that the response of these latter groups to institutionalization would differ as well.

Drawing on what we know about the dimensions of the prior sexual adjustments of men who go to prison, our first major sense of the experience is actually how little sexual activity of any sort occurs within the prison.[10] Thus, even after the shock of imprisonment has worn off (and often for the recidivist this occurs quickly), there is no sudden burst of sexual activity of any type. Confirming these impressions is the low order of complaint one hears about sexual deprivation, even when prisoners are presenting a list

---

8. Alfred C. Kinsey, Wardell B. Pomeroy, and Clyde E. Martin, *Sexual Behavior in the Human Male* (Philadelphia: W. B. Saunders Co., 1948), pp. 327–93.

9. Paul H. Gebhard et al., *Sex Offenders* (New York: Harper & Row, 1965).

10. From a preliminary analysis of the differences between the preinstitutional and the institutional sexual outlet of adult male prisoners interviewed by the Institute for Sex Research, the institutional rates are only one-tenth to one-fifth of noninstitutional rates. For some males the institutional rates are nearly zero.

of grievances after a riot or outbreak of some sort. Part of this is surely due to the closeness of custody in the institution and the fact that men move and live in close proximity, and, except for certain moments of the day, there is very little privacy—not so much from the custodial staff as from the inmates.

However, another cause of this reduction is that sexual activity is normally potentiated by or channeled through an existing set of eliciting social situations that do not exist in prison. The man in prison finds himself without the appropriate stimuli which suggest opportunities for sexual activity or situations that are appropriate for such activity. Without the existence of these social cues, the biological substratum for sexual activity is never aroused.[11] The absence of females, the sheer sensory monotony of the prison environment, the absence of those social situations that call for sexual responses (being out on the town, going to bars to drink, etc.) serve as effective inhibitors of sexual responsiveness. The most successful aphrodisiacs seem to be an absence of anxiety, the presence of available sexual cues, an adequate diet, and plenty of rest. Of these, only the latter two are common in the prison environment, and in some cases only the last is.

The other source of sexual cues is fantasy, those remembered or desired sexual experiences that commonly serve as the basis for masturbation. However, as a result of the social origins of the bulk of the prison population, there is a major taboo against masturbation and a paucity of complex fantasies that would sustain a commitment to sexual experience.[12] Thus, unlike the middle-class male who learns and rehearses sexual styles in the context of masturbation, the usual prisoner is drawn from a population in which sexual experience is concrete and not symbolic; in which there is a taboo on masturbation; and, finally, in which much of heterosexual experience is structured around the need to have sexual encounters that validate his masculinity among other men. In this environment it might be said that men have sex with women in order to be able to talk about it with other men.

The Kinsey evidence is that even among lower-class men who do

11. For a discussion of the necessity of socially facilitating cues for sexual arousal and performance, see chapters 1–3.
12. Kinsey et al., *Sexual Behavior in the Human Male*, pp. 497–509.

masturbate, there is often no conscious fantasy accompanying the behavior and it serves primarily as a mechanical release of felt physical tension. This is quite unlike the middle-class situation, in which masturbation occurs at relatively high rates and is accompanied by fantasies of sexual experience. These fantasies then begin to facilitate further masturbation and a continuing commitment to this sexual outlet. This adjustment rarely happens in the lower-class environment and, along with the sensory poverty of the prison environment, accounts for the ease with which strong commitments to sexuality are abandoned. Thus, prisoners may complain about sexual deprivation in terms such as, "I would really like to have a piece," but often this is a continuation of lower-class male talk about sex, not a passionately felt drive that will eventuate in sexual activity.

Homosexual Adjustments in Male Institutions

Since most prisoners do not seem to feel an overwhelming sexual need, male homosexuality in this context must be seen as something more complex than merely the outcome of sexual desire or the need for physical release. There are varying estimates of the number of males who have homosexual contact during their periods of imprisonment. The range is probably somewhere between 30 and 45 percent, depending upon the intensity of custody in the institution, the social origins of the population, and the duration of the individual sentence. Donald Clemmer, in the only published study of interviewed prisoners concerning their own sexual behavior, determined that 60 percent of the prisoners restricted their sexual behavior to continence, nocturnal emissions, or masturbation, while the remainder had some homosexual experience usually in addition to solitary masturbation.[13] Joseph Fishman estimated this latter percentage to be from 30 to 40 percent;[14] Gresham Sykes from his study of one penitentiary estimated 35 percent;[15] and researchers at the Institute

13. Donald Clemmer, "Some Aspects of Sexual Behavior in the Prison Community," *Proceedings of the American Correctional Association,* 1958.
14. Joseph Fishman, *Sex In Prison* (New York: National Library Press, 1934).
15. Sykes, *The Society of Captives.*

for Sex Research concluded that the proportion of inmates ever having homosexual experience in long-term felony penal institutions ranges from 35 to 40 percent.

The composition of this 40 to 50 percent of penal population who have homosexual experience in the prison can also be estimated in terms of their preinstitutional homosexual experience. From the interview data of the Institute for Sex Research on a group of 888 white prisoners who were not sex offenders, about 7 percent had homosexual experience for the first time in prison.[16] This would suggest that, of the total prison population, between 5 and 10 percent of the total population having homosexual experience did not have homosexual experience prior to incarceration. About 25 to 30 percent of the population will be having homosexual experience, but will have been modestly experienced prior to incarceration. Between 5 and 10 percent of the prison population will have been extensively or nearly exclusively experienced as homosexuals in the free community.

Even with these relatively high incidence figures, it seems quite clear that the frequency of homosexual contact is usually quite low, even among cellmates; and in no sense does it approach the rates of heterosexual or homosexual behavior of these same prisoners on the outside, except possibly for those prisoners who come into the institutions with well-developed homosexual commitments and who become the "passive" partners in homosexual liaisons.[17] In some prisons, usually those with a very low order of custody inside the

16. Gebhard et al., *Sex Offenders.*
17. The notions of "active" and "passive" in homosexual relationships are more obscuring of the actual conditions of the behavior than they are enlightening. The psychiatrist Irving Bieber has suggested the words *insertor* and *insertee* by substituted for *active* and *passive,* since these latter words assume that role behavior in a sexual act has major meaning in psychological personality terms. *Homosexuality* (New York: Basic Books, 1962), pp. 238–54. For an attempt at clarification of this confusion, see chapter 4 of this volume. It must be pointed out that homosexuality in prison is quite a different phenomenon from homosexual experience in the outside community. Thus, the image of homosexuality as consisting of masculine-seeming men who are always "active" derives primarily from both journalists and scientists observing homosexuality in prisons and then extending their observations unchecked to the outside world.

walls, high rates of homosexual behavior may be achieved; however, these are not the prevalent conditions in most prison systems.

More important than the sheer incidence or frequency figures are the complex series of roles involved in the homosexual experience in prison. Males with no experience or only incidental homosexual experience prior to imprisonment and who have homosexual experience in the penal institution are a group Clemmer calls quasi-homosexual.[18] These two groups, those who begin homosexual experience in prison and those who continue a previous minimal adjustment, are that portion of the prison population that inmates describe as "jockers" and "punks." Those persons with noninstitutional extensive homosexual experiences fall into the sexual argot roles of "fag" and "fairy."[19] It is important to recognize that some males with extensive nonprison homosexuality may be sufficiently aggressive to fill "jocker" roles as easily as those with less experience.

The sources of this homosexual activity for the predominantly heterosexual and aggressive male seem to be twofold. One element is certainly a search for meaningful emotional relationships that have some durability and serve as a minimal substitute for affective relationships that they normally have on the outside. This is not unlike the chance homosexual contact between men during combat or in other situations of all male communities under circumstances of fear and crisis. It represents an attempt to counter the effort of the prison to atomize the inmate community in order to reduce the potential for collusion, which could result either in conniving for goods and services or in attempting escape.

One of the collective responses to this institutional attempt to control behavior is the development of a resistant inmate community. At the individual level, one of the responses is the establishment of homosexual liaisons. A second motivation underlying many of these relationships transcends the level of affectional need and essentially becomes a source for the continued validation of masculinity needs and a symbol or resistance to the prison environment. The male whose primary source of masculine validation in the outside

18. Clemmer, "Sexual Behavior in the Prison Community."
19. Sykes, *The Society of Captives.*

community has been his sexual success (rather than work, family, etc.) and who has conceived of himself as aggressive, competent, and dominant in his responses to his world (commonly expressed in sex with women), finds that in prison he is deprived of these central supports for his own masculinity. In reaction to this, he enters into homosexual relationships in which he can be conceived as the masculine, controlling partner and which for him and for other males in the system validate continued claims to masculine status. A complicating factor here is that some men suffer a profound psychological crisis when the supports for their masculine identity are removed. In these cases either a severe homosexual panic or falling into a "passive" homosexual role can be likely results.

The homosexual adjustment in prison, as opposed to continence or masturbation, has the important advantage of being social and demonstrative. And, from an inmate point of view, if the homosexual behavior is not "passive," it may well be wrong, but it is certainly not totally abnormal. It is the location of homosexual behavior on continuation of activity-passivity, masculinity-femininity, and aggression-submission that define the "normality" of the adjustment. Indeed, certain sexual techniques are defined as passive or feminine in the penal institution, and these are what Iruing Bieber has described as insertee roles (active fellatio and passive anal intercourse).[20] In these cases the male who ejaculates is the masculine, aggressive partner. Robert Lindner argues, quite persuasively, that the prison is a dependency-creating institution where males are stripped of their initiatory capacities.[21] One reaction to this dependency (which is perceived as enforced "unmanning") by the aggressive male is taking the "wolf" or "jocker" role. Lindner says that this homosexual behavior is not "real" homosexuality, by which he apparently means that it does not have the same etiology as the homosexuality which one observes in most noninstitutionalized males. The homosexual behavior of these imprisoned males is essentially acted out in terms of dominant or predatory relationships. The aggressive males in adult prisons have been com-

20. See footnote 17.
21. Robert Lindner, "Sexual Behavior in Penal Institutions," in *Sex Habits of American Men*, ed. Albert Deutsch (New York: Prentice-Hall, 1948), pp. 201–15.

monly recruited from boys who had the experience in juvenile institutions, or from "hardrocks" in adult institutions. One of the most interesting findings in Paul Gebhard *et al.* was that a much larger proportion of offenders charged with rape had their homosexual experience only in penal institutions and in these aggressor roles than did any other sex offense group, or indeed the general prisoner control group.[22]

In the penal situation the insertee or passive partner is considered a member of one of two groups. First, there are those who are described as "born" homosexuals—persons who are homosexual on the outside and homosexual on the inside. A portion of these males are overt and obvious, and they often appear in misdemeanant institutions for minor offenses. A 1934 study of an eastern urban municipal penitentiary reported that there was a brothel stocked with such males who presented themselves as females.[23] In 1952 in a long-term penitentiary much the same arrangement existed, with a group of well-known males operating as "female" prostitutes. Their cells were fixed up as fancy cribs, and they sexually entertained other males for contraband funds. In these situations the masculine heterosexual image of the active male is well protected through a clearly defined prostitute-customer relationship in which the other male acts and plays the role of a woman. In prisons in the South, the overt homosexual often promotes a homosexual relationship with an aggressive male in order to protect himself from the tradition of violence that exists in these institutions. This tradition of violence includes exposing homosexuals to gang rape by large numbers of other males by whom this gang rape is then defined as a heterosexual experience. Two such experiences in southern penal institutions, widely separated in time and place, have been described by James Blake and by George Devereaux and M. C. Moss.[24,25]

22. Gebhard et al., *Sex Offenders.*

23. George Henry and Alfred Gross, "The Homosexual Delinquent," *Mental Hygiene* 25 (1941): 420–42.

24. James Blake, "Letters from an American Prisoner," *The Paris Review* 13 (1956): 8–44.

25. George Devereaux and M. C. Moss, "The Social Structure of Prisons and the Organic Tensions," *Journal of Criminal Psychopathology* 4 (October 1942): 306–24.

The second major group of males who are the passive recipients of homosexual contacts in penal institutions are those who are called in inmate argot "punks" or "made" homosexuals. Two major subtypes exist in the institution—one such adjustment is often a more developed and a later historical consequence of the other, and therefore a clean line between one and the other is often hard to locate. The first type is the prostitute, a male who sells himself to a number of others in the penal institution, but who is generally heterosexual in the free community. Often these males were homosexually seduced during a prior incarceration in a training school or other prison and then embarked on a career as a homosexual prostitute. There is a second group of males who do not sell themselves, but who are each currently attached to a single male. Most of these inmates have experienced the process of seduction. If they have future sentences, they may become prostitutes or be reintroduced into homosexual experience with a single other male. The general technique of seduction involves an older inmate picking up a younger prisoner and—through constant companionship, the giving of favors and teaching him the "ropes"—creating an indebtedness on the part of the younger man. There then begins a process of introducing the new prisoner to conventionally "married" couples in the penal institution—those "jockers" and "punks" who are living together and who are well-known to the inmate population. The purpose of this introduction is to generate the belief that this pairing is a common situation in the penal institution. Prison-made pornography is available to stimulate arousal, and there are certain situations in which preparatory body contact can be produced, such as a rubdown. These overtures, hopefully for the "jocker" at least, ultimately generate a situation of sexual contact which involves either "leggin's" (interfemoral intercourse), anal coitus, or fellatio with the "jocker" in the insertor role. The process may vary in speed, in the amount of time at each stage, or even the success of the approach. However, the frequency of its occurrence and the ubiquity of its existence in various institutions makes it appear to be a widespread product of male imprisonment.

A more sensational, if rarer, event is homosexual rape which is more likely to occur in penal institutions where the custodial staff only controls the outer walls of the prison. It also occurs in short-

term detention institutions where there is a highly transient population and an extreme mix of males of all types in a closely confined
situation. In the situation of the jail, highly aggressive males with
considerable prison experience may be housed with mentally re-
tarded or physically immature younger males who become victimized.[26] This is also a characteristic of loosely run institutions
where social services for inmates are practically nonexistent, and in
which the older "jocker" has some control of goods and services of
the institution. These goods and services are used for seduction and
when seduction fails (but the younger male is in debt) rape may result. Homosexual rape can also occur during riots when the whole
social fabric of the institution tends to collapse and immature and
mentally unstable males are assaulted. Homosexual rape is not a
very frequent occurence, and at time there is some question (as in
heterosexual situations) as to whether the situation is really in fact
rape or whether it is a seduction which has simply gone wrong.

  One of the central problems of homosexuality among males in
prison is the management of the emotional content of the sexual situation. The mechanisms by which males who conceive of themselves as heterosexual and who conceive of themselves as aggressive
and dominating can involve themselves in homosexual situations
are unclear. Lindner de-emphasized the affectional element in the
relationship and suggests that the basic need for the "jocker" is to
subordinate other males to his will.[27] Among lower-class men in the
free society, the presence of females and the activity of coitus defines "maleness," and the promiscuity of these males suggests a
need for continuous masculine validation. In prison such validation
can only occur through creating a surrogate heterosexual relationship. Ernest W. Burgess (noted in Devereaux and Moss) has described this as a "romantic gesture" which attempts to recreate the
structure of a heterosexual relation through an affair with a male:
the "jocker" dominates the "punk" and in homosexual behavior
acts out his masculinity. By doing so, he is also resisting the prison
administration.[28] In this sense, homosexuality for the aggressive

  26. Alan J. Davis, "Sexual Assault in the Philadelphia Prisons and Sheriff
Vans," *Transaction* 6 (December 1968): 8–16.
  27. Lindner, "Sexual Behavior in Penal Institutions."
  28. Devereaux and Moss, "Social Structure of Prisons and the Organic
Tensions."

male takes on certain aspects of a social gesture against the stripping procedures of the prison. In the prison, toughness may substitute for intercourse as a measure of *machismo*. There is support for this view in the work of Lionel Ovesey, in which he suggests that many homosexual conflicts and symptomotology may result from other than sexual needs and may, in fact, arise out of conflicts in power and dependency needs.[29] Patients produce pseudo-homosexual ideation when they have been attacked in their sphere of maleness (quite often this is the occupational sphere for middle-class males). Jack L. Ward has argued that the acting-out delinquent who has also been attacked in his masculine spheres through the stripping process of the prison acts out his power drives against the "punks" instead of dreaming of homosexuality.[30] The "punks" are those who don't fight, who are dependent, who are "queer." It is the physical weaklings against whom the masculinity of those who are stronger is pointed. In many cases this quite clearly substitutes for both the heterosexual and heterosocial life which is no longer available.

Homosexual Adjustments in Female Institutions

Existing material on the social structure of the penal institution is strongly biased by the imagery of institutions for men. The prison for women is ameliorated primarily by a general societal commitment to a belief in the myth of the weaker sex. Women's prisons often have no walls, utilize dormitory or even private room arrangements in cottages, and are of considerably smaller size than institutions for men. At the same time, there is a greater opportunity for heterosocial contacts, since there are substantial numbers of men working around the institutions—if not as guards, then as maintenance men or other employees. These institutions seem, at least from the physical arrangements, to be far less coercive and more enlightened than comparable all-male institutions. Nonetheless, they remain penal institutions with many of the same commitments as do all-male institutions. Women's prisons are like men's prisons

---

29. Lionel Ovesey, "The Homosexual Conflict," *Psychiatry* 17 (1954): 243–50.
30. Jack L. Ward, "Homosexual Behavior of the Institutionalized Delinquent," *The Psychiatric Quarterly Supplement* 32 (1958): 301–14.

in that a publicly defined "good" institution is one that is quiet, undisturbed, and efficient, whatever these virtues may cost in terms of treatment programs. Like the all-male institutions, they exist in a precarious equilibrium of power distributed between the administration and the inmates.

There is a further complication as well: by and large, our society is biased against committing females to prison, especially when any alternative is available. Thus the women's prison often has within it women who have either committed major crimes (most commonly homicide) or had long careers in crime and who have been recidivistic. Thus, in a certain sense, the female institution is composed of some women who have had no prior link to delinquent lifestyles and a larger number who had long-term ties with such a life.

As we have noted before, the major dimension which differentiates between the sexual adjustment of persons in the larger society is gender; that is, men and women differ fundamentally in their sexual commitments. While this is obvious, the consequences for the differential sexual adaptation of the males and females in prison are not.

The sexual adjustment of these women to imprisonment is strongly linked to the general goals to which most women are socialized in the larger society. Probably the most significant difference between men and women in this regard is that women are socialized in the language of love before they learn about sex, while men are socialized in the language of sex before they learn about love. The consequence of this is that women commonly show considerably fewer problems managing the physical elements of sexual deprivation than do men. While there is little evidence, one might expect that the frequencies of any ameliorative behaviors, such as masturbation and homosexuality, are considerably less frequent for women than for men in prison. There is considerable evidence that such behaviors are less frequent among women in the free society than among men, and one should not be surprised that such continuity would be found inside the prison. In addition, women seem to tolerate the absence of overt sexual activity far better than men do, and thus the rates of overt sexual behavior in the female institutions should be considerably lower than those found in male prisons.

The typical response of women to the depersonalizing and alienating environment of the penal institution differs substantially from that of males. Almost universally in juvenile institutions, and in some observed cases in institutions for adult females, female prisoners appear to form into pseudo-families with articulated roles of husband and wife. Then, especially in juvenile institutions, they extend the family to include father, mother, children, aunts, uncles, and cousins.[31] These family systems seem to arise from three sources. One source is a process of compensation; the majority of females in these institutions are from severely disordered homes, and the creation of the pseudo-family often compensates for this lack. Spencer Stockwell and others have reported that practically all of these females involved in homosexual family structures had prior histories of exploitation or brutalization by older males.[32] This is a very valuable observation, since these characteristics are also found in the histories of daughters in father-daughter incest cases, and in the cases of chronic runaways where the running away has been suggested in an attempt to prevent such incest experience. A new family is desperately recreated in the penal institution to substitute for the disintegrated family, which seems so characteristic of the female delinquent. The content of these pseudo-family experiences is extremely limited in emotional character. Sidney Kosofsky and Albert Ellis reported on the stereotyped romantic content of illegal letters which were sent between girls in a girls' school.[33] They pointed out that the content of the letters contained very little real sex or references to genital sexuality—most of the discussion related either to family structure or to love and affection of the sort portrayed in sentimental popular songs.

A second source of pseudo-familial organization results from the

---

31. See Seymour L. Halleck and Marvin Hersko, "Homosexual Behavior in a Correctional School for Adolescent Girls," *American Journal of Orthopsychiatry* 23 (1962): 911–17; Rose Giallombardo, *Society of Women: A Study of A Women's Prison* (New York: John Wiley & Sons, 1966); David Ward and Gene Kassebaum, *Women's Prison: Sex and Social Structure* (Chicago: Aldine Pub. Co., 1965); Sidney Kosofsky and Albert Ellis, "Illegal Communications Among Institutionalized Female Delinquents," *The Journal of Social Psychology* 48 (August 1958): 155–60.

32. Spencer Stockwell, "Sexual Experiences of Adolescent Delinquent Girls," *International Journal of Sexology* 7 (1953): 25–27.

33. Kosofsky and Ellis, "Institutionalized Female Delinquents."

socialization of women. Unlike males, who form gangs in self-defense, women tend to form families, the basic institution in our society that offers them stable and legitimate roles. Finally, the pseudo-family serves to stabilize relationships in the institution. It establishes orders of dominance and submission, the primary models for which come from family relationships with fathers, husbands, and children. Since all social systems require some form of articulation which is hierarchical in nature, it is not odd that women model their experience on the institution that they know best in the outside community. There is some evidence that the pseudo-family is not as prevalent in institutions largely populated by older females, and it is possible to speculate that in these institutions dyadic friendship patterns are more frequent and may be more similar to those in male institutions.

Inside the context of these familial structures there is the potential for and the acting out of overt homosexual contacts. In the two most recent studies of female prisons there are varying estimates of the number of women who are involved in homosexual practices. This variation is probably a function of differing definitions, with one definition limiting the estimate to overt physical contact (yielding a rate of about one-half) and the other probably referring to the proportion of the population who are currently involved in roles in pseudo-family structures (yielding a rate of about 85%).[34]

A minor part of the overt female homosexual contacts may arise from deprivation of sexuality, but the primary source is the lack of emotionally satisfying relationships with members of the opposite sex and the desire to create the basis for a community of relationships that are stable and predictable. The overt homosexuality derives somewhat from the conventional sexual content of the role definitions of husband and wife, but also partially from the fact that a certain proportion of females who come into these institutions may well have experience with lesbian relationships (often through experience with prostitution in the free community). This is not to say that female homosexuals become prostitutes, but rather that

34. The two volumes are Ward and Kassebaum, *Women's Prison* and Giallombardo, *Society of Women*. For an excellent comparative discussion, see the joint review of these volumes by Sheldon Messinger, *The American Sociological Review* 23 (February 1967): 143–46.

among prostitutes homosexual relationships are sought because of the degraded conditions of paid contacts with men. The processes of induction into homosexual activity in the women's prison are part of a search for affection and stability in personal relationships, and follows the same principles of that observed in male institutions. The homosexual relationship offers protection from the exigencies of the environment, and the physical homosexual contacts are less sought for the physical release that they afford than for the validation of emotionally binding and significant relationships.

Interracial Homosexual Contacts

A special complicating problem for the American prison is the existence of racially integrated institutions for both men and women. The oppressive characteristics of race relations in the society as a whole penetrates the relationships between whites and blacks inside the prisons. In some states there is a disproportionate number (and in some institutions even a majority) of blacks in penal institutions relative to the number of blacks in the areas from which the prisons draw, due to higher black arrest rates. This movement of the Negro minority into a near parity of numbers or even majority status brings the racial conflict into the confines of the penal situation. Further, there are cultural disparities in terms of pre-institutional attitudes toward sex in general, and homosexuality in particular, which are also productive of specific conflicts about sexual adjustment.

Black males, deprived in the outside society of even more methods of validating masculinity than the most economically depressed of white males, find even greater need for continuing validation of masculinity in relationships to women. In this sense the black male, even more than the white, finds continuing validation of masculinity needs in aggressive homosexual relationships in prison.

Black homosexuality in general, and black homosexuality in prison particularly, seems different from the white experience. The black male is less likely to express the degree of repugnance to homosexuality that white males do. In like measure, he will be less likely to express strong positive sentiments toward homosexual experience if he has had it. This lack of strong positive or negative feelings characterizes black homosexuality both in the free community and in the prison. The motivation of the Negro prisoner to have homosexual contact is more directed by dominance needs and sexual access than by strong needs for affective investment. Indeed, these needs may tend to involve the Negro prisoner more often than the white prisoner as the aggressor in homosexual rape.[35] Another conflict-producing element is the desire of some of the overt white male homosexuals for relations with black "jockers." This desire on the part of the white male is commonly a result of the general problem in male homosexual relations of wanting an object who is somehow different from the self, but also male. This desire is also reflected in contacts of male homosexuals with men in military uniform or in an interest in sadomasochistic experience as well as an interest in men of other races. All of these contacts are pointed toward a differentiation between the two sexual partners. These contacts of white males with black males produce an intense potential for violence. Part of this potential arises from white "jockers" who are jealous of the black "jocker's" increased status resulting from having a white "punk" (since the relationship is viewed in heterosexual terms, one can read "white woman" for "white punk"). But another element in this possibility of violence is the fact that black males generally have a more emotionally detached attitude toward sex. In this situation, the white male often has much more intense sexual and emotional investments in the black male than the black partner is prepared to reciprocate. If the black male leaves the white male for another lover, there is a much greater possibility of violence resulting from the jealousy and anger on the part of the deserted passive homosexual. Homosexual contact between white males may also result in violence, but the relationships are not imperiled from so many sources. The jealousy of white "jockers," the fickleness of the black "jocker" and "punk" contributes to the instability of these particular liaisons.

This cross-racial situation is also observable in many female institutions, but it takes the form of family organization that has been noted before. Even in segregated southern institutions cross-racial

35. Alan J. Davis, "Sexual Assault in the Philadelphia Prisons and Sheriff Vans."

sexual feelings between females are quite apparent. In these situations, a complex family constellation is created by the female inmates. In practically all such cases the black females are defined as
male and the white females defined as females. The masculine partner is described as a "stud" or a "daddy," and the female partner is
described as a "baby," a "vot," a "wife," etc. For the black females,
as with black males, the institutional homosexual experience is less
affectively loaded. Hence, there is often the potential for violence
on the part of white females because of the greater emotional investment in the sexual experience. This black-white family structure
has been observed in training schools in Illinois, in Ohio, California, and New Jersey, and in other institutions across the United
States.

Conclusion

This conceptualization of the pattern of homosexuality in the
prison for men suggests a number of problems that face the prison
in dealing with sexuality. It means that, as long as the prison is an
environment which is largely devoid of situations where legitimate
affectional ties can be established, there will be a tendency for the
formation of homosexual relationships, especially among those men
serving long sentences who have concomitantly lost contact with
meaningful persons in the free community. If, in addition, the prison does not allow legitimate attempts of the inmates to control their
own lives and does not give an opportunity for expressions of masculinity and self-assertion that are meaningful among men at this
social level, there will be homosexual relationships created to fulfill
this need. The proposal for conjugal visits does not meet this problem, in part because such an outlet is available for only the number
of inmates who have intact families. There is little evidence that the
society will tolerate sexual relationships for prisoners when these relationships are not sheltered under the umbrella of a marriage.

What is clear is this: It is not the sexual drive itself that makes a
prison full of unrest, in fact, most males survive the deprivation of
sexual outlets and normally survive transitory homosexual commitments to return to more or less conventional heterosexual lives on
the outside. What the sexual problem in the male prison does repre-

sent is a series of land mines—some for the administration, more for the prisoners. Inmates get into relationships which have some potential for shaping their future commitments to sexuality, which leave them open to exploitation, and—especially for those who take the passive role—the possibility of distortion of their self-conceptions. Further, there is some tendency for these relationships to create problems of sexual jealousy. When a relationship deteriorates or when a transfer of affection takes place, there is a distinct possibility of violence. The violence that does occur often is extreme. At this point it becomes a serious matter for prison management.

The dilemma for the prison manager is that often he is not aware of the relationships until they erupt into violence. Attempts at intervention in this process through getting inmates to aid in the identification of those involved may result in serious scapegoating of these persons out of the sexual anxieties of the other prisoners. The segregation of these prisoners has also been attempted. However, one major difficulty with this measure seems to be that, when the most obvious homosexuals are removed from the situation, there is a tendency to co-opt other persons to take their place. This tendency is also noted when the aggressive male is removed, though the policy has usually been to remove only those men who are conventionally obvious—that is, those who appear excessively effeminate.

Probably the only long-term solution is to adopt the policy of home visits at intervals during incarceration and to provide alternative modes of self-expression for those social and psychological needs which, because of the current structure of the male prison, result in homosexuality.

From the arguments posed above, it is suggested that what is occurring in the prison situation for both males and females is not a problem of sexual release, but rather the use of sexual relationships in the service of creating a community of need-satisfying relationships that the prison fails to provide in any other form. For the male prisoner homosexuality serves as a source of affection, a source of the validation of masculinity, or a source of protection from the problems of institutional life. Similarly, the females tend to create family structures in an attempt to ward off the alienating and disorganizing experience of imprisonment; the physical homosexual relationships are merely part of the binding forces of these relationships.

Therefore, the problem for the prison administrator becomes considerably more complex than merely the suppression of sexual activity—it becomes a problem of providing those activities for which the homosexual contacts are serving as substitutes. The inmates are acting out their needs for self-expression, control over their own behavior, affection, and stability of human relationships. The homosexual relationship provides one of the few powerful ways of expressing and gratifying these needs. Unless these needs are met in some other way, there is little opportunity for adequate control of homosexual activity in the prison environment. It might be hypothesized that any attempt to become more coercive and controlling of inmate behavior in order to reduce homosexual contacts may result not in a decrease in activity, but perhaps in an increase. By increasing coercion one increases the pressure to divide inmates from one another, and one decreases their capacity for self-expression and self-control. As the pressure builds, there may well be a tendency for homosexual relationships to increase in importance to the inmate population as a reaction to the intensity of the pressure.

Imprisonment and the concomitant sexual deprivation of inmates obviously have some serious consequences, at least during imprisonment and have a minor potential for complicating post-institutional life. Little systematic research exists that links the prior non-prison experience of the prisoner (both sexual and nonsexual), methods of institutional management, and the consequences of the interaction of these two elements for the inmates' future functioning. The fact that many inmates adjust easily to the climate of deprivation in the prison may be a measure of their pathology and inability to get along in the outside community rather than a measure of healthy functioning. Just because we can manage to make people conform to a climate of deprivation, both sexual and nonsexual, is no reason that we should.

9

Pornography: Social Scripts and Legal Dilemmas

Nowhere is the semanticist's injunction against overloading words with multiple meanings and ambiguous emotions more applicable than in the confusion surrounding the applications of the term *pornography* and, to a lesser extent, the related term *obscenity*. While it is commonly recognized that the processes of deciding what to include and not to include in the category of "pornography" or "obscenity" are extremely difficult, it is rarely noted that the very use of these terms in the process of labeling an event or thing as sexually stimulating can produce a psycho-sexual response in the labeler and his audience very similar to that produced by the pornographic object itself. The very act of labeling generates a sense of sexual anticipation and engages our fantasies about the business of pornography and the erotic character of those who produce it. In the same manner that the social apparatus which surrounds other unconventional sexual expressions is conceived as being motivated sexually, the production, wholesale distribution, and retail sale of pornography are viewed as erotic enterprises. This process of simplification by which persons and situations are defined as totally sexual when they are marginally connected to sexuality is perhaps one of the major sources of the potency of pornography itself. Everything is grist for the mill of sexual fantasy because the process of that fantasy strips away the hulls of reality, seeking only those kernels that fit its needs.[1]

Partly because of the capacity of this fantasy to use the widest range of materials in its routine organization (from *Studs Lonigan* to *Fanny Hill,* from the *Sears, Roebuck Catalogue* to *Playboy),* it is assumed that sexual fantasy and its objective correlative—pornography—have a magical capacity to push men into overt sexual action. In this view of sexuality the sexual impulse lies like the beast in every man and every woman (though less so among the latter), restrained only by the thinnest tissue of social repression. Underpinning most of the discussion of sex in this society (and one of its minor expressions, pornography) is an intense feeling that there exists some kind of Hobbesian contract to protect us against natural (and bestial) sexual man. On some ultimate level, it is held that sexual activity requires no explanation; it is, in a sense, explanation in itself. If, as Steven Marcus maintains, the sexual behavior described in hard-core pornography occurs in a socially and psychologically denuded landscape, so does much of the scientific thinking about sexuality.[2]

At the same time, human sexuality—however closely it appears to be tied to biological processes—is subject to the sociocultural molding to a degree surpassed by few other forms of human behavior. While the number of forms that sexual activity may take on a physical level is restricted by the fixed limitations of the human body (there are, after all, only a fixed number of concave and convex surfaces available), the objects that may be defined as desirable, the social locations within which such activity may take place, and the specific activities to be defined as pleasurable vary over social life to a profound degree—indeed, to a degree that dwarfs the uniformities of biology. And, of course, on the level of imagination —that is, on the level of the purely symbolic—the restrictions or limitations of biology prove to be at best temporary barriers.

1. It should be noted here that the publicly available content of sexual fantasy is almost totally defined by male needs, as is the content of pornography.
2. Steven Marcus, *The Other Victorians* (New York: Basic Books, 1964).

The Social Dimensions of Sexual Arousal

It is the authors' contention, perhaps more explicitly in this chapter than in others, that all human sexual behavior is socially scripted behavior. The sources of sexual arousal are to be found in sociocultural definitions, and it is extremely difficult to conceive of any type of human sexual activity without this definitional aspect. Thus, while there is frequently an almost hysterical concern on the part of many males over being embarrassed by uncontrolled arousal in situations involving social nudism, the fact is that this is an extremely rare occurrence. The structuring of the social nudist situation so self-consciously screens out an erotic content that arousal rarely occurs. The sexual potential of any situation becomes effective for most males and females only if the situation is defined as appropriate and the partner as sexually available. From these definitions both the possibility of sexual activity and, to a considerable measure, the specific kinds of sexual acts follow. It is also equally clear that the sources of the sexual scripts—the elements of definition—find their origins not in biology or even training for sex itself, but in the application of social attributes to both the situation and the actors. It is not the physical aspecs of sexuality but the social aspects that generate the arousal and organize the action, or, in other words, provide the script.

The problem may be approached in another way. In U.S. society—and perhaps in most Western societies—to learn about sex is to learn about guilt. To develop a commitment to sex is to learn techniques for the management of guilt. While personality problems for many individuals in the Western world are directly linked to problems of managing guilt in the sexual area, it is difficult to assess the degree to which sexual behavior also receives its sense of intensity and potency from this same source. At any rate, the permeation of the sexual area with a high guilt-provoking potential is a reason for the need for, and an element in the shaping of, sexual scripts. Sexual scripts not only elicit sexual responses, but they also establish the legitimacy of ordered sets of behaviors; they become the conventionalized strategies for managing guilt.

Freud in his essay on erotic degradation deals essentially with this problem.[3] His discussion of the need to distinguish sharply between the erotic and the maternal, and the use of symbols or rituals of degradation as a basis for facilitating this distinction, is in fact a discussion of one aspect of the need for sexual scripts. The problem Freud recognized—that is, the inability to be erotically attracted to what one loves or being unable to love that to which one is erotically attracted—is somewhat extreme. Considering that the largest portion of sexual activity in our society occurs within the context of a marital union—rather than in pre-, extra-, or post-marital relationships—it becomes clear that most individuals manage some degree of integration of both elements, the erotic and the sentimental, in a single dyadic relationship. What we know little about are the processes that facilitate this integration of conflicting elements. Sexual scripting, which takes many forms, ranging from the most symbolic representation, the sexy nightgown, to the integration of behavior and fantasy by one or both partners, may well play this facilitating role.

The critical characteristic of pornography is not merely that it deals with explicit representations of sexual activity; recall its original definition: the language of, or works about, prostitutes.[4] Pornography is not arousing or exciting merely because it deals explicitly with sex, but because it deals with illicit sex. It is a challenge to find a single pornographic or erotic work that has as its major focus the description of conventional sexual activity that occurs within a marital relationship. The rule is: if the activity is conventional, the context is not (the relationship, the motives, etc.); if the context is conventional, the activity is not. The landscape of pornography— "pornotopia" as Steven Marcus named it—contains prostitution, homosexuality, rape, incest, sado-masochism, adultery, etc., as its most familiar contours.[5] Pornography deals almost exclusively with deviant social or sexual behavior. One consequence of this is that the need for social scripts to organize the encounter with pornography is as great as, if not greater than, the need for comparable scripting in actual sociosexual behavior. For, as a whole line of so-

---

3. S. Freud, "The Most Prevalent Form of Degradation in Exotic Life," *Collected Papers,* vol. 4 (London: Hogarth, 1949).
4. Wayland Young, *Eros Denied* (New York: Grove Press, 1964), pt. 3.
5. Marcus, *The Other Victorians.*

cial thinkers running from Durkheim and Freud to the present make perfectly clear, people must not only learn how to manage guilt derived from things they do, they must also learn to manage the guilt that derives from the things they think about.

In a society characterized by a reasonably integrated normative system, it is almost as difficult for most people to engage in vicarious deviance as it is to engage in an act of overt deviance. However, it is obvious that more acts of deviance occur vicariously—through fantasy or identification with actors in one or another of the cultural media—than occur on the level of overt behavior. We can be sure that virtually all persons have on numerous occasions engaged vicariously in major acts of deviance, both sexual and non-sexual. What makes this possible is that the resources for the managing of guilt and for the appropriate elaboration of accompanying social scripts are much greater on this symbolic level, through the modification and transformation of social identities and social relationships. In consequence, opportunities for rituals of expiation and a return to conventional moral postures are more available at lower costs on this level than in the real social world.

Just as people rarely engage in overt acts of incest, vicarious participation in an act of incest is also extremely difficult. Offered the possibilities of identification with an actor in a literary work who is about to commit an incestuous act, readers find that identification is made difficult by the anxieties that their feelings about the act would generate. The organization of sexual arousal and the capacity for vicarious participation would be disrupted by crippling ambivalences. However, the world of vicarious action may be reordered. For example, if the characters involved in a novelistic depiction of incest truly do not know of the familial bond and as a result they do not commit incest for themselves, the reader may have his passions stirred by his knowledge of that bond, but still share the innocence of the characters. (This is one of the frequent themes of the gothic novel.) Or the reader can know that one partner, the one he does not identify with, engages in this behavior with a cruel and wicked purpose, making the actor with whom he identifies essentially a guilty victim whose later sufferings will prove to be adequate to justify a return to the moral community. In other words, the world of symbolic representations has a conspicuous advantage over the "real world." In the latter, the commonsense observation that becomes the basis of Talcott Parsons' pattern-variable scheme—that "you can't have your cake and eat it too"—clearly operates.[6] In the former, the logical impossibility becomes a sociological possibility.

Nevertheless, there are fundamental limits to the flexibility of the world of vicarious experience or symbolic representation. When the reordering of social life or social values becomes excessive, representations cease to be plausible and identification becomes difficult or impossible (which is the reason why most of the Marquis de Sade fails as pornography except for the manifestly pathological personality), or we become unable to manage guilt and organize sexual tension. There are limits to the power of sexual scripts.

The Ethnography of Pornography

This necessary intrapsychic relation between the world of pornography (and in a direct sense the world of potential sexual arousal) and the world of social roles, values, and social structures is also shaped by the kinds of pornographic materials that are available and the social contexts in which they are seen. This is *not* to follow the arguments of Marshall McLuhan about the primacy of the media, but to examine the ethnography of apprehending pornography and the social contexts in which it may be seen. Not only do psychosocial elements predominate in the organization of the pornographic object itself—the social context in which pornography is perceived controls many dimensions of the sexual response, whether one shares in a group presentation of pornographic materials or sees them alone.

The stag film is an excellent example of the way in which we tend to ignore the social context within which pornography is used and from which a large part of its significance for the individual consumer derives. Out of context, the blue movie is rarely more than a simple catalogue of the limited sexual resources of the human body. Prior to 1968, stag films were seldom seen by females and were most commonly enjoyed by two kinds of male groups: those living in group housing in colleges or universities and those

6. Talcott Parsons, *The Social System* (New York: Free Press, 1951).

belonging to upper-lower class and lower-middle class voluntary social groups. More recently, both the private trade in stag films and in longer and equally explicit films in movie theaters and arcades have increased, especially in large urban centers. It is now possible for many persons in the United States to walk into a theater on a well-lit street in a reasonably decent neighborhood and see films showing mouth-genital contact and intercourse, both heterosexual and homosexual. These relatively recent developments serve to bring previously restricted sexual resources to new audiences in new situations. The stag movie remains a staple in young male college groups and among voluntary organizations, but it serves both similar and different functions for the major categories of persons who see them.

The critical continuity between past and present is that most audiences are still all-male. For the male college student, the stag films are a collective representation of mutual late adolescent and young adult heterosexual concerns and, to a lesser degree, they instruct in sexual technique. For this group the exposure in a group situation is either concurrent with or prior to extensive sociosexual experience. The group context serves to reinforce adolescent masturbatory fantasies in an all-male context. As a transitional experience, it may relieve tensions associated with greater heterosocial intimacy and the movement from an all-male to mixed gender social commitments. From all observational data, such males comprise only a small proportion of the attendees at the "X"-rated film theaters. Exposure comes later in life for the second group—after marriage or, at the very least, after the development of sociosexual patterns. For this audience the group experience itself provides validation of sexual appetites in social milieus where other forms of validation, such as extramarital activity, are inaccessible by virtue of age and social skills and, in addition, may be subject to severe sanctions. The primary referent of the films in this instance is in the area of *homosocial* reinforcement of masculinity and hence only indirectly a reinforcement of heterosexual commitments. This reinforcement of heterosexuality is reflected in the way the films portray the obsessive myths of masculine sexual fantasy. They emphasize, for example, that sexual encounters can happen at any moment, to anyone, around almost any corner—a belief that is a close parallel to the romantic love fantasy so very characteristic of female arousal. In the case of the male, however, sex replaces love as the central element. These films also reaffirm the myth of a breed of women who are lusty and free in both surrender and enjoyment. Given the kind of social context within which the films are shown, there is little reason to assume that their sexual arousal is not expressed through conventional sexual or social actions.

The body of newcomers to the audience for blue or near-blue movies appears to be made up of males over the age of thirty, of middle- and lower-middle income populations, for whom the experience is essentially private. The degree to which they are drawn from the viewers who belong to fraternal and other voluntary organizations, is unclear, but the functions of the two situations appear sufficiently different so that there is no reason to assume recruitment from one group to another. What is most likely is that this group of males is using the film as an occasion during which they can masturbate or as a supplement to their regular sexual diet. This use varies by location; theaters in New York City's Time Square and similar bright light areas have more masturbators than "X"-rated theaters in the suburbs. The private use of film erotica is linked more closely to the private consumption of literary pornography than it is to all-male group showings.

There is a small body of evidence that these films are also being used as an adjunct form of sexual arousal among the small subgroup of persons in U.S. society who are involved in collective forms of heterosexual behavior involving orgies, wife-swapping, and the like. The use of the stag film in this context commonly occurs after the original involvement of individuals in this form of behavior. Its utilization as a specific source of sexual arousal is secondary to its mere presence in defining the situation as being more erotic. It is the fact of the film's social definition as arousal producing that is important rather than its specific content. Indeed, this may be another instance of life imitating bad art. The use of erotica "to get things going" is an ancient convention in pornography. However, this use is probably as statistically rare as the behaviors that it accompanies.

Noncinematic pictorial representations of sexual activity lend themselves to the same kind of analysis; unlike films, and more like written materials, their use is essentially private. Nonetheless, patterns of use remain congruous with other patterns of social life and process; they represent anything but the triggering mechanisms through which the social contract is nullified and raging, unsocial lust (whatever that might be) is unleashed. The major users of pictorial erotica are adolescent males. If these materials have any use, it is as an aid to masturbation. There is no evidence, however, that the availability of "dirty pictures" increases masturbatory rates among adolescents. This is a period in life when masturbatory rates are already extremely high, particularly for middle-class adolescents. Indeed, in the absence of hard-core pornography, the boys create their own stimulation from mail-order catalogues, magazine ads, and so on. In middle-class circumstances, many young men and the majority of females in all social classes can enter early adulthood without ever having seen hard-core pornography.[7]

If exposure to this kind of pornography, while facilitating masturbation, does not substantially affect masturbatory rates, it is still possible that such materials may shape the content of the masturbatory fantasy in ways that create or reinforce commitments to sexual practices that are harmful to the individual or to others.[8] While no research in this area meets the most stringent of scientific criteria, research that does bear on the topic indicates that exposure to pornography is most commonly a transient, trivial, and diffuse event. It is explainable as an accidental by-product of normal adolescent socialization or as a more direct consequence of conventional sexual success among males. It may be observed that most pornographic materials share with the masturbatory fantasy a sense of omnipotence, but the acts represented are rarely homosexual, and they are not sadistic beyond the general levels of violence common in contemporary kitsch. Once again, one suspects a reinforcing or facilitating function rather than one of initiation or creation.

The pornographic book, in contrast to photographs and films, represents a very different consumption situation. Few books are

7. Alan D. Berger, John H. Gagnon, and William Simon, "Pornography: High School and College Years," Commission on Obscenity and Pornography, vol. 9 (U.S. Government Printing Office, 1972).

8. George Steiner, "Night Words" in *Language and Science: Essays in Language, Literature and the Inhuman* (New York: Atheneum, 1967).

read aloud in our society, and it is very unlikely that this would occur with a book of descriptions of overt sexual activity. In fact, prosecutors take advantage of this by reading sections of allegedly obscene books aloud in court with the aim of embarrassing the jury into a guilty verdict. The privately consumed erotic book almost universally provides nothing more than novel content for an existent fantasy structure or reinforcement for fantasies that are already established. Few books lead to overt action of any kind, and the erotic book is unlikely to be an exception.

The most difficult problem in defining the legal margins between pornography and nonpornography is the rapidly changing fringe literature found on public newstands: the pulp books, national tabloids, men's magazines, and pinup collections which line the racks in drugstores, bus stations, and rail and air terminals. It will be recalled that it was the girlie magazines that were most often under legal attack for nude pictures in the recent past. (It must be noted that the frequency of legal attacks is decreasing rapidly with the increasing disarray of the moral ideologies in support of sexual censorship.) The most recent magic line of censorship to be breached is that of pubic hair, though recently it was the bare breast or exposed nipple. Not so very long ago, navels were ruthlessly airbrushed away and Jane Russell's cleavage was a negotiable issue in securing the censor's approval of the movie *The Outlaw.* The Gay Nineties were made gayer with pinups of strapping beauties clad in tights revealing only the bare flesh of face and hands. The current limit of visual materials in the nationally advertised, publicly mailed magazine is the simulation of coitus or mouth genital contact, but without including the genitals of either gender. These boundaries are, of course, trangressed in materials sold in off-street book stores where a self-selected audience handles materials in their private reverie. In winter of 1971 the magazine *Trans-Action* included a photograph of someone making a pornographic photograph (including a photographer and a couple in physical contact, but obeying the concealed genitals rule), and *Playboy* now routinely includes pubic hair and photos of concealed sexual action.

The period of most rapid change has been the quarter-century since 1945, with a constantly accelerating pace culminating in a rush over the five years prior to 1971. Pictorial material of nude males and females, and mixed gender photos limited by the concealed genital rule when body contact occurs, are relatively widely available. More difficult to come by are photos of sexual action, but the determined adult purchaser in a large urban place (especially in New York City and San Francisco) can find them. In our era the pulp book, available on the newsstand, freely describes most physical sexual activity with an increasing degree of accuracy, commonly only slightly less explicitly and more metaphorically than hard-core pornographic pulp books. Indeed, the margin between the respectable pulp novel and the hard-core novel is more and more permeable. Scenes previously described just "off-camera" in the pulp novel have become more elaborated and frequently include the conventional language of the erotic literary subgenre. There are still, however, representations, frequently self-advertising, in pulp novels that are designed to set them apart from the rest of the newstand materials. The books that are most similar to the hard-core pornography of the past still do not mingle freely with all other pulp books. Porno books are clearly published for their capacity to elicit sexual arousal, and they are purchased by an audience that knows what it is buying.

To view examples of fringe or even hard-core pornography exclusively in terms of their sexual function is misleading. Since we tend to overestimate the significance of sexual activity, we see the trends of representation in these works as indicators of sexual behavior in the community. An increase in works about homosexual love is taken as an indication of an incipient homosexual revolution or even as the cause of a homosexual revolution. If we find more books about adultery, sado-masochism, or fast-living teenagers, we believe that there must be more adulterers, sado-masochists, and fast-living teenagers in our midst. With a dubious logic reminiscent of primitive magic, many people believe that if the availability of such representations increases, so will the frequency of such acts, and conversely that the way to cut down on this antisocial behavior is to suppress the pornographic representations.

While it is conventional to see most pornographic representations as being without nonsexual meanings, either internal to the representation or in the external situation of use, it is apparent that both of these considerations are in error. It is perfectly apparent from what has gone before that for varying kinds of erotic objects to elicit an erotic response there are situations of consumption which define both the sexual and nonsexual meanings and payoffs of that consumption. Correlatively, the pornographic object itself is given its sexual meaning by being embedded in conventions which are largely sexual or by having its own internal conventions of presentation which link to nonsexual culture elements. Hence, Morse Peckham quite successfully argues that the erotic photograph or drawing which seems totally detached from nonsexual life is a culturally bound object deriving its erotic and aesthetic presentational values from nonsexual conventions in social life.

Historically, the evidence for the socially scripted quality of sexual activity was more evident in the fringe literature—men's magazines, tabloids, etc.—with hard-core texts often shorn to a minimum of social signs. As it became possible to use publicly more explicit sexual material there was a merging of these two domains, fringe and hard-core, both in films and in literature.

Currently, there is a greater attempt to place sexual activity in the context of a social script, with a greater concern for nonsexual social relations and social roles, and a more direct treatment of appropriate social norms. Some part of this, particularly its common trait of compulsive moralizing, is an attempt to establish a spurious —but legally defensible under the Roth decision—"redeeming context." This may also represent the producer's awareness that more than simple lust is involved, that the consumer may bring to the work a complex of motives, many of which are nonsexual.

As Kenneth Burke observed over thirty years ago, the Freudians have too simple a model when they seek expression of the sexual in various social activities—economic, political, religious, artistic, etc. —and it is equally appropriate to seek expression of economic, political, religious, or artistic motives in sexual activity.[9]

For example, the psychiatrist Lionel Ovesey links many of the homosexual fantasies of his male homophile patients not to their "latent" sexual commitments, but to their problems of managing

9. Kenneth Burke, *Permanence and Change* (New York: New Republic, 1935).

other personal relations, particularly in their jobs.[10] In these cases
the management of dominance or aggression in nonsexual spheres
of life, or the management of ideologies and moralities of social
mobility, may be the underlying and organizing sources of fantasies
whose sexual content provides an accessible and powerful imagery
through which these other social tensions may be vicariously acted
upon. Attacks on a male's occupational self-esteem produce feelings
of weakness and impotence, a weakness and impotence normally
assigned to submissive women or to homosexuals. The dreamer selects the imagery of homosexual submission to stand for occupational submission.

These symbolic transformations are not random, but have a cultural pattern, and the use of the sexual symbolic in American society—especially for males—is commonly linked to problems of
efficacy and achievement. Sex is a domain of activity where the individual male can conceive of himself as being plausibly efficacious,
even though he may be relatively nonefficacious in other spheres of
social life—spheres that might well be far more important to him as
sources of self-validation. Sexual scripts and sexual fantasies found
in and evoked by the pulp sex novel or "X"-rated film might then
be viewed as ways of easing nonsexual tensions or vicariously
achieving nonsexual gratification through the utilization of a sexual
imagery. In line with this, William and Marlene Simon found in an
analysis of detective fiction that problems associated with uncertainties of social mobility were a frequent theme in the establishment of
plausible motives for deviant acts.[11] And William Simon, in an essay on the political novel, observed that a number of political
novelists such as George Orwell, Eugene Zamiatin, or Norman
Mailer, who found themselves in personal positions of relative power-
lessness, often resorted to sexual images, symbols, or descriptions in
order to act out their politics in particularly "powerful" ways.[12]

10. Lionel Ovesey, "The Homosexual Conflict: An Adaptational Analysis," *Psychiatry,* 17 (August 1954): 243–50.
11. William and Marlene Simon, "Past the Visceral Sleuth: Reflections
on the Symbolic Representation of Deviances," *Studies in Public Communication,* 1:1 (August 1962).
12. William Simon, "The Political Behavior and the Political Novelist,"
Mankind (August 1957).

Two themes lie at the heart of the use of pornographic and semi-pornographic materials consumed in private: the definition of situations and actors that make sexual action possible (in particular, on how such scripts facilitate the management of guilt deriving from engaging in deviant behavior); and, somewhat related to the first, the nonsexual themes that inform sexual activity in pornography.

The basic question in the integration of the sexual element in the social script is: Who does what to whom in what kind of relationship, to what consequence? Here it is evident that of the five key terms—*who, what, whom, relationship* and *consequence*—only one —the *what*—is essentially sexual, and that the other four, frequently in a rather complex interrelationship, determine the fifth.

This may be seen more clearly by briefly describing a not untypical literary work—*Sin Struck,* which is organized around what appears to be a major theme in the land of pornographic prose—sex and social mobility. All societies must establish norms surrounding opportunities for social mobility that not only restrict aspirants by and large, to the use of a nondeviant means but that also provide the nonmobile with potential sources of consolation: ways in which the nonmobile find self-validation in their nonmobility. The common phrase: "I could get ahead if only I. . . ." appears and then follows some opportunity or offer that makes our hero feel extremely virtuous for having rejected it. It could have been cheating or stealing or being dishonest or ignoring the basic virtues and joys of family life or being ruthless and exploitative in relations with other people. Using sex is clearly part of this group. Yet it remains a fairly common temptation, even if most persons are perceptive enough to avoid a genuine test.

The initial question of the story *Sin Struck* is whether a young, aspiring, and untalented actor from a small mining town in Pennsylvania can find happiness and success by being a stud for an aging and insatiable actress. The answer very clearly is no. Interestingly enough, the world of the theater and Hollywood are very frequently settings for such novels. This is appropriate as it is widely believed that these worlds are depraved and the ultimate examples of magical mobility.

The character in *Sin Struck* will be punished for his use of sex to

achieve his goal by failing as an actor, punished for several explicitly described sexual encounters which clearly prove that even aging
actresses can be great fun. Next, he will move into a world of crime
in collaboration with a professional thief whom we know is untrust-
worthy because of his consistent abuse of prostitutes. The persons
to be robbed are a wealthy Broadway producer and his nympho-
maniac wife who deserve to be robbed anyway because they use
their wealth to sponsor orgies at which all kinds of aspiring young
actors and actresses will be misused. Already, the suggestion of easy
expiation of our hero is suggested by the social justice implicit in
the crime. Enter a female in crisis; she has been deserted on her
honeymoon by her upper-class husband who is unable to face his
own impotence. The husband promptly dies in flight, making our
heroine both sexually and morally available. Our hero services our
heroine, convincing her that sex can be fun, and, at the same time,
establishes his dominant masculinity which was called into question
by his subservience to the aging actress. His partner in crime is
promptly killed by the police while trying to double-cross our hero;
he goes to his death without implicating our hero—which will make
our hero's ultimate atonement for crime psychological rather than
penal. The hero's positive act of rehabilitation will be to rescue our
heroine, who, while languishing in a highly suspect hotel, has been
seduced by a multi-millionaire lesbian from Alaska who wants to
take her away to a life of depraved comfort in her wilderness empire.
The novel ends with our hero, now secure in his masculinity, walking into the sunset with our heroine who is now equally secure in
her femininity; they are walking in the direction of a secure and exclusively heterosexual life among the working class of some small
town. They have "found their place in the order of things."

The plot is trite; so is the sex. But the social environment of the
sexual action is not incidental. Nor is it merely a flimsy attempt at
meeting the Roth decision's requirement of a redeeming content.
(The social plot is necessary to a more unambiguous enjoyment of
the sex detailed within.)

Historically, it was the materials on the fringe that contained the
most evidence of social scripts. However, evidence for minimal social scripting can be found in nearly all pornographic materials,
and, with the decreasing boundary between the two, more rather

than fewer elements of social scripts are to be found. Indeed, the
rapid onset of boredom with stag films when they are viewed without other persons present probably derives from the absence of sufficient social cues internal to the film for integrating the presented
materials and motivating arousal.

Perhaps the most significant aspect of these items that exist in the
literary fringe world of pornography is that they are most often the
center of concern when community standards are formulated. The
girlie magazine, the pulp book, the "X"-rated film, are visible and
priced within the range of the mass market. Because such items are
sold at transportation depots or in locations that tap neighborhood
markets, they are the most visible portion of the problem and are
the source of the discontent among those who are committed to policing sexual activity either directly or through the censorship of sexual materials.

The Legal Situation of Pornography

When any of the materials which are defined as pornographic enter
the public domain (apart from any questions of private utility) they
attain their most serious aspect, for in this realm they attract the attention of law enforcement agencies, and if those arrested are sufficiently affluent they require the attention of the United States Supreme Court. The behavior of this judicial body in setting standards
in what is increasingly a national society deserves the most attention.

The Supreme Court decisions handed down on March 21, 1966
(Memoirs of a Woman of Pleasure v. *Massachusetts, Mishkin* v.
New York, Ginzburg v. *United States),* are the landmark decisions
on the present limits of legitimate expressions of sexual behavior in
the publically available media.[13] The three decisions, especially
Ginzburg, aroused a new affection for the Supreme Court among
those who desire repressive control of such materials and considerable regret among those who find themselves on the permissive side
of the censorship issue. However, the court itself showed less than

---

13. *U.S. Law Week,* 34: 36 (March 22, 1966), Washington, D.C., Bureau
of National Affairs, pp. 4236–67. All quotations are from this document.

unanimity, since only three judges concurred with the majority decision in all three cases. This lack of consensus on the part of the court, resulting in a total of fourteen separate opinions, is only a slight reflection of the pluralistic ignorance of the larger society on these same matters.

The court reversed the state of Massachusetts suppression of *Memoirs,* better known as *Fanny Hill,* under the Roth test of 1957 —that is, "whether to the average person, applying contemporary standards, the dominant theme of the material taken as a whole appeals to a prurient interest." One of the indicators of the social worth of *Fanny Hill* was the translation of the book into braille by the Library of Congress.

The conviction of Edward Mishkin, owner of tht Main Stem and Midget book stores in New York City, was upheld. In the words of the court, "Mishkin was not prosecuted (by New York State) for anything he said or believed, but for what he did." What he did was commission, publish, and sell such illustrated books as *Mistress of Leather, Cult of Spankers,* and *Fearful Ordeal in Restraintland* for an audience interested in sado-masochism, transvestitism, and fetishism. It is apparent in 1972 that the state of New York would no longer prosecute Mishkin for these materials, indicating a substantial drift in standards without court intervention.

But Ginzburg is the key decision. Ralph Ginzburg was being tried on postal charges of obscenity for three publications: *The Housewife's Handbook of Selective Promiscuity,* an issue of the biweekly newsletter *Liaison,* and a volume of the hardbound magazine *Eros.* In this case the court departed from earlier rulings by considering not the obscenity of the specific items, but rather the appeal to prurient interest made in the advertising campaigns. The court remarked: "Where the purveyor's sole emphasis is on the sexually provocative aspects of his publications, that fact may be decisive in the determination of 'obscenity.' "

To the court, one of the proofs of Ginzburg's motives was his request for second-class mailing privileges at Intercourse or Blue Ball, Pennsylvania, before obtaining them at Middlesex, New Jersey. Three of the justices voting for reversal filed written dissents in which they argued that the court was creating a new crime—that of pandering, exploitation, or titillation—which Ginzburg could not have known existed when he committed it. Furthermore, the dissenters said, if a statute creating such a crime had come before the court, it would be found unconstitutional.

It is the Ginzburg decision that gives us the primary thread to follow in seeking to understand "obscenity" as it is now seen by the Supreme Court and how these institutional decisions relate to the sexual arousal caused by what is conventionally termed pornography. With this decision, the court has moved—in a way that may be inimical to the conception of law as abstract principle—toward the arguments made earlier in this chapter about the factors that are relevant to triggering a sexual response. The court's sociological discovery (whether intentional or not) is that, in sex, the context of the representation is the significant element in eliciting the prurient response. That is, the physical activity of sex and its symbolic representation have no power outside a context in which the erotic elements are reinforced or made legitimate.

In doing this, the court did not change the rules under which any work will be considered outside this context of presentation. If a book is charged—as *Fanny Hill* was—with being obscene in and of itself under the Roth decision, it will be treated in exactly the same way as it would have been in the past. When aspects of the context of advertising or sale—the acts of labeling—are included in the original charges, then the Ginzburg rules will be applied. This was demonstrated in the court's decision in May, 1967, on a number of girlie magazines. Obscenity convictions against the magazines were overturned because, as the court stated, "In none was there evidence of the sort of pandering which the court found significant in *Ginzburg* v. *United States.*"

Whether the majority of the court was aware of the significance of the change it made in the definition of obscenity is not clear. from the tone of the opinions, it is obvious the court felt it was dealing with a problem of nuisance behavior—not only to the public, but to the court itself—quite analogous to keeping a goat in a residential area or urinating in public. By making the promotion of the work a factor in determining its obscenity, the court was reinforcing the right of the person to keep his mailbox clean and private, not to mention the likelihood that the court was cutting down the amount of misleading advertising.

The Supreme Court apparently considered pornography to have two major dimensions. The first can be defined as dealing with sexual representations that are offensive to public morality or taste. This concerned the court most importantly in the Ginzburg case. The second centers on the effect of pornography on specific individuals or classes, which is the focus of most public discussions and prior court decisions on pornography. This dimension was mentioned only twice in the array of decisions of 1966, but much of the confusion in discussions of pornography reflects a difficulty in distinguishing between these dimensions or a tendency to slip from one to the other without noting the change.

The first dimension—offenses to public morality—not only appears more objective, but also has a cooler emotional tone. The problem becomes one of tolerating a public nuisance, or defining what constitutes a public nuisance. This issue becomes complex because the heterogeneity of an urban society makes it difficult to arrive at a consensus on what the limits of public morality might be. We might also add the complicating factor of our society's somewhat uneven libertarian tradition, a tradition which affirms the theoretical existence of the right to subscribe to minority versions of morality. This entire issue obviously touches upon important issues of constitutional freedoms. As important as the implicit issues may be, however, the explicit issue is public nuisance, a misdemeanor, that usually brings only a fine or, at most, up to a year in county jail. Talk of offense to public morality or public taste is relatively remote from the old fears of serious damage to the community or its members.

The second dimension—effects upon persons exposed to pornographic productions—generates more intense emotions. Claims are made that exposure to pornography results in infantile and regressive approaches to sexuality that can feed an individual's neuroses. At the other extreme, it is alleged that exposure tends to fundamentally and irreversibly corrupt and deprave. The latter argument asserts that exposure to pornography either awakens or creates sexual appetites that can only be satisfied through conduct that is dangerous to society. More simply stated: Pornography is a trigger mechanism that has a high probability of initiating dangerous, antisocial behavior. There also exists what can be called a major counter-argument to these, but one that shares with them a belief in the effectiveness of pornography. This argument is that pornography serves as an alternative sexual outlet, one that releases sexual tensions that might otherwise find expression in dangerous, antisocial behavior. For the proponents of this view, pornography is seen as a safety valve or a psychological lightning rod.

These serious views of pornography appear to lead directly to the formulation of empirically testable questions. These center about the general hypothesis (stated in the null form) that those exposed to varying amounts of what is described as pornography (what is represented in what media, in what amounts is variable) at varying points in the life cycle (from childhood to old age) in varying sociocultural milieus will *not* be more likely to engage in deviant behaviors (criminal or merely deviant, sexual or otherwise) than those not exposed in parallel circumstances. Stated this way, what appears to be a simple causal picture turns out—as usual—to be complex. As we have noted before, the evidence collected by the Commission on Obscenity and Pornography seems to support this null hypothesis. What is significant is that no dramatic changes in behavior appeared to follow exposure in any study. A parallel set of findings is reported in the book *Sex Offenders:* "It would appear that the possession of pornography does not differentiate sex offenders from nonsex offenders. Even the combination of ownership plus strong sexual arousal from the material does not segregate the sex offender from other men of a comparable social level."[14] The authors of this book sum up their feeling that pornography is far from being a strong determinant of sexual behavior and that the use of pornography tends to be a derivative of already existing sexual commitments. It has been observed: "Men make the collections, collections do not make the men."

Nevertheless, given the intensity and frequency with which the argument of pornography's corrupting powers is raised, one might wonder whether any amount of negative evidence would be believed. Indeed, we suspect that compelling evidence about the limited power of pornography will be greeted with disbelief, not only by

14. Paul H. Gebhard et al., *Sex Offenders: An Analysis of Types* (New York: Harper & Row, 1965), p. 678.

Puritans, but by sexual revolutionaries as well. Thinking about pornography comes very close to being an antonomous sexual act, an act that enhances and elaborates on an image of men and women making them more sexual than they really are.

This major distinction of public nuisance versus public corruption results in two different images of the pornographer and his occupation. Projected through the rhetoric of public corruption, we see him as someone self-consciously evil: a representative of the antichrist, the Communist conspiracy, or—at the very least—the Mafia. We also tend to see him in terms of the obscenity of ill-gotten wealth because he deals in commodities that are assumed to generate high prices.

Thought of as a public nuisance, the pornographer appears in somewhat more realistic terms. Here we find not a sinister villain, but a grubby businessman producing a minor commodity for which there is a limited market and marginal profit and which requires that he live in a marginal world. Furthermore, our collective displeasure may be derived from his association with a still greater obscenity—economic failure. However, whether the pornographer is Mephistopheles or a Willie Loman, he is one of the few in our society whose public role is overtly sexual, and perhaps that is reason enough to abandon any expectations of rationality in public discussions of his role.

The significant social dilemma is the formulation of community standards, and this has been the dilemma of the courts themselves. One interesting attempt to strengthen enforcement of conservative standards is the interpretation of federal law to allow prosecution of a seller in the jurisdiction in which materials are received rather than in the ones from which they are mailed. Thus, in the rather liberal jurisdiction of New York City, where the judge must compare the sale of obscene materials to all the other crimes that come before him, the seller may well be seen as a small-timer and his crime may be judged a misdemeanor. However, in a rural jurisdiction where religious standards are more conservative and a pornography offense is viewed more seriously—especially when compared with the strayed cows and traffic violations that make up most of the court docket—the seller is a heinous criminal.

The accumulation of decisions by the Warren Court indicated a wish to establish a national standard, allowing some jurisdictions to be more liberal but none to be more conservative.[15] Thus the Supreme Court of that era attempted to build a floor under the right of materials to be protected under the First Amendment, at the same time constraining—through the use of the Ginzburg decision —the importation of materials into conservative communities through wide mailing campaigns. In its more recent decisions, the court indicated (somewhat Delphically) that its concern in the future would be with three areas, none of them directly concerned with the content of any works charged as pornographic. These were sales of smut to minors, obtrusive presentation, and "pandering" a la Ginzburg. The court's decisions, however, may well be too conservative in a period when a national society is being created through penetration by the mass media into larger and larger elements of society. Indeed, it is likely that most legal revolutions have been imposed from above and that communities will fall back to the set floor, if allowed to do so. To trust to local innovation may be to trust to nothing.

The category "pornography" is as elusive as mercury. Its content in the past no longer meets our present definitions. The use and users of contemporary pornography vary. Indeed, it might be said that sex itself would not change if there were no more pornography. Pornography is only a minor symptom of sexuality and of very little prominence in people's minds most of the time. Even among those who might think about it most, it results either in masturbation or in the "collector" instinct.

What is most important about pornography is not that it is particularly relevant to sexuality, but that it elicits very special treatment when it confronts the law. In this confrontation the agencies of criminal justice, and especially the courts, behave in a very curious manner that is quite dangerous for the freedom of ideas as they might be expressed in other zones of activity such as politics,

---

15. No major obscenity case has come before the Court newly dominated by President Richard M. Nixon's appointees. While that new body of Justices may wish to more severely limit the use of sexually explicit media, the increased tolerance in the last few years of both consumption and changed general standards without a concurrent social breakdown would seem to reduce their freedom of operation.

religion, or the family. Our best protection in this regard has been the very contradictory character of the courts which carefully excludes the consideration of sexual ideas from the general test of the expression of ideas: Do they give rise to a clear and present danger? Our problem is not that pornography represents such a danger —it is far too minor a phenomenon for that—but that the kind of thinking prevalent in dealing with pornography will come to be prevalent in controlling the advocacy of other ideas as well.

Afterword

The bulk of this chapter was written during 1967 and 1968 and revised in 1971 prior to the publication of either the general report or the technical volumes of the Commission on Obscenity and Pornography, created by the United States Congress. Much of the work of that commission was quite valuable and supports the null hypothesis about the power of pornography. Perhaps the most interesting single study was that of Berl Kutschinsky, which found declines in certain classes of sex offense behavior in Denmark following the liberalization of their pornography laws. Both the timing of the reductions (the first after literary pornography was made legal, a second after pictorial and film pornography was freed) and the specific offense groups who were affected are generally instructive about the character of sexual behavior. It is the detailed analysis in Kutschinsky's work that is instructive since it brings to bear on sexual behavior a relatively complex social psychological model and suggests the great variation that exists in the categories "pornography" and "sex offender."[16]

We find nothing in these new findings to change our view of the scripted nature of sexual behavior nor of the relatively minor role pornography plays in psychosexual development. The relationship between depictions of sexual activity in every media, when there is no special category called pornography, is difficult to conceive. So much of our concern with pornography results from its secret, degraded, and excluded status that it is impossible to predict a response in the absence of guilt and anxiety.

16. Berl Kutschinsky, *Studies on Porography and Sex Crimes in Denmark*, (Copenhagen: New Social Science Monographs, 1970).

10

Social Change and Sexual Conduct

During the last quarter-century, and especially during the last decade, U.S. society has appeared to undergo an accelerating change in its sexual practices. While the central focus of our attention has been on the young, since they appear most vulnerable to the forces inducing change, changes have been found in all age groups. Whatever the specific reasons for change among the youthful population, our attention since the early 1960s has been directed to examples of a revolutionary potential that includes political, familial, chemical, and sexual elements.

The current state of confusion about interaction between sexual conduct and other aspects of social change stems from four main sources. The first of these is that, as a society, we are saddled with and delighted by an imagery of change—indeed, of revolution—when we talk about sexuality. This climate of opinion clouds our ability to judge accurately whether or not there is change and, if there is, what direction it is taking. The demand for novelty, even in scientific research, distorts the process of data collection. It highlights the dramatic to the detriment of the pedestrian and forces the creation of theories that are overweighted in the direction of change. At the same time, the imagery of change becomes a variable not only in scientific activities, but in social life itself. For those who are changing, the experiences of change becomes a mark of "being with it"; for those not changing, change becomes both a danger and a measure of being "out of it." The idea of change has become as important to the twentieth century as the idea of progress was to the nineteenth.[1]

The second and perhaps even greater difficulty which affects any discussion of sexual behavior is our profound lack of information. Not only do we not know very precisely the social statistics of sexuality (how many are doing it, with whom are they doing it, at what ages and with what frequencies), but, more important, there is even less information about the connection between sexual activity and the social and psychological contexts in which such sexual activity occurs. Research efforts are fragmentary and often ill-founded, influenced by fantasy and desire, and—worst of all—are pornotopic in design, seeking to analyze the sexual without reference to the social or psychological circumstances that turn sexual behavior into sexual conduct.[2]

It was this lack of prior data that made the original interpretations of the books *Sexual Behavior in the Human Male* and *Sexual Behavior in the Human Female* such curiosities.[3] Without prior baseline figures, the cross-sectional data in these volumes were interpreted in any fashion that their readers wished. Unfortunately, no one interpreted the data conservatively by taking the viewpoint that, according to the Kinsey reports, there was a decline in sexual activity from a promiscuous and licentious nineteenth century. (Even though the decline in the rates of purchasing sexual contact with females by males could have been viewed as a humanizing process in the society.) Since there were no prior data that anyone was willing to examine, it was presumed that the Kinsey data stood for a vast eruption of sexuality, despite the fact that the amount and directions

1. See J. B. Bury, *The Idea of Progress* (New York: Dover Publications, 1955).
2. For the distinction between sexual behavior and sexual conduct see E. W. Burgess, "The Sociologic Theory of Psychosexual Behavior," in *Psychosexual Development in Health and Disease,* eds. Paul H. Hock and Joseph Zubin (New York: Grune and Stratton, 1949), pp. 227–43. Another insightful notation of this distinction is in Paul Bohannon's book review of *Human Sexual Behavior,* eds. D. S. Marshall and R. C. Suggs (New York: Basic Books, 1971) in *Science* 173: (September 17, 1971): 1116–17.
3. A. C. Kinsey et al., *Sexual Behavior in the Human Male* (Philadelphia: W. B. Saunders Co., 1948); and A. C. Kinsey et al., *Sexual Behavior in the Human Female* (Philadelphia: W. B. Saunders Co., 1953).

of short-run changes were small and—even when they existed—
were muted in the reporting of the data.

The third source of error is perhaps more problematic than is a
lack of data. It is the flawed interpretative mechanism of theoretical
scheme or conceptual apparatus through which sexual phenomena
are commonly viewed, analyzed, or gathered.[4] This flawed intellectual framework derives from two sources. The first is experiential:
the sexual actor in our culture lives in schizophrenic detachment
from his nonsexual life. He feels that his sexual impulses are autonomous, even though reflection on most of his experience will show
him that his sexual commitments are under extremely good control
or are often of little importance to him. Without such reflection, the
sexual world appears to be self-starting and self-motivated. It seems
to exist *sui generis* in experience. However, it is demonstrable that
sexual activity is in fact not a very powerful drive, and the word
drive itself may be a misonomer. One can show that the felt experience during sexual activity is quite distinct from the importance of
sexual activity during the rest of waking or even sleeping life. At
the same time, the major theoretical and intellectual apparatuses
for interpreting the role of sexual behavior in social life see it as an
imperious drive that presses against and must be controlled by the
cultural and social matrix. The dominance of this drive reduction
model, mediated by cultural and social control, is preeminent in the
bulk of psychoanalytic, anthropological, and sociological literature.

The explanation of sexual change that flows from this intellectual
posture is very simple. The sex drive exists at some constant level in
any population age group; its intensity follows a rising and ultimately falling trajectory in any individual life cycle. It presses for expression and, in the absence of controls (whether existing in the external laws or mores, or in appropriate internalized repressions
learned in early socialization), there will be outbreaks of sexual

---

4. It is not at all clear what the relation of this intellectual attitude or
apparatus is to what Thomas Kuhn has referred to as "paradigms in science." It might be fruitful to examine the difference between a set of ideas
that cohesively structure research and thought and loose overarching intellectual metaphors. Any examination of Freud's own work and that of his
followers will demonstrate this. In sociology the best exemplification is
Kingsley Davis "Sexual Behavior" in *Contemporary Social Problems,* eds. R.
K. Merton and R. Nisbet (New York: Harcourt Brace Jovanovich, 1970),
pp. 313–60.

behavior.[5] The drive presses, society and culture constrain it, and when constraints are loosed sexual change occurs. This control-repression model of sexuality has influenced the majority of discussions of the impact of social change of various kinds of sexual behavior—it has yielded rather simpleminded consequences. The introduction of the automobile, teen-age dating, going steady, dancing close together, dancing styles related to rock and roll music, and short skirts all have been asserted to be changes which would result in sexual excess. The discovery of adequate treatment for venereal diseases and the widespread availability of birth control devices were attacked because they would reduce the dangers of sexual activity. The availability of sexually stimulating material (pornography) has been attacked from the time when a nipple was the danger point (1950 or so) to the emergence of pubic hair. All of the following reactions are based on variants of the same faulty reasoning —that mutual sexual access among the young will result in coitus, that sexual behavior is only constrained by its dangers, or that the sexual beast can be aroused with instant success by the mildest stimulus.

The fourth source of confusion is the self-interest of various onlookers. There is a certain commitment to finding the world more sexual than it is, more exciting, more pornographic. This pastime serves the self-interest of both sexual radicals and sexual conservatives. The sexual radical and the sexual conservative are, of course, in disagreement about consequences of lowered controls over the sexual drive—the former believing that there will be a genuine flowering of a more human, more natural way of life, and the latter believing that there will be a degeneration of the cultural fabric in all areas of social life. What they agree upon is the transcendent power of sexuality when released. The entire older generation, which is generally nonideological about sex, is in a sense the ambivalent embodiment of these opposing radical and conservative ideologies. They are the losers if sexual change occurs, one way or the other. If sex is a therapeutic truth which they have hidden from themselves, they will have been cheated of participating in it. If it is a corruption, then all they have worked for will go the way of the Roman

5. Prescott Lecky described analytic psychodynamics as psychohydraulics— hence the metaphor.

Empire.[6] Hence, the increased level of cosmetic sexuality in the society, especially on the part of the young, makes the older generation both jealous and angry. They are jealous because of what they think they have missed; they are angry because the young appear to be having such a good time. It is nearly impossible to live in this society and fail to share some of these emotions when watching the youth revolution as portrayed by the mass media.

While corrections can be made for the problems of data, self-interest, sexual ideology, and for the current climate of mandatory change, without changes in the faulted model of sexuality no serious discussion can be had about the future of sexuality. As we have argued, the theoretical framework is fundamentally in error. Even with the best of data, faulty interpretations would be made. Without the application of a more complex, alternative model of sexual development, our interests will continue to be dominated by the epiphenomenal aspects of sexual change.

Sources of Change

Changes in the sexual component of the human condition can result from changes in the biological, technological, and psychosocial domains of life. It is evident to us that, at the present time, the biological substratum is very nearly a constant in human sexual affairs. Except for specific classes of genetic and hormone failures, the vast majority of humans are biologically equipped to perform sexual acts. There probably are more people suffering from sterility and infertility than there are people with sexual performance inadequacies resulting from physical difficulties. This does not obviate the fact that there are many persons with socially defined performance difficulties in the sexual area, but these are rarely due to biological defects.

While technology is the most visible engine of change in Western societies, it affects the sexual aspects of life only through those institutions and persons which link technological change to that process which we have described as the *gender identity-sexual identity-*

6. Margaret Mead has remarked that the only thing the modern United States has in common with ancient Rome is good plumbing, but the analogy tends to stick.

family formation-reproduction cycle. Developments in medical science involving venereal diseases and birth control are the most powerful developments that specifically relate to this cycle and do so by reducing the risks of sexual intercourse in the latter case and all forms of sexual contact in the case of venereal disease. It does not appear that these developments have had widespread impact on illegitimate sexual behavior (though the substitution of the pill for the condom may have increased the spread of venereal disease). They probably have had more impact inside of marriage, where birth control devices are most frequently used. Other technological developments have not turned out to have as much impact on sexuality as was originally anticipated. The automobile has not increased sexual activity even among the young, though it has resulted in an increase in privacy for noncoital sexual contacts. It has, however, become another element in the masculinity package, resulting in higher rates of car theft and accidents. It is also part of that successful consumer identity package which makes car ownership both a measure of personal success and a tie to the conventional social structure. In these same ways other technological developments affect emergent sexuality, but only through the intervention of psychosocial processes.

In the psychosocial arena the following processes seem to be most significant in their impact on the family replacement cycle that we have described previously:

The economic movement from scarcity to affluence

The movement from scarcity to affluence in the society has clearly varied in its direct effect on individuals, but the sheer existence of long-term affluence in a large sector of the society indirectly affects those who are not affluent. The central consequences of affluence on sexual activity seem to be threefold: (1) it increases role flexibility throughout the life cycle, especially after the age of twenty;[7] (2) it changes the attitude of the affluent toward the value of objects and ownership, while not reducing the desire to consume. As affluence reduces the value of things, they become more dispos-

---

7. We emphasize after age twenty since the youthful period has always had a set of larger options in Western societies.

able, replaceable, and lose their uniqueness; (3) it increases the attachment of all members of the society to societal norms primarily through consumption rather than production values.

The emergence of social movements with sexual side effects

A large series of social movements have emerged in the society that do not have goals specifically aimed at sexual change but whose implementation carries with them (either as general rhetorical baggage or as a specific commitment to liberalism) a required assent to greater sexual freedom. One of the most significant of these is clearly the so-called "youth movement," beginning with the hippies and moving through the commune and other current events in youth culture. The political freedom of the young, the eighteen-year-old vote, and the experience of the Vietnam War or political protest increased commitments to general anti-adult values. These oppositions can be expressed through sexual activity during a time when the early experimentation with sexuality is heightened by a reduction in adult controls over the behavior of the young. The second major movement is women's liberation, in which two major elements are intertwined—gender politics and sexual politics. It is possible to think of a society with both a sexual double standard and equality between the genders in occupational and social domains; however, given the complex intermixture of gender or sexual politics in American society, changes in one will affect the other, so that the woman's movement in both its gender and sexual dimensions should have some effects on sexual activity; but they will clearly not be simple ones. A third source of change is the general political revolt of blacks, Chicanos, and American Indians which has created a series of smaller possibilities of sexual change. The sexual relations between ethnic and racial groups can more generally be used by all participants to work out motives representing exploitation, power, guilt reduction, and the like. Revolutionary romanticism can enhance the sexuality of members of previously suppressed and degraded classes and groups.

The emergence of specifically sexual social movements

There are a number of sexual movements in the society whose ends are the legitimization (legalization or normalization) of specific sexual or erotic minorities. The thrust of these changes have come either through "disinterested" legal reformers or through members of erotic minorities using legal redress or confrontational politics. The goals of some groups are more radical than those of mere reform. They seek not only the legalization of their behavior, but its right to exist as a nonstigmatized public alternative to conventional marital or nonmarital heterosexuality. At the same time, there are other groups that seek to increase the freedom of heterosexual relationships (e.g., kinds and numbers of partners, techniques, feelings). These are often, but not always, related to the encounter and sensitivity group movement. The legal reform movements seek to change the laws affecting large classes of sexual behavior, moving ultimately to a legal situation in which the only offenses are those that offend the public taste and those that involve great disparities in age (with fixed lower floor), force, or close blood relationships. The more radical legal reformers would remove incest from the prohibited list if it did not involve great disparities in age, and there is some serious debate about ages of consent and what is a public nuisance. Indeed, the Sexual Freedom League and other heterosexual groups are working beyond sex law reform toward the celebration of what are currently deviant sexual practices. The Gay Liberation group is the most powerful of the erotic minority groups; it seeks both change in the general image of homosexuality and an improved self-image for the homosexual. The slogans "Gay is good" and "Out of the closets and into the streets" suggest the concerns of these groups. Other erotic minorities—transsexuals and transvestites, for example—have done some organizing, but the impact of these groups is unclear. There is no evidence that there has been internal organization among female prostitutes and the various occupational subcategories attached to this profession.

The erosion of rigid gender differences

The ritual use of Dr. Spock by the middle classes in child-rearing, with the involvement of middle-class fathers in family household activities, and the existence of the mother who is also a professional career woman exemplify the processes that have begun to erode some of the rigid male-female gender difference in early childhood training. This erosion occurs most strikingly in middle-class populations and among college students, thanks to the influence of youth culture and changing parental commitments and models. Hair styles, unisex clothing, and nonsexual coeducational living arrangements are outgrowths of this early experience and the effects of increasing affluence and role flexibility. Among those with more traditional early gender training, the current more permissive gender atmosphere of adolescence presents alternatives to a more rigid set of role specifications.

The eroticization of the social backdrop

While more fundamental processes are changing, we are also experiencing a cosmetic sexual shift in the society. The backdrop of daily life and life as experienced in the media has grown more erotic or, at least, what an older generation considers erotic. There has been movement in sexually stimulating pictures from the *Sears, Roebuck Catalog* corset ads of the 1940s to fellatio in three dimensions in the 1970s. Today, we have a larger volume of erotic literature, photography of naked people (mostly women), a literature celebrating sexual athleticism, and (in person) braless, miniskirted, or bikinied females. (It is significant that increasing eroticism partly increases the "object" quality of women, an aspect of change that is opposed by another change-oriented group—women's liberation. The no-bra look is serving both males' fantasies and a return to naturalness.) While there is a heightened sense of the sexual in today's daily life, this backdrop only affects behavior indirectly, without supplying the social networks for acting out the behavior. And although it does not directly affect behavior, the shifting of the backdrop does create new sexual expectations in both older and younger generations.

It is apparent that changes in these psychosocial processes will not affect all sectors of the population at the same time or penetrate them at the same rate. In terms of change, whether individuals or social groups are in the avant garde or at the end of the parade will have both structural and psychological consequences. At the psychological and individual level, being the first to change means dealing with certain kinds of anxieties and ambivalences; being the last to change poses still another set of problems. At structural-collective level, change can be defined as valuable, if it occurs within the affluent or central components of the society. If change occurs among the disadvantaged and abused, it is regarded as the harbinger of revolution. The problems of sequencing and rate of change, and of social position are central not only to the character of change, but to the existential experiences of those involved in the process of change.

Changes in Gender Identity

Today's change pattern in softening gender identity lines seems to take most of its force early in life: parents are more strongly curbing aggression among males, are having children of both sexes dress more alike (i.e., pants for boys and girls), and are de-emphasizing the occupational dimension of male life in child-rearing. These patterns are supported by child-rearing experts and have most of their effect in middle-class and upper middle-class families, with far less significance in the white working class, among ethnic minorities, and in lower-class populations.

These gender softening factors affect some children early in life, but they are more widely felt in early adolescence when many young people adopt clothing fashions that reduce the differences between the sexes. Here, in the world of youth culture, there is far more opportunity for such gender softening to have cross-class consequences. During this period, conventionally gender-trained young people come into contact with unisex themes and either comply with the styles or resist them. After adolescence, the major attacks on rigid gender difference are being carried out by either the women's liberation movement or in the occupational domain itself, where the content of occupational activity has become unrelated to those activities that were conventionally the goals of male socialization. Most occupations no longer require large amounts of aggression or physical strength. Furthermore, the increasing numbers of bureaucratic and service occupations require the management and manipulation of people rather than things. In many of these occupations, women may be equal to or superior to men. Changes in gender difference, training, and maintenance emerge at three time points and through a number of different processes: (1) early in life, during gender identity formation, there are varying and changing child-rearing practices; (2) during adolescence there are reductions in the gender differences due to the youth culture; and (3) during adulthood both political and occupation factors work toward the reduction of male or female differences in the world of work, both in terms of work content and in terms of access to the positions themselves.

If there is a central theme in gender-identity training or definition at these three life cycle points, it is that—from the point of view of an older set of rules concerning the relations between men and women and the content of gender roles—the present convergence between roles will have males moving further toward the female role than females will move toward the male. It is clear that the content of these gender roles has never been fixed, and it is only through using descriptive categories that originate in an older perspective that we can describe this shift. In one sense, this sort of comparison is partly meaningless and partly obscuring. No future individual of either gender who possesses a new combination of gender-defining elements that will be then labeled as gender specific will experience himself or herself merely as a recombination of older elements. There will not be the sense of dissonance between culture and self that the present woman's liberation participant feels, but the new combination (say, total equality of sexual access) will be experienced as the natural outcome of socialization and the sociocultural situation of that moment.

The decrease in accentuated gender-role differences has a number of potential sexual changes built into it. One of these is the possibility that males whose early rearing is in such a tradition will have lowered commitments to what Evelyn Hooker has called the "male alliance" during early adolescence. They may be less exclusively homosocial in their relations during this period. At the same time, they will be able to relate more easily to females, could have lowered rates of early adolescent masturbation, a lowered level of genital focus, and have lessened commitments to aggressive fantasies as a part of sexual arousal. For these males the experience of early adolescence and later adolescence will contain lowered levels of anxiety about sexual performance from the genital point of view, and a lowered pressure toward premarital coitus as part of a male achievement syndrome. There may even be slightly elevated rates of coitus as a consequence, partly because such males will be seeking intercourse in much the same terms that females will be.

For those males more conventionally reared, the impact of gender-role softening will appear during adolescence through the cosmetic impact of youth culture. Both stylistically and in the existence of persons of middle-class status who exhibit and voice a different pattern of attitudes toward sex and women, it is possible to generate an interpersonal set of relations among young men which support a change in relations between young men and women. It is important to note that concomitant patterns of gender change do not seem to be occurring among women; that is, there do not seem to be new child-rearing practices emerging early in life, and during adolescence the changes among females seem quite slight. Changes among females are more likely to result from a decrease in the rigidity of male's definitions of what females should be. This change will result from changes in the training of males rather than of females. It is likely that, in the face of reductions in male sexual assertiveness, women may have to be more self-directive in defining themselves sexually, because the act of defining women as sexual will be less important to men. While many of these early changes are occurring in middle-class populations, it is important to note that they do not seem to be occurring among white working-class males or in large sectors of other racial-ethnic subgroups in the society. It may be possible that there will be a great deal of tension between males in the society as some portion of the male population adopts newer gender role commitments while other populations, often marked by differences in class and ethnic/racial status, do not.

During adulthood the sexual consequences of gender-boundary softening will be unclear. It could make for lower rates of extramartial coitus among some groups of men because of stronger familial attachments, while there could be a counter-movement among women. If there is a single most likely outcome, it is that there will be movement toward a less penis-oriented sexual encounter between men and women. There is already some evidence for this in the popularity of the encounter groups movement (experience each other as people, not sex objects), and in the sensualist movement, which is moving toward a more total body concern in sexual activity (a definition which again is feminine in an older sense of that word). The water bed is an example of this shift in sexual focus. It changes the kind of physical structure on which coitus can occur, eliminating the fixed surface, and creating a flowing, moving environment that denotes flexibility rather than rigidity in sexual performances.[8] If these movements imply anything about sex, they imply pattern of sexual athleticism with a commitment to a wider variety of sexual activities between sexual partners.

As a process operating independently of all other changes, a decline in gender identity accentuation would produce males with a greater capacity for emotional commitment to females earlier in life, with a lowered pressure for direct sexual gratification and with a wider interest in total bodily commitments. At the same time, males would be more capable of responding positively to changes in women's roles as they occur. There are some historic indications that those males who make this adaptation early in the general process of change will have some problems in maintaining a softened gender identity that will be free from external identifications —being called "queer" or "different" (as "hard hat" sexuality views long hair). They may even encounter internal doubts and reactions similar to pseudo-homosexual adaptation, since there will be continuing pressures toward the conventional definition of masculinity.[9] Some women find that their older self-definitions of femininity will not be enhanced in interactions with males who are not as domineering and assertive.

In large measure, there do not seem to be as many kinds of changes occurring to female gender roles at this point as there do to males. It is likely that many changes in women's roles will emerge in reaction to changes in male's roles—hence, the timing of changes for women will be later for men. As women move to a more central occupational economic role in the society, the changes in their behavior (sexual and nonsexual) will be less reactive in character.

8. Rigidity and flexibility are not value words here, they are descriptions of styles of experience which can be differentially evaluated.
9. Lionel Ovesey, *Homosexuality and Pseudohomosexuality* (New York: Science House, 1969).

The Emergence and Confirmation of Sexual Identities

At the present time in U.S. society a confirmed sense of sexual identity as distinguished from gender identity begins to emerge at puberty as the surrounding environment begins to treat differently the newly pubescent child. While for some children this emergence into a new definition will be built on the less restrictive gender identity pattern we noted above, for the most part the integration of new sexual selves will continue to be built on relatively conventional models. The changes that seem most significant for this period appear to be caused by the mass media's involvement with the youth culture and by changes in the family produced by increasing role flexibility on the part of adults rather than children.

It appears that adults are reacting to young people in early and latter adolescence as being sexual—indeed, as being more sexual than they really are. Thus, in the fantasy life of adults, there is a kind of constant eroticism among the young and the overreaction of adults to youth's cosmetic sexuality begins to confirm its acting out. This means that young women in early puberty who dress in sexually provocative styles appear not as girls, but as women. While this shift in social identity has always been the pattern in adolescence, and while the reactions of others have always been the process through which the young of both genders have combined the new sexual roles with prior gender commitments, the feedback loop now seems to occur somewhat earlier in development, with adults reacting to young people's dress and styles closer to puberty.[10] This is explicitly true for young girls whose dolls now have breasts, boy friends, beauty contests, and rock concerts. While the gender role definitions of the children's toy world are conventional, the sexual implications are far more intense and significant. The young are more exposed to a wider range of explicit sexual stimuli in the me-

10. This is not the same as the past with early marriage or early definition as sexual in pre-industrial and early industrial societies. In those situations, reproductive maturity and sexual maturity were coterminous with marriageability, and such culturally approved transitions are vastly different from emergent sexual identity without legitimate sexual behavior, marriage, or reproduction.

dia than has ever been the case in this society, and they are presented with images of their own sexuality—images which, at this point, actually characterize a relative minority of the young.

While the young are becoming more eroticized cosmetically, they nearly all share or reject vicariously (and in some cases are involved with) other social movements (women's liberation, students' rights, sexual liberation, anti-war activities) which enhance the conences and the supposed moral inferiority of their elders. Such specific issues, whatever their transience, operate to strengthen the imcific issues, whatever their transience, operate to strengthen the image of rebellion and to foster other forms of guerilla warfare against parents and authority figures. Sexual activity and participation in drug subcultures begin, in part, for most young people as personal vendettas with parents and then become, for a minority, political in character (that is, a testing of the ultimate basis of the parent-child relationships which rest in part on the physical and economic power of the former). As this political rhetoric of the family emerges it can become, for a few young people, a serious alternative allegiance to familial authority. For others, each separate cause can become a mixture of justification and rationalization falling short of ideology.

At the same time that these events are occurring, events which should enhance the probability of sexual activity on the part of the young, there is not a great deal of evidence that such activity actually is being acted out by the current generation of high school students. While the temperature of the adolescent hothouse seems to be higher now than ever before, there has not been a concomitant increase in early sexual activity on the part of the young. In short, the earlier and more intense definition of the young as sexual does not seem to be acted out by the young themselves; that is, there is not any direct conversion of a new level of erotic identification into specific forms of behavior. It is likely that this is in part a function of the continued existence of prior conventional gender-role commitments on the part of the majority of the young, as well as the continued commitment of both young men and women to the rhetoric of love, interpersonal attachment, and, ultimately, marriage. At the present time there is little social or interpersonal payoff for sexual activity of any sort during early adolescence, and minimal payoff for coitus during later adolescence. Outside of the conventional routes to marriage, the payoff for young women in both periods is close to zero, though for males some rewards of homosocial adulation for sexual success do exist (though these pleasures are not unalloyed). Sexual activity during this period can become symbolic of anti-adult attitudes and be performed by either gender, or young women can drift into sexual activity at the behest of young men who are still acting out of an older male sex exploitation ethic. In any case, there is no other specific societal linkage or payoff system that makes the behavior appropriate. Until the ideology of "sex is fun" or "sex is good in itself" is more widespread, the acting out of sexual commitments does not seem to be likely in early adolescence. When these young people enter later adolescence, however, and especially the early period of serious mate selection, it is likely that these earlier (in the life-cycle sense) definitions may well tend to increase the amount of premarital sexual activity on the part of the young. During the mating period, the definition of sex as a pleasure to which the young have a right can be combined with a pay off system (dating-mating-marriage) that is currently in existence.

A new element that will affect this period of development is the increasing flexibility of parental figures. While the adaption of youth movement customs by parents is greeted with derision by the young, the amusement is often mixed with more than a little anxiety. During the early 1960s parents who did the twist were figures of fun, but now the serious sexuality of older persons is becoming more apparent to young people. Using the conventional language of psychoanalysis, the central problem of adolescence can be seen as an attempt to solve again the Oedipal dilemmas of early childhood and to come to terms with an independent sexual identity. During childhood parental figures were assumed to be stable objects, if not inside themselves, at least in their representation to their children. Indeed, from the Freudian point of view, the objective correlative of the superego had parents remaining parents to their children throughout their lives, providing a continuity of moral character that could serve as a firm basis for either acceptance or rejection of parental values. The emerging role flexibility supplied to adults by affluence has eroded both the fact and illusion of this phenomenon, and parents have become increasingly ambiguous figures for their adolescent children. In this struggle, children often revolt in an attempt to coerce their parents into remaining the same. As a result, there is a mutual identity struggle between parent and child, with the latter often having a more rigid definition of the parent's behavior than the parent has of his child's.

It may well be that the significant sexual changes occurring at the present time are more apparent in an older generation whose responses to the increasing sexual openness of the society can be acted out with fully formed sexual commitments. The existence of these commitments are more apparent to the young in this generation than they were previously, and the young are rarely prepared for the dynamic changes that can occur in adults. This does not mean that the young will not get used to them; it means only that the transition period for the adolescent will grow more complex until sexual identity concepts change. In the long run (one to two generations away) it is likely that there will be a great deal more heterosexual activity in early adolescence and perhaps an increase in eroticism among the young. It is also likely that there will be an increase in sexual activity between persons of a wider range of ages, which will serve to introduce sexual activity more widely among the young.

Changes in Early Adulthood and Marriage

In general, it is likely that all the forces we have mentioned will lead to an increase in sexual activity prior to first marriage on the part of the young. At the present time, and for a number of years into the future, the boundary between the sexually active young and those younger will be stable in the middle teens. It appears that there will be a steady increase in the proportion of young people who will have premarital coitus; however, for the present (the next decade) there will be no great increase in the number of sexual partners for large numbers of women. While the institution of marriage is in disrepute in certain circles (more among those who have lived in it than those who have not), the institution of romantic love and its concomitant dyadic regression is not. Intense dyadic attachments are still the norm among the young, and they still represent the primary situation in which young women engage in heterosexual activity prior to marriage. If these are the main conditions that currently determine whether premarital coitus will occur among young women, then most males would be restricted by them. The current pattern is a steady increase in the proportion of young women who are not virgins at marriage, but who have coitus in the context of love and mate selection. Clearly, the increase in the proportion of women who have had intercourse under these conditions will also, as a result of misadventures, result in an increase in the number of women who have had intercourse with more than one male. This proportion should increase somewhat over the next ten years (say from 15% now to 30% by 1980). Larger increases in the numbers of sexually active women prior to marriage is probably a generation or two away. Large increases will require that women's economic lives not be tied directly to those of men, as well as a major ideological change in the way women view their own bodies as sources of pleasure. In part, such a change can take as its ideological starting points the language of women's liberation (which will become somewhat more meaningful to women just prior to marriage who may be joining the labor force), the increased level of sexual content given to women's identity during early adolescence, and an environment of males who seem less exploitative sexually.[11] These are the elements that are required to produce changes of this type, but it will take some time for them to be developed. In this case, it would seem that the more conventional patterns of mate selection will stay the dominant style for the next fifteen to twenty-five years. Most young people will continue to get married after relatively limited premarital sexual careers. This does not mean that there will not be increases in the numbers of nonvirgins, or that the frequency and incidence of premarital coitus will not increase. It merely means that the emotional and normative content of premarital sexual life will be relatively traditional for the vast majority of the young. If this is the case, this group of young people will not be the cutting edge of societal change.

11. Thus Gloria Steinem can be conventionally erotic, which is the usual content of the late normal adolescence, and liberated politically as well. It is the novel joining of these formerly disparate individual themes on a collective level that is significant to social change.

The potential for change is somewhat greater during the periods of early marriage and later marriage. One factor that may contribute to change during this period is an increasing divorce rate. Much as failure in love relationships can produce females who have an increased sense of their sexual selves, so divorce can—for some women, if it does not erode entirely their sense of self—produce persons who are more available sexually both to themselves and others. An increase in the number of sexually active women in our society can be produced in this manner and by the failure of other nonmarital forms of dyadic sexual relations between men and women. This process will create a larger population of sexually experienced women who will be more open to the language of women's liberation, both occupationally and sexually, and who will be more prepared to act out a newly acquired sexual commitment. With the backdrop provided by the heightened level of eroticism available in the media and with an increased commitment to a sensualist ethic, it is possible for larger numbers of women to seek out sexual activity rather than wait passively. If the number of young, divorced women (those twenty to twenty-three years old) is large, they can revert to being part of the never-married population and become personal models for a different pattern of sexual activity for never-married younger women. The difficulty of transmission of behavior models between the divorced woman and the never-married woman in the past has been the stigma of failure attached to divorcees, since they have failed in the activity to which never-married women were devoting nearly all their time and energy. The divorcee (or the failed affianced) in the past has failed in woman's most precious goal—getting and staying married. However, this pattern has begun to change, thanks to larger numbers of divorcees and failed fiancees and because of the emergence of a rhetoric supporting divorce and the single life as an acceptable alternative to marriage.

The recently observed decline in the number of children per family could also have direct and indirect consequences on sexual activity during and between marriages. With fewer children or no children in a marriage, there are fewer economic, social, and moral obligations to hold the marriage together during periods of stress. Smaller families and especially childless families are more likely to increase the pool of divorced men and women. In childless marriages the absence of children could reduce the conflict between the erotic and the maternal, and males could continue to conceive of their spouses as exclusively erotic creatures rather than having to share them with children. This could increase the rates of sexual activity in marriage and increase the economic resources that support a more flexible young life style. At the same time, children do increase the emotional and social complexity of marriage, providing novel experience for both males and females—because children do develop the number of roles available to adults, not only in relation to children, but to the surrounding social world as well. Marriages without children, or those which have a short child-rearing period as a result of decline in total numbers of children in the family, will have to find alternative sources of emotional and social novelty in other activities, some of which can lead to more extensive nonmarital contacts for each partner.

It seems that, as part of a general reduction of the economic and social costs of marriage failure and a decline in the number of children, there will be an increase in extramarital activity on the part of both men and women. The general form of extramarital coitus will remain relatively stable; that is, as private adventures on the part of the marital partners, though in some cases there will be mutual extramarital coitus (one of many varients of "swinging"). There will be ideological support for increases in extramarital coitus, both in attitudes expressing limitations of conventional marriage and in a rhetoric supporting sexual expression as a necessary part of human fulfillment. There will probably be a flowering of extramarital coitus sometimes in the 1970s (the parents of our typical fifteen year old) as part of the general crisis among middle-class marriages. Whether or not the practice will become a normative standard for the society is unclear. Any increase in extramarital intercourse will reinforce the parents' more prominent sexual identity for their adolescent children. In this case, there will be completion of a series of feedback loops between the generations with increasing role flexibility on the part of parents, allowing an increased commitment to nonmarital coitus, followed by a further impact of a new set of sexual standards on adolescents.

Activity and Affect

Because of the factors discussed above, we believe that adolescents will be more sexually active than their parents or even any generation that has reached the age of thirty in 1970. Such aggregate changes that will occur among them, however, will be relatively slow in occurrence, and the increases in the sexually active proportions of the adolescent population will be smooth rather than eruptive in character. There will be more of a steady increase of premarital sexual activity, mostly after the age of sixteen. The incidence will increase among women, and the frequency will rise among both women and men rather continuously over the next twenty-five years. Toward the end of that period there will begin to be steady increases in heterosexual activity among young people who are under sixteen, and general increases in erotic behavior during early adolescence. Most of the young will continue to get married, but there will be both a larger number of divorces and a higher frequency of extramarital coitus during marriage, though the two processes are not necessarily related. The cosmetic level of sexuality in the society will probably increase with the increased availability of reproduction technologies—inexpensive home television recording equipment for example—that allow private creation of erotic materials. The general level of the society's erotic character will probably increase a good deal in terms of the availability of commercial erotic materials. What the current availability of erotic material will do to the young person's long-term appreciation of erotica is unknown, but there will remain a substantial market for most public forms of erotica among men for at least another generation.

Given these changes in sexual activity, there is a parallel shift in the affective dimensions of sexuality that is perhaps more important —and, indeed, central—to shifts that are not merely aggregative in society, but reflect a fundamental difference in consciousness. Along with the increasing role flexibility that has occurred with the rising affluence of Western society, there has been a concurrent, but not necessarily related, drift toward the increasing secularization of the society. Sexuality, which was deeply linked with sin and norma-

tive transgression and the problems of legitimacy in the minds of
most Western Europeans since the rise of Protestantism and the
Counter-Reformation, was historically linked to the working out of
social metaphors. That is, the sexual act was linked to experiences
larger than the self and, even though these strictures probably did
not descend very far into isolated peasant populations, the posture
of the major religious institutions of the West toward sex was, at
least, roughly known and observed. With the emergence of capitalism and the rise of European culture as a worldwide phenomenon,
the prior social metaphors linking individuals to collective and cultural forms developed new thematic characteristics. The restraining
hand of Puritanism was not only set upon the economic world, but
upon the sexual in such a way that the emerging metaphors for sexuality in the eighteenth and nineteenth centuries were those of con-
servation as opposed to excess—metaphors which utilized a merging of a capitalist symbolic with psychic and bodily functions and
organs, and which required the increasing privitization of sexuality
from the rest of social life. The economic metaphor of sexuality became dominant, while the sexual commitment was private in action,
it remained social in its meanings. With the emergence of sexual
revolutionaries in many forms at the end of the nineteenth century,
the battleground for sexual metaphors still remained in the social
arena. The rhetoric from Freud to the Esalen institute, from D. H.
Lawrence to Norman Mailer, from Comstock to Spiro Agnew
agrees on the social significance of sexuality. When one behaves
sexually, one is acting out the metaphor of sex as power, sex as
transgression, sex as reinforcing of natural masculine and feminine
roles, sex as the apocalypse.

While this rhetorical pattern still exists, it has lost a great deal of
its power to persuade because at the same time society was being
generally secularized, sex was being secularized as well. The experience of the sexual as being powerful was a natural concomitant of
cultural arrangements which carried with them a belief in the dangers of transgression of legitimacy or (in its enlightenment correlate)
the dangers of chaos and disorder. Once these larger sets of cultural
meanings had been overthrown or had evaporated, the experience
of the sexual that was dependent on them lost its viability as well.
Only those who saw sex as having an autonomous meaning or as

giving meaning to the rest of life could believe that, when all other things were changing, sex and the feelings related to it would remain the same.

At this point sex is close to having escaped from the world of the social metaphor. If it does not exemplify health and illness, good and evil, excess and restraint, the essence of the masculine and feminine if it lies not only in the domain of personal morality, but in the domain of personal choice, then sex can no longer stand for significant social or personal oppositions. The correct modern metaphor has been suggested by Nelson Foot, who was usefully commenting on Kinsey in the early 1950s, when he suggested the phrase "sex as play."[12] If sex is merely a form of play, then our concerns with who does it, how old they are, or the marital status of the participants is misplaced (unless we are concerned with disease or pregnancy). Sex is fun and subject to the morality of fun. It is entered into by choice of the two or more partners; anyone may do whatever good manners dictate; the rules are made up by partners who—in the Piagetian sense—are autonomous. We may wish to restrict sex between children and their elders, but what objection do we have to older people teaching younger people about games or sport? These are the essential meanings of the phrases, "doing your own thing" and "whatever turns you on." Play is nonconsequential, except for professionals whose livelihood depends on the activity. There is an interest in skill, but only to improve the intrinsic quality of the game itself.

If one of the present characteristics of sex is that it is experienced powerfully by many people who have a great deal of emotional commitment, then the drift of sexuality into the world of play will begin to reduce this emotional intensity. Sex will be experienced like eating—an important and indeed luxurious experience in some circumstances, but not the emotional center of experience. It cannot stand for fidelity and infidelity, probably its most common social connection today, nor can a woman's surrender of her virginity be a major gift any longer. Among the romantics, sex cannot stand for passion and constraint or for the tension between ruling and submission. It is perhaps appropriate that the movie *Love Story,* which

12. Nelson Foote, "Sex as Play," *Social Problems.*

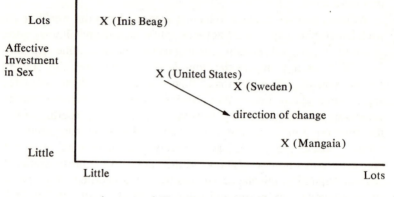

FIGURE 10.1

Activity and Affect in Sexuality in Four Societies

includes both copulation and the flattened emotional affect of the 1930s films, should be a major work of the late mid-century. This indicates how much we have changed since Romeo and Juliet.

It should be clear that these cool feelings about sex are not dominant in the social scene today. But increasingly, the rhetoric of sex as a matter of personal choice, as being good for one's happiness or as being of no one else's concern is an increasingly important value in our society. It is embodied in the sex law reform that is stumbling forward in our society. The remainder of the sexual domain can scarcely survive the revolutionary impulse. While the young still exhibit romanticism early in adolescence and slightly later, this romanticism is not now linked to sexual exclusivity. And although there is still a belief in marital fidelity, its practice is fading in at least some portions of the population.

The relationship between the intensity of affect attached to conventional sexual behavior and the amount of sexual behavior in any society is difficult to determine. It does seem that there is no necessary connection between them. It is perfectly possible to envision a society where there is low affective attachment to sex and yet a great deal of sexual activity. It is equally possible to think of a society where there is a lot of affective investment is sex and not very much sex behavior. Affective investment means that the society and individuals in it see sexual activity as important and central to their concerns and that sex behavior is normatively linked to larger collective concerns. Figure 10.1 suggests the varying relation between the amount of sexual activity and the intensity of affect related to heterosexuality in four exemplary cultures. The arrow suggests the future direction for U.S. society in the relation between these two highly abstract attributes.[13]

What we mean to suggest here are two things, neither of which will make sexual conservatives or revolutionaries very happy. It seems to us that there will be a general increase in the amount of heterosexual activity in the society over the next twenty-five years (this will make the liberals happier and the conservatives more unhappy) but that this sexual activity will not be experienced as immensely therapeutic, nor will it be used in revolutionary changes in morality and equity between genders, the classes or the races (which will make the liberals unhappy and which will prompt the conservatives to say, "I told you so").

Afterword

What is essential in the creation of a scenario for the future is to recognize that the participants in any future landscape will not behave in any way that we can dictate. While present-day males may view a future increase in the number of sexually active females with a sense of envy, it is very difficult to predict how the males at that future moment will respond. Similarly, females may feel that women in the future will be better off than today's women, thanks to fewer aggressive and exploitative men and greater equality between the genders, but what the women who are alive at that moment will feel may not be satisfaction. At the same time, we must not submit to the opposite tendency—that is, to degrade change by saying, "They will be doing it more, but enjoying it less." The critical posture to maintain is that the future will not be better or worse, only different.

13. For descriptions of Inis Beag and Mangaia see respectively: John Messenger, "The Lack of the Irish," pp. 41–42 and 68, and Donald Marshall, "Too Much in Mangaia," pp. 43–44, 70, 74–75 in *Psychology Today* (February 1971).

Index

social organization of, 236-40
Promiscuity
 among heterosexuals, 146-47
 among male homosexuals, 146
Prostitution, 217-34
 apprenticeship, 227-28
 -client talk, 228
 defined, 217, 218
 departure from, 233
 in different culture, 218, 219
 entry into, 225-27
 history of, 219-22
 and rise in premarital sex, 223,
  224, 225
 the world of, 229-33
Prostitutes
 personal relationships of, 229-30
 and pimps, 231
 male use of, 223
Psychoanalysis
 and sexual images, 9, 10, 11
Psychoanalytic theory, 5
 flaws in, 17-18
 and homosexuality, 135
Psychosexual development, 99-103

Rainwater, Lee, 44n
Ramsey, Glenn, 155, 116
Redlich, F. C., 137n
Reiss, Albert J., 72n, 81
Reich, Wilhelm, 67
Reiss, Albert, 135, 136n, 170n
Religion
 and homosexuals, 159-61, 214
Research on sex, 284-85
 on male homosexuals, 132
 problems with, 13-14
 see also, Clinical research
Rhiengold, Joseph C., 59, 176n,
  179n
Rolph, C. H., 226n
Romantic love
 and lesbians, 208-10
 and prostitution, 222
Rose, Arnold, M., 137n
Ross, H. Lawrence, 172n
Rossi, Alice, 180n

Schachtel, E., 13n

Schachter, S., 21
Schaffer, Dora, 176n
Schmidhofer, Ernst, 120n
Schofield, Michael, 135, 136n
Schools
 and sex education, 121
Scripts
 and human behavior, 19
 see also, Sexual scripting, Social
  scripting
Sears, Robert R., 32n, 42n, 44
Self-acceptance
 among lesbians, 210-15
Self-hatred
 among homosexuals, 164
Sex
 as "natural" or "unnatural," 4-5
Sex education, 31-34, 50, 126-28
 common methods of, 115-16
 content of programs in, 121-23,
  124, 125
 and the media, 123-24
 need for, 113-14
 by parents, 32, 33, 115-20
 by peers, 39-41
 possible sources of, 117, 120-21
 and the schools, 121
Sex drive
 theories of, 11
"Sex play," 35-36
Sex roles
 learning of, 42-44
 and X-rated movies, 266-67
Sexual activity
 change in rate of, 299
 among male homosexuals, 146
 periods of intense, 103-4
Sexual behavior, 107-9
 authors' view of, 9
 in literature, 8
 problems of studying, 5
 theories of, 5-7
 see also, Sexual conduct
Sexual conduct
 changes in, 283-84
  and gender roles, 292-95
  predictions about, 303-7
  research on, 284-85
  sources of, 287-92